# San Francisco Bizarro

A guide to notorious sights, lusty pursuits, and
downright freakiness in the City by the Bay

## By Jack Boulware

St. Martin's Press

New York

After moving to San Francisco in the 1980s, bedazzled by what he thought was the city of opportunity, Jack Boulware assumed a series of extremely low-paying occupations: dishwasher, Time/Life book salesman, improv comedian, actor, audio-visual technician, graphic designer, bank clerk, musician, magazine editor, and one ignoble moment where he dressed up like John Hancock and handed out bookmarks in the lobby of the Fairmont Hotel. He somehow recovered to write about the city for *SF Weekly, British Esquire, New York Times Magazine,* and the *Washington Post,* and is the author of *Sex, American Style: An Illustrated Romp Through the Golden Age of Heterosexuality.*

# Introduction

For decades, San Francisco has been known as the City By the Bay, a fabulous and sophisticated oasis of cosmopolitan culture, lingering on the edge of the continent like a twinkling jewel. Thousands of conventioneers and tourists flock to its borders annually. It consistently ranks among *Condé Nast Traveler's* favorite cities, enlivened with an ethnic and cultural diversity as well as incomparable vistas, sumptuous dining, the wine country, no wonder Tony Bennett sang that song about the cable cars...etc., etc., blah blah.

We've all heard this before. Entire sections of bookstores perpetuate this romantic notion, punctuated by tired quotes from long-dead personalities. This town has been sold and resold so many times, we've completely lost touch with whatever drew people here in the first place. Spend a month here and you'll realize the real San Francisco appears petty, narcissistic, and selfish, clinging to its old press clippings like an aging Norma Desmond.

But by the same token, San Francisco is a complex town that lets you be yourself, that accepts you even if your family doesn't. No matter how uncomfortable your own skin feels, you can move to this city, discover who you really are, and plant your feet on the ground, and before you know it, one of two things will happen:

1) You'll become a visionary, resistant to all authority. Others will beg to learn a tenth of your knowledge. Uniqueness will bubble from your core. You will forever have a hand in great things that will impact the world; or

2) You'll meet a bunch of like-minded individuals and soon be either attending meetings, or dancing down the street in a parade somewhere. Again, uniqueness will bubble from your core, and you'll have a hand in great things that will impact the world. And a web page will be involved.

Along with this singular sense of tolerance and acceptance comes a celebration of the eccentric, from entrepreneurial to just plain weirdo freak. We supply the world with blue jeans, boxer shorts, and LSD. Our Satanists, piercing, and tattoo shops make international headlines. Our politicians still get in fistfights and throw S/M parties. We publish more zines per capita than any other city. Television and the slot machine were invented here. The United Nations began here, as did topless dancing and Victoria's Secret lingerie, the martini and Irish coffee.

This book will shine the light into these bizarre, dark corners of the city — the alternative histories, the little-known (and some would say best-forgotten) facts and trivia that help fuel the reputation of San Francisco as Kookville, America's Campground of the Damned. Learn how lunatic the Bay Area really is, and realize how sane you really are in comparison. And if you're offended, there's always Tony Bennett.

SAN FRANCISCO BIZARRO:
A GUIDE TO NOTORIOUS SIGHTS, LUSTY PURSUITS, AND
DOWNRIGHT FREAKINESS IN THE CITY BY THE BAY

Boulware, Jack.
San Francisco Bizarro: A guide to notorious sights, lusty pursuits, and
downright freakiness in the city by the bay / Jack Boulware

This book was designed by Karl O'Melay
www.omelay.com

ISBN 0-312-20671-2

First St. Martin's Griffin Edition: May 2000

10 9 8 7 6 5 4 3 2 1

# Acknowledgments

A book like the one you're holding pretty much writes itself, especially if you're talking about a civic freak show like San Francisco. This guide could easily be three times the size. We'll have to wait for next time for the senior-citizen nudists group and the diseased eyeball exhibit. If you have a zesty idea that you'd like to see in future editions, please send it to:

San Francisco Bizarro
c/o Jack Boulware
PMB 101
530 Divisadero St.
San Francisco, CA 94117

Any project this diverse couldn't possibly get produced without lots of help. First of all, big thanks to all the magazine and newspaper editors who printed my articles about this weird city over the years, especially the *SF Weekly*. Thanks also to the dozens of people who contributed great suggestions, from friends who got dragged along on strange field trips, to the guy on a bar stool, slurring about how the book will be an absolute failure unless it mentions the place where his uncle used to work.

Thanks be to Karl O'Melay, who did an enormous and terrific job of designing everything, and cranking out layouts from the house in Berkeley with the toilets in the foyer. Thanks once again to Deborah Lewis for looking over the text.

An extra special thanks to the photographers who ran around the Bay Area, snagging many of these images. In particular, Paul Trapani, Anthony Pidgeon, and Sharon Selden. All of them are total pros, and graciously contributed these shots for a fraction of their worth, so you should hire them.

Payola-type thanks to all who loaned photos and artwork, from the folks included in the chapters, to Lazlo at San Francisco Rock Posters and Collectibles, and Cloud Source, for the extended loan of their fancy digital camera.

Thanks to Bonnie Nadell for making it all happen, and to Patrick Hughes, whose idea this was in the first place.

And finally, thanks to my family, who wondered why in the hell I would ever want to move to San Francisco. I hope this book in some way explains.

# San Francisco Bizarro

# Table of Contents

# Chapter One

# It's A Living

It's said the reason that California harbors more flakes than anyplace else in the country because somebody tilted the continent and all the nutbags ended up here. But however method the flakes arrive, like everybody else, they eventually have to get on with their business. The Bay Area has long been a safe haven for the ideologically pure visionary, where people's twisted passions have become their livelihood. Behavior that puzzles or disgusts other regions of the nation, is not only employable here, but often revered, and people travel great distances to be within proximity of it. Strange notions often fester here first, before erupting and spewing all over the rest of the nation — hippies, beatniks, blue jeans, nuns in drag, roller derby, Folger's Coffee, Corn Nuts, mountain bikes, human potential groups, satanists, Apple computers, Hells Angels. So what's the deal? Is it the fresh air? The scenery? The lack of a decent freeway system? There's no agriculture, no manufacturing, and unless you count the recent invasion of computer nerds, no main industry to speak of. You could argue that our minds wander into bizarre areas because we refuse to have real jobs. Or maybe it's that we'll do anything for a buck as long as we can keep paying the steep rent. Or perhaps we see somebody else hurling all their energies into the weirdest scheme imaginable, and we accept this blind passion as the normal way of living our lives. Whatever the reasons, a majority of these ideas have become quite successful. As Martin Mull once said about golf, if you're real good at it, you can end up making a shitload of money.

# Roots Rock!

Looking for a natural solution to Viagra? Convinced that a plant can cure your diabetes? Need a quick pick-me-up without waiting in line at the gourmet coffee shop? You're obviously in the market for ginseng, the miracle plant from China. First brought to the modern world by a British explorer in 1713, ginseng now is available globally, from natural food stores to corner liquor markets.

But to get the real deal, you need to check out the World Ginseng Center, on the border between Chinatown and North Beach.

Photos: Anthony Pidgeon

This flagship store operates in a chain of four, has been in business for 20 years, and moves the heaviest concentration of ginseng in Northern California. Much like a small supermarket, the owners sell ginseng in every form imaginable, from open bins of roots to tea bags, capsules, candy, and gum. A Mr. Coffee machine sits on a counter, percolating fresh tea for the customers. A middle-aged woman sits on a stool, sorting the dirty-looking roots into piles. An antlered deer's head, wrapped in Christmas lights, surveys the scene from above. All the signs are in Chinese; you need to ask around for someone who speaks English.

Store manager Jane Chow says almost all ginseng in America is grown via cultivation on ginseng farms in Wisconsin. Most of her sales are to tourists, who pay from $30 to $200 a pound for gift packs and bags of the gnarled roots.

"Americans don't like it," she says. "They like the capsules."

Americans are extremely picky when it comes to ginseng. Although the home-grown Wisconsin variety is more potent, we prefer ours to be imported from China or Korea, because if it's from the Far East, it must be good, right? At the same time Americans buy up the Asian ginseng, most of the Wisconsin ginseng is sold and shipped to relatives in mainland China. So this means that somewhere out on the Pacific Ocean, ships loaded down with ginseng are passing each other in opposite directions.

Big jars of clear fluid sit in the display cases, filled with tentacled ginseng roots that look as though they're ready to burst out of the glass and into a PIXAR animation film, singing in the voice of Bette Midler and dancing down the street. These are actually special gifts sent to the store from its Wisconsin supplier. Jane says they're full of vodka, but nobody's ever tried to drink it.

The store sells other food products — from dried clam meat, bamboo shoots, and abalone to honeysuckle crystals, cuttlefish, and analgesic balms — but it's ginseng that brings in the customers. The store will turn over from completely empty to bustling with 20 patrons in the span of 15 seconds. The arguments over ginseng age and quality are fun to eavesdrop on, even if you don't understand Chinese.

Wild ginseng grows in places like New York and Ohio, and is displayed behind the counter in red velvet boxes. The wild roots, thinner and more gangly than their cultivated cousins, can date back 70 years, and are priced up to $4,000 a pound. Is wild ginseng any better than the other?

Jane Chow smiles. "It's older," she replies helpfully.

**World Ginseng Center**
**801 Kearny Street**
**(415) 362-0928**

# Birth of the

**S**an Francisco's North Beach is generally credited with giving birth to the Beat Generation — not the 1990s goatees, but the real true-blue beats of the 1950s, with dirty kids hanging out at coffee shops, playing bongos, and reading the new literature inspired by Benzedrine and bop jazz. Jack Kerouac would later write about frenetic road trips in his novel *On the Road*, and Lenny Bruce would riff on religion and politics in nightclubs. But one night in 1955, a skinny kid named Allen Ginsberg lit the pilot light for everyone with his first-ever reading of his new poem entitled "Howl."

In the 1950s, poetry as a form was turning more verbal. Writers were discovering the difference between the spoken and written word. Dylan Thomas traveled around the country performing to crowds, and released recordings of his readings. Ginsberg moved to the Bay Area in mid-1955, writing and tripping on peyote, attempting to snag the cadences of human speech, trying to capture, as he would later put it, "an extreme rhapsodic wail I once heard in a madhouse." He lived at 1010 Montgomery Street, working on portions of a new poem, and finished the second section while sitting in the cafeteria at the Sir Francis Drake Hotel.

Eventually it was time to freak out his friends, and perform it in public. An event called "6 Poets at 6 Gallery" commenced on October 7, 1955, at a performance art space at 3119 Fillmore Street, near Union. Other poets on the evening's bill were Gary Snyder, Michael McClure, Philip Whalen, and Philip Lamantia, hosted by Kenneth Rexroth. But it was "Howl" that got everyone's attention. Ginsberg's first line would become permanently etched in the brains of future generations of Contemporary Lit majors:

"I saw the best minds of my generation destroyed by madness, starving hysterical naked, dragging themselves through the negro streets at dawn looking for an angry fix."

The crowd was stunned at the poem's power. Passing wine in the audience, Kerouac was yelling, "Go! Go!" "Howl" eventually appeared in print and on albums, and pop-culture bigshots like Bob Dylan were floored by this weird, wild rant at American society, and the phrase

THE POCKET POETS SERIES

HOWL
AND OTHER POEMS
ALLEN GINSBERG
Introduction by
William Carlos Williams
NUMBER FOUR

# Beatniks

"angel-headed hipsters."

At that time, America's beat scene revolved around the City Lights bookstore, the nation's first paperback-only shop, opened two years before by Lawrence Ferlinghetti and Peter Martin, and named both for a small literary magazine published by Martin, and the Charlie Chaplin film.

City Lights published "Howl" in 1956, with an introduction by William Carlos Williams that concluded, "Hold back the edges of your gowns, Ladies, we are going through hell." At least some people thought it was hell. Customs officials and San Francisco police both seized copies of the slim volume, claiming it was degenerate homosexual filth, and arrested Ferlinghetti and his store manager on obscenity charges. (Ginsberg happened to be out of the country at the time.)

City Lights went to court in San Francisco, in a very famous First Amendment obscenity trial that lasted throughout the summer. Poets and scholars rushed to testify on behalf of the poem and the store. Although the SFPD juvenile division declared it was "not fit for children to read," the judge eventually returned a verdict of not guilty, saying the poem did indeed have redeeming social value. The case established obscenity criteria for the future, and

**JACK KEROUAC STREET**

On January 25, 1988 The City of San Francisco approved a proposal by **CITY LIGHTS BOOKS** to rename 12 streets for S.F. writers and artists including this alley.

paved the way for the distribution of saucy titles like Henry Miller's *Tropic of Cancer* and D.H. Lawrence's *Lady Chatterly's Lover*. Ferlinghetti still owns and runs the City Lights store, and was recently named the Poet Laureate of San Francisco.

Over 40 years after it first appeared, 815,000 copies of "Howl" have been printed — not bad for a filthy little poem. Ginsberg kept in the public eye during the hippie and punk eras, all the way up until his death in 1997. His literary archives, now housed at Stanford University, contain old tennis shoes and bags of his pubic hair.

"Howl" location
3119 Fillmore Street

City Lights Bookstore
261 Columbus Avenue
(415) 362-8193

# Hippies and

I n the 1960s, Haight Street transformed from a sleepy residential neighborhood into a circus atmosphere of long-haired, braless freaks waltzing down the sidewalks with flowers painted on their faces. Gee, it couldn't have been because they were all *stoned out of their gourds.* To capitalize on this insanity, the Thelin brothers opened the Psychedelic Shop, the world's first head shop, selling pipes, rolling papers, posters, and issues of *The Oracle,* a groovy hippie-dippy newspaper printed with multi-colored inks and scented with jasmine. The Thelins set up theater seats in the window of their store, so customers could sit and watch the parade of humanity pass by. A bus company offered tours through the Haight so tourists could stare at the disgusting hippies out the windows. Hippies followed the bus along the street, holding up mirrors to the occupants.

This odd new scene had to spawn from someplace special. And that place was often under the tongue, an ideal spot to ingest a dose of lysergic acid diethylamide (LSD), a drug that was manufactured in a bathtub.

Grandson and namesake of a Kentucky senator, Augustus Owsley Stanley III was also a whiz-kid eccentric. Nicknamed "Bear," he ate no vegetables, only meat. He wore flamboyant clothes, and pontificated in restaurants for hours on any subject that came up. And he became one of the world's first acid chemists.

Owsley's acid achieved legendary status. His first batches were capsules, then he switched to a light blue liquid called "Mother's Milk," to be placed on sugar cubes. And then he invested in a pill press and started manufacturing tablets of acid.

Acidheads found his product always extremely potent, a wild ride to the core of the soul that stripped away all the filters of perception, and made you quit your job and go with the flow, man. People referred to Owsley as "the unofficial mayor of San Francisco." The doses that first turned on the Haight-Ashbury were cooked in his bathtub in Berkeley. But this clandestine laboratory didn't last long.

On February 21, 1965, federal narcotics agents burst into Owsley's apartment at 1647 Virginia Street, tipped off to a possible methedrine lab. Even if they were looking for LSD, acid would not be illegal for another year. There was no meth lab, so the swashbuckling Owsley immediately hired the deputy mayor of Berkeley as his attorney. After the charges were dropped, he sued the police for the return of his lab equipment — and won.

He then left town to set up other labs, one in Los Angeles and later, back in the Bay Area, in Point Richmond. It was said his operations manufactured 4 million hits, and probably gave away just as many.

Other Bay Area chemists saw the potential of this exciting new industry, and cranked up their own labs. Some dipped sheets of paper in LSD to make blotter squares. Others put the chemical into tiny microdots, or "orange sunshine" pills.

A bathtub startlingly similar to Owsley's

One group added their liquid acid to a clear gelatin solution, then rolled the mixture out into sheets and cut it up into squares. The Clearlight operation took their name from a phrase in the *Tibetan Book of the Dead*, and shipped millions of these 250-microgram "windowpane" doses all over the world. From 1970 to 1972, they manufactured all this LSD in an office building, smack in the heart of North Beach.

"Very aesthetic, very pleasing," remembers one tripper of the Clearlight experience. "No other acid had that quality."

Clearlight's North Beach lab took up two floors of the building, one for the lab and the gelatin cutting machine, and the other for offices and sleeping cushions (this was the hippie era, after all). The crew conducted their reactions during noisy rush-hour traffic on Columbus Avenue. Ceiling fans blew the chemical stench out a vent in the roof, and supplies were loaded in and out of the building in the early-morning hours. At the end of the night, an assistant would sweep up the floor, get hundreds of free acid hits, and hand them out at parties.

But the party couldn't last forever. In 1977, nine Clearlight members were convicted for conspiracy to manufacture, distribute, and possess LSD. Some turned legitimate and got out of the business, and a few disappeared completely.

Owsley also is no longer in the business, and at last report is designing and selling a line of expensive brass sculptures from his home in Australia. But he recalls the acid days with great fondness.

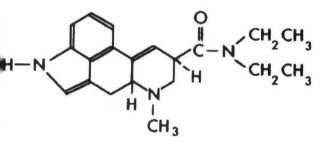

"I always trusted what happened on acid," he wrote recently. "Everything that happens to you on acid is real. Everything you see is real, everything you experience is real, everything you think about is real. The thing about it is, that a lot of the stuff you see is not stuff you see when you're straight, because when you're straight you're limited. The acid removes the 'filters' and lets the noise through. That 'noise' is as real a part of the universe as the other part that you do allow to pass through, it just hasn't been important for you."

Current tenants of Owsley's Berkeley apartment all understand the historical significance of their bathroom, and actually pay rent to the same landlord. The original Psychedelic Shop on Haight Street is now a pizza parlor, but the store's name lives on, via another head shop on Market Street.

**Psychedelic Shop**
**(now Cybelle's Pizza)**
**1535 Haight Street**

**Owsley's LSD bathtub**
**1647 Virginia Street, Berkeley**

**Clearlight LSD lab**
**222-234 Columbus Avenue**

# Boomer Baubles

**A**ny self-respecting yuppie knows that an office uncluttered with high-tech gadgetry is not just lacking in zest, it's also *embarrassing*. Without fancy toys lying around in plain view, it's very difficult for visitors to guess the vast resources of your disposable income, and let's face it, there is no bigger shame. It's also more of a challenge to talk like a bigshot on the phone when there's nothing to fiddle with in your hands. Fortunately, to help us through such crises, we have The Sharper Image.

In 1977 Richard Thalheimer was a nobody office supplies salesman in San Francisco. But he had two things going for

Courtesy: The Sharper Image

him: He was confident, and he was observant. Sensing a burning need for joggers to own a fancy digital stopwatch, he found a bunch of such timepieces, and marketed them through magazine ads for $29.95. He sold out immediately, and started thinking. If people liked to spend money on an unnecessary yet expensive stopwatch, they might also be interested in unnecessary yet expensive telephones and calculators. Thalheimer kept collecting unnecessary yet expensive gadgets, and selling them by mail-order. In 1979 he published his first Sharper Image catalog. By 1981, he was raking in so much money he opened his first store, a sleek, round-shaped building in the middle of San Francisco's Financial District.

Thalheimer's timing was perfect. It was the go-go '80s, and the nation was crawling with status-seeking yuppies, flush with disposable cash and on the hunt for inconsequential baubles with which to impress each other. The Sharper Image eagerly served up the latest glittering trinkets to catch the yuppie eye — Uzi machine gun replicas, household robots, rowing machines, suits of armor, reproduction jukeboxes that looked *just like the real thing*. Starting with one stopwatch, the empire has now grown to over 90 stores worldwide, with net sales over $200 million annually.

The flagship store in downtown San Francisco is set up as a playpen for rich guy executives, who visit on their lunch breaks to tinker with the samples. Recent additions to the catalog include The Truth.Seeker, a sculpture that flashes lights in reaction to stress in a human voice, and the Ionic Hair Wand hair renewal system, which employs cleansing ion energy.

This shop is definitely worth a visit. How many times do you get the chance to monkey around with an Ionic Hair Wand? Another great feature of The Sharper Image is a polar-opposite worldview 20 feet away from its front door. As you walk out of their building, you immediately detect pot smoke drifting over from the sidewalk, where the city's bike messengers congregate on a concrete wall between deliveries.

The Sharper Image
Sutter at Market Streets
(415) 398-6472

# Cookies of Chance

Too many times we have sat in a Chinese restaurant at the end of a meal, cracked open that little cookie, inspected the piece of paper, and 1) played a silly guessing game with everyone; 2) traded it for someone else's; or 3) taken the paper home to post on our refrigerator or place of employment. But while we snicker at the accidental accuracy of this broken-English message contained in a stale sugar cookie, most of us have no idea that the entire concept is a big fat lie. The fortune cookie isn't Chinese, and it wasn't brought over from China. It was invented in San Francisco by a Japanese man. Go ahead, it's okay to take a moment. Heavy, isn't it?

The Japanese Tea Garden in Golden Gate Park was originally called the Japanese Village, and is the only surviving concession from something called the Midwinter Fair, held in 1894. When the exposition wrapped up, the operator, an Australian named John Marsh, sold the concession to park commissioners. The commissioners, in turn, hired a native Japanese man named Makota Hagiwara to tend the gardens and operate the teahouse.

Hagiwara supposedly came up with the idea of a folded piece of baked dough, containing a little prophetic piece of paper. Having no vision of the future himself, he never patented the idea. He just served the cookies in the teahouse. White people, of course, went nuts over the mystical-prophecy aspect of it all, and came down to the tea garden to try the cookies. Hagiwara's family ran the tea garden until 1942, when all Japanese Americans were sent off to detention camps, and the city assumed operating responsibilities for the garden and teahouse.

Hagiwara's legacy to the world is now standard issue for Chinese restaurants worldwide, but you can still visit the tea garden for tea, and enjoy the descendants of the first fortune cookies. And if you're feeling a bit frisky, you can check out the X-rated versions available at the Golden Gate Fortune Cookie factory, located in a Chinatown alleyway.

Japanese Tea Garden
Tea Garden Drive in
Golden Gate Park
(415) 752-1171

Golden Gate Fortune Cookies
56 Ross Alley
(415) 781-3956

# Rock and Roll Potty Training

**M**ill Valley, just north of San Francisco, is not only home to many famous guitarists and musicians, but is also the residence of the world's most prolific toilet-seat guitar manufacturer. In 30 years, Charlie Deal has designed and built 115 functioning models, using mail-order parts and old seats he has recycled from the trash.

Originally from the Minnesota/North Dakota area, Deal moved out to California and worked odd jobs until 1969, when he got a gig performing comedy with musician friends at the Vacaville Medical Facility. He put together a guitar from a toilet seat, and that night was introduced as the "world's crappiest guitar player." Deal passed out toilet paper to the crowd, and a new cottage industry was born.

Courtesy: Charlie Deal

He attempted to register a patent, but the patent office refused, saying it was simply a modified toilet seat. He was forced to prove it was actually a working guitar, and now holds two patents on the idea.

He gets his seats from flea markets and garage sales. Some people save them for him. One environmentally aware company produced a water-saving toilet, offered rebates for used toilets, and turned over their trade-ins to Deal. He bought a number of toilets from one woman who had been putting together a toilet art project.

"I like the old ones," he says of his toilet seats. "They're much nicer — birch, poplar, oak, alder."

One is featured on the cover of the album *Sports*, by Huey Lewis and the News. Deal makes primarily six-string electrics, but has also produced a "Four Flusher" bass model, and a left-handed "Reverse Flush" design. The necks come from a mail-order company in Ohio, and he says he likes to use vintage pickups whenever possible. He will make the toilet in customized colors to match any decor. Prices start at $700, but he says he'll offer a discount if the customers laugh at his jokes.

**Charlie Deal's Toilet Guitars**
**45 Plymouth Avenue**
**Mill Valley, CA 94941**

# Gnome Central

L et's just say, for argument's sake, you're nuts for gnomes. All kind of gnomes, pixies, and/or fairies. You can't get enough of 'em. Gnomes gnomes gnomes. If people are looking at you kind of funny, don't feel like you're a *freak* or anything. Just get on board the Bay Area's International Gnome Club. American membership is just 12 bucks a year, and boasts members all over the world, who collect or make gnomes for a living.

Through her *Gnome News* newsletter, Liz Spera provides gnome geeks all sorts of necessary tidbits: Updates on gnome sightings, new retail-store gnomes, gnome-related products like books and calendars. Readers send in photos of their gnomes, and the stories that go with them. Like London's Ron "Ron the Gnome" Broomfield, whose gravel yard and garden support more than 700 cement and plastic gnomes, the culmination of over 30 long years of gnome-hunting.

Owning and maintaining a yard-full of gnomes isn't as easy as it seems. Plastic/vinyl gnomes can develop black sunburns, or mildew. Club members will know instantly that these unsightly blemishes can easily be removed with bleach and a toothbrush. Conventional gnome wisdom says you should place the little fellas in groups of three or four. A *Gnome News* reader adds: "Gnomes tend to do well when partially hidden behind foliage or low branches, appearing to peek from behind plants."

Photos Courtesy: Tom Clark / Cairn Studios

**The International Gnome Club
22814 Kings Court
Hayward, CA 94541-4326**

# Don't Tell Mom

A s a young doctor in 1960s San Francisco, David Smith kept watching the numbers increase of overdoses and drug-related medical problems. In June 1967 he opened America's first free medical clinic, in the Haight-Ashbury district. Staffed by volunteers, the clinic had one primary policy — to accept everyone, from teenagers with crabs on down to indigent addicts. People now knew there was an affordable place to go where they wouldn't feel embarrassed or ashamed. In 1972 the clinic founded the Rock Med ("Rock Medicine") mobile emergency care clinic, to provide medical assistance at hippie concerts. In talking down kids from bad acid trips, Rock Med staff use three basic tenets: 1) "You're okay," 2) "You're in a safe place," and 3) "No, we're not going to tell your mom."

The clinic has grown to include HIV testing and outreach, meth programs, women's health, and jail psychiatric services, among others. When Nirvana came to play a gig in the city in 1989, the young Seattle grunge kids acted snot-nosed. And in fact they were. They had the flu. While getting treated at the clinic, Kurt Cobain and company noticed a city campaign to insist that IV drug addicts bleach their needles, so they named their new album *Bleach*. Or so the story goes. Maybe they just thought of it when they were doing laundry.

Photo: Anthony Pidgeon

**Haight-Ashbury Free Clinic
558 Clayton Street
(415) 487-5632**

# New Age Golf Geeks

**A** golf organization that meditates before walking onto the tee? A group that refuses to keep numerical score, and encourages members to instead write down a word that best describes how they felt about each hole? Only in Northern California could there exist the Shivas Irons Society.

This peculiar golf brotherhood spun from the 1972 novel *Golf in the Kingdom*, by Michael Murphy, which described a fictitious game of golf played between the narrator and a Scottish character named Shivas Irons. Dazzled by the book's combination of New Age mysticism and sports philosophy, golf nuts gobbled up hundreds of thousands of copies.

Steve Cohen read the book while working as a Gestalt therapist at Esalen, the Big Sur human potential resort founded by Murphy. He thought of combining his own ideas and Murphy's mystical philosophies into the game, so that it wouldn't be just for guys in ugly slacks — it could also be a metaphor for your life.

"What was always clear was that the game is addictive is some way," Cohen says. "It feeds some part of the being that needs nurturing."

In 1988 Esalen first offered a "Golf in the Kingdom" workshop. It was so popular that three years later Cohen expanded the idea into the Society. He put a newsletter together in his home in Carmel, came up with a little infinity symbol for the logo, and says he went from zero to 1,400 members without any effort. Close to 2,000 people

have joined up over the years, paying $50 or more annual dues. Members include professional golfers, golf writers, even celebrities like Tommy Smothers. Cohen's newsletter chronicles the Society's movements, and sells jackets, golf balls, Murphy's books, and cassettes of golf inspirational talks. Although his *Golf in the Kingdom* was the genesis of the entire organization, Murphy is not involved, other than to lend his name to the board of advisors.

The Shivas Irons Society attempts to rediscover the original essence of the 600-year-old game. They dress up in traditional costumes, and play with antique clubs and a ball stuffed with feathers. And they layer on their New Age hippie grooviness.

They don't keep numerical score. During official Society events, they hire classical musicians to set up and play along the fairways. They meditate before going to tee off, and afterward talk about their feelings. They creatively visualize a goal for the ball, and sometimes play an entire hole without anybody speaking. The group's little maxims encourage everyone to have fun and feel better about themselves.

"Make a game of the game."

"98 percent of golf is between shots."

"You gotta feel good about the swing because when it's in the air it's out of your control."

**Shivas Irons Society**
**P.O. Box 222339**
**Carmel, CA 93922-2339**

# Treats for the Tree

S an Francisco is home to many transgressive subculture movements: circus freaks and Satanists, pornographers and sadomasochists, piercers and tattooists, or giant industrial machines that do battle with each other. But an even more terrifying subculture exists, the sort of extremist obsessive behavior that defies rational explanation, a parallel universe of reality that even if witnessed only once, makes one bring a damp cloth to the forehead, lie down on the floor, and hope the convulsions go away soon. We're talking the work of Christopher Radko, the world's most famous Christmas ornament designer. The Bay Area's outlet for all things Radko is a Financial District gift shop called The Glass Pheasant, whose centerpieces are two garish Christmas trees jammed with Radko pieces, towering to the ceiling in a permanent display.

Radko's designs are handblown eyeball assaults of multiple blinding colors, the sequin-soaked shapes dizzying in their variety: kitties, ducks, doggies, dolphins, bears, clowns, unicorns, pigs, sea horses, skiers, angels, alligators, elephants, wise men, King Tuts, genies coming out of bottles, gnomes in front of tree stumps, astronauts standing on satellites, Santas under giant mushrooms, Santas in tennis outfits or football uniforms, and something best described as a double-amputee Captain Hook, where one hand is obviously a hook but in place of the other hand shoots out a silver-sequined, cane-like, almost vaguely penile appendage that drops to the floor between his buckled shoes.

Each ornament sells for between 15 and 45 bucks, and takes a week to make in Radko's shops in Poland, Germany, Italy, and the Czech Republic. His celebrity ornament customer list includes Al Gore, Katharine Hepburn, Liz Taylor, Bruce Springsteen, Dolly Parton, and Elton John. And Barbra Streisand.

"This is where it's at," says Gary, owner of The Glass Pheasant, gesturing to his store bristling with Radko ornaments. "The quality, detail, uniqueness — he's Mr. Perfection."

At a special book signing in San Francisco a few years ago, Radko gestured to some limited-edition ornaments that sold for $25 but in three years would be worth a thousand bucks each. "There's a huge secondary market," he said. "It's insane what people will pay for that." Indeed it is.

Christopher Radko Ornaments
The Glass Pheasant
239 Grant Avenue
(415) 391-8377

# Tanks a Bunch

Our nation will never forget World War II. To many, it was the last great war. Double U Double U Deuce, the big one. America was attacked, fought back, and preserved liberty for the free world. Veterans help keep the memory alive, as do historians and Hollywood filmmakers. And since 1992, so have the Bay Area Tankers.

This local group of radio-controlled tank enthusiasts meet up throughout the year to show off their tanks and stage mock battles in dioramas with miniature villages. Membership is around 30, spread out from San Jose to Sacramento, and their larger events can attract up to 300 people from around the Bay Area and the country.

Because tanks really came into their own in WWII, BAT favors vintage models from the 1940s. "German Panther and Tiger tanks from World War II will always be the cat's meow," quips BAT Public Information Officer/Secretary Rich Upton.

Although the club has its fair share of talented engineer and machinist types, who spend hours creating the complex functioning tracks, turrets, and guns, Upton emphasizes that most Tankers are just regular-guy hobbyists who want to buy the kits and drive around a bunch of tanks: "We're not talking rocket science here."

The group meets monthly to discuss gearbox problems, power train upgrades, the difficulties of approximating the Sherman suspension system, or the types of tanks used in the 1951 WWII film *The Tanks Are Coming*, which influenced many members in their youth.

In addition to meeting in the Bay Area, small pockets of radio-controlled model tank fans gather around the globe, from New Zealand and Britain to Canada, Holland, and Germany. A dedicated few travel between countries to attend large-scale radio-controlled armor shows, and see what people are up to in the field. One German model club in particular puts on a big show, charging and firing their meter-long battle tanks, and setting off gas bombs and rockets for effect. Members even dress up in jumpsuits with insignia.

Not only do imaginary battles rage in the radio-controlled model armor industry, there are battles between the two primary model tank manufacturers. The Tamiya company builds its models to 1/16 scale, but its competitor Bandai insists upon 1/15 scale. Add to this discrepancy the fact that in Germany and Japan historical vehicles are built to 1/10 scale, but some private builders' models are 1/8 or even 1/4 scale, a size so large that the garage won't have room left for the car.

But it doesn't have to be that confusing. A few hundred bucks will get the fledgling started with a basic model tank and radio equipment, and then it's essentially how much time and money you're willing to spend from that point.

BAT dues are $20 for the first year, which includes a baseball logo cap and a subscription to the members-only *BAT Bulletin*. Upton also publishes a *Recon Report* newsletter for the general public, and says his group will soon develop a hierarchy system for awards, plaques, and pins. Future plans for BAT include

Bay Area Tankers
P.O. Box 7734
Oakland, CA 94601

# Inventor's Paradise

I n 1894, Charles August Fey began developing various coin-operated gaming devices in his Market Street lab. Four years later he invented the first three-reel bell slot machine, which immediately caught on with the gambling public. Fey's basic design is still in use in most slot machines today. He naturally fueled others with inspiration. In 1910, the Mills Novelty Company of San Francisco came up with the "Operators Bell" slot machine, the first device that featured the fruit symbols on the reels. Each fruit stood for a different flavor of chewing gum; they were included to promote the sales of gum and the machine, so as to circumvent the prohibition against payout machines. Today, the Mills Novelty Company is the world's largest slot machine manufacturer, headquartered in Las Vegas. And Charles Fey got a marker in the heart of San Francisco's Financial District.

Another mad inventor who earned a historical marker was Philo T. Farnsworth. In his laboratory on Russian Hill, this 21-year-old whipped up something he called the "image dissection tube" in 1927, and successfully transmitted the first all-electronic television image. Known as "The Genius of Green Street," Farnsworth had to wait until 1948 to see his dream manifest into a Bay Area reality, when San Francisco's first television station, KGO-TV, aired its premiere broadcast. He died in 1971, which meant he probably caught a few episodes of *Zoom* and *The Electric Company* on PBS, and was spared the launch of the WB network.

Photo: Sharon Selden

Slot machine invention location
406 Market Street

Television invention location
202 Green Street

Courtesy: Rich Upton

locating a piece of private property where they can meet and run their tanks every month, and working on improving the technology. Eventually they hope to use sound modules to simulate engine sounds, cannon and machine gun fire, and install guns that can fire either talcum or lasers. On the larger machines they plan to affix actual video cameras with transmitters. There's even a faction that wants to shoot 10mm paintballs, but the BAT club charter has a strict policy — no projectiles.

"This is California," sighs Upton.

# Footrace of Fools

E ach year, on the third Sunday in May, the city shuts down. Helicopters patrol overhead, streets are blocked off, neighborhoods are paralyzed. It's time for the Bay to Breakers, when 80,000 fools run the width of the city, along a 12K (7.46 mile) course, and end up at the ocean. Originally started in 1912 to lift the city's spirits from the big earthquake, now it's a parade of organized wackiness. In 1988, the *Guinness Book of World Records* declared it the largest footrace in the world — over 102,000 people. But most of these aren't athletes. The few thousand serious runners are allowed to start the race first, and then it's time for the jackasses.

Costumes are encouraged, from giant Viagra pills to marijuana leaves, mad cows, blow-up dolls, stupid hats, or jackets made from duct tape. Wheelchairs, strollers, and wheeled beer kegs are allowed. Public drunkenness and nudity is permitted.

At the end of the day — and for some, it takes a full day to run the width of the city — everybody ends up at a big party in Golden Gate Park, called Footstock, with awards, and a live concert. The *San Francisco Examiner* prints up the race results, so the top 10,000 runners get their names in the paper. And every single person who runs (or walks) the race gets a free T-shirt, and the feeling of satisfaction that can only come from participating in a race that provides more hangover than workout.

**Bay to Breakers Hotline**
**(415) 808-5000, ext. 2222**

# Swim Insanity

T his organization has nothing to do with dolphins, and everything to do with collective brain damage. Since 1877, members of the Dolphin Club have been waking up early and celebrating their collective insanity by swimming every morning in the freezing waters of San Francisco Bay. Originally limited to 25 members, this bunch now numbers nearly 900, and the all-volunteer group runs on membership fees only.

Their big annual event is the Escape From Alcatraz Triathlon, an exercise in mental illness that is tiring even to describe here in words. Participants begin by taking a ferry boat to Alcatraz Island, then leaping off and swimming the 1.5 miles to Aquatic Park — no wetsuit or fins allowed. People crawl out of the water, immediately hop onto a bicycle, and haul ass 14 miles across the Golden Gate Bridge to Mill Valley. They ditch the bike and run up and over Mount Tamalpais to Stinson Beach, then turn around and run back over the mountain to Mill Valley, a 13-mile trip. Those whose hearts haven't exploded receive an official Escape From Alcatraz belt buckle. Another annual shindig, the Old-Timers' Crab Feed honors the club's older members, some of whom have been doing this for over 60 years.

Photo: Mary Beth Barber

**Dolphin Club**
**502 Jefferson Street, Aquatic Park**

# Ersatz Christ

**A** long time ago, way back in the 1980s, a San Francisco guy named Larry got dumped by his girlfriend. Despondent, he built a human-shaped sculpture out of wood and invited a few friends to Ocean Beach, where they torched the man as some sort of ritual joke. Okay, fine. They thought it was pretty cool, so they did it again the next year. And again, and again, and soon more people started coming, and so they found a location in the desert, and then it became an entire weekend retreat, and then more people started coming, and as the man was lit on fire every year he grew larger and larger in size, and it began to take on a religious significance for people across the world, and bands and artists and dance troupes would come and perform, and there were so many people attending that they would have pre- and post-Burning Man events in San Francisco, for weeks and weeks on either side of the show, and the yet-to-be-burned man would be on display, and they would have photos and photos and videos and videos of previous Burning Man events, and soon every single solitary journalist working in the 20th century would get the plumb Burning Man assignment, and get naked and stoned and roll around in the mud with all the other people in the desert, and articles appeared, and books were published, and web sites were created, and as people would try to establish some kind of utopian, alternative society/community, a circular shape of a city/commune was agreed upon, and the digital computer geek crowd discovered this raw and untamed getaway for the weekend, where they could act like pagans and communicate with others and talk and laugh and not have to spend time hyping somebody on the amazing features of a brand-new time-saving computer application, and people brought computers to do live instant chatroom messages

Photo: Paul Trapani

and sent them to the rest of the world hungry for such information, and they dragged in more booze and took more hallucinogens, and then a few years ago somebody drove a motorcycle straight into a truck and died, and somebody else drove a vehicle into a tent where people were sleeping, but it didn't change much of anything, really, and the event kept growing, and although some of the original organizers started arguing between themselves, it hasn't really showed any signs of slowing down or stopping at all, and every summer the same question is on everyone's lips in San Francisco: "So, like, are you going to Burning Man?"

Burning Man Project
www.burningman.com

# A Church

**W**alking through the Western Addition on a weekend morning, pedestrians will detect live jazz drifting out of a storefront. Not the yuppie white-guy jazz, but furious, extended jams that make you stop in mid-step and listen as it spills out onto the sidewalk and the street, a sonic flash flood of love, the kind of jazz played by people who have lived life on many levels, reached up to stroke the face of the devil, and then transcended beyond it. This is Sunday mass at St. John's Cathedral African Orthodox Church, the only church in the world devoted to saxophonist John Coltrane.

In his youth, Coltrane would have laughed at the idea of a church bearing his name. He was much more in league with demons than any god. Divorced, with both alcohol and heroin problems, he was a compulsive overeater, often fell asleep during concerts, and was fired from Miles Davis' band.

St. John Will·I·AM Coltrane

Image: Deacon Mark Dukes

But then in 1957, Coltrane found God, and cleaned up his act. He formed his famous quartet, with McCoy Tyner on piano, Jimmy Garrison on bass, and Elvin Jones on drums, and began a quest for the higher truth. He would play a solo for 45 minutes. He rehearsed 12 hours a day, even practicing between sets of his own shows, straining for that perfect sound. During the 1960s, Coltrane recorded some of his best albums — *Giant Steps, Live at the Village Vanguard, A Love Supreme.*

Simultaneously, a Bay Area hairdresser named Franzo Wayne King was inviting people into his living room, for a regular "listening clinic" he called The Yardbird Club, named for Charlie "Yardbird" Parker. The idea was to educate the black community about African jazz music.

Coltrane played one of his last gigs in San Francisco, just before he died of liver cancer in 1967. King caught a show at the old Jazz Workshop club, and remembered the experience as a "baptism in sound." With this religious awakening, King picked up the saxophone, and went on to play at the Berkeley Jazz Festival and at clubs around the city. He also realized that what he really wanted from his living room group was a Yardbird Temple, a place of prayer, where they could discuss deeper transcendence into evolved beings. Coltrane was pointing the way. The Temple raised some money, and in the early 1970s opened their space on Divisadero Street as the One Mind Temple Evolutionary Transitional Body of Christ.

For the next 10 years, the church studied ancient Indian religious writings, pushing their curiosity into other faiths, much like Coltrane did. In 1980 King studied under Archbishop G.D. Hinkson of the African Orthodox Church in Chicago, and was soon consecrated as a bishop. Since the African Orthodox Church is a part of the Eastern Catholic Church, they believe there is only one actual manifestation of God. No deities

# Supreme

other than the one — not even Coltrane. King simply made Coltrane a saint instead, and the church changed its name to St. John's.

The 30 core church members are required to listen to Coltrane's *A Love Supreme* at least three times a day, but most of the week, the storefront is quiet, empty except for a Hammond organ sitting in one window. Like many churches, they pursue many ongoing community projects, from counseling and computer classes, to giving away clothing and food. Every Tuesday afternoon, a church member hosts a Coltrane-themed radio show on KPOO, 89.5 FM.

And on Sundays everybody fills up the joint for the jazz jam session — pierced hipsters and their parents, business suits, teenagers, little children, mothers and their babies. Musicians wander in and unpack their gear. Don't worry if you're not a hotshot. If you're not very good, just don't play very loud. The last three rows are taken by white kids, many of whom will skip out before the sermons begin.

First-time church visitors will stare at the walls covered with artwork: A portrait of a black Jesus above the altar, surrounded by candles; Henri Dauman's photograph of a sweaty Coltrane, blowing; colorful murals by Deacon Mark Dukes, depicting John Coltrane holding a saxophone, the bell of which is ablaze in roaring flames.

A rotund man named Brother Reggie comes out to welcome the congregation, and tells everyone it's okay to slap, shout, stand, sing, however the spirit may move you. He then smiles and says, "You are in for a treat."

According to the program, Frederick Harris is the man who starts it off on piano, a mellow improvised groove that gets heads bobbing. The other musicians lay back, let him run it out a bit, and then they slowly pick it up and fall in, rising up and up,

growing louder and louder. Wearing priest robes and a sax around his neck, Bishop King can blow like hell, actually. He trades solos with a white guy in a suit in the front row, until it's all up and running.

A couple of *really long* jams later, Harris disappears. The room still cooks away on a theme, folks are standing and clapping along to the beat. Where's Harris? Bishop King wanders to the back of the room, and suddenly the unmistakable sound of a Hammond B-3 organ cuts into the rhythm, the solos ripping up and over the rest of it. The sound is stunning. People turn around, and see Harris jamming on the Hammond organ in the window, and standing there in front of him, Bishop King, former hairdresser and founder of the world's only church devoted to Coltrane, sticking his cordless mike into the Hammond's speakers, and hollering, "YEAH! YEAH!"

As this book goes to press, the church enters a transition period. They can best be found via their web site..

**St. John's Cathedral African Orthodox Church**
**www.saintjohncoltrne.org**

# Hell's Bells

Years before Black Sabbath's Ozzy Osbourne screeched the immortal heavy metal lyric, "Satan laughing, spreads his wings, OH LORD YEAH!" a dedicated few were already laughing — and conducting Satanic rituals — in a Victorian living room of San Francisco's quiet Richmond district. For over 30 years, the city has been world headquarters for the Church of Satan.

After touring the country, working as a burlesque organist and circus lion tamer, musical prodigy Tony Levey returned home to the Bay Area, and kept his circus name of Anton Szandor LaVey. While raising a family, he continued playing organ

and started giving a weekly series of lectures in his living room, on eclectic topics like cannibalism, circus sideshows, and lycanthropy. Evenings became so crowded that on the advice of a friend, he combined his eccentric interests into a cohesive philosophy, and in 1966 launched the world's first church devoted to the devil. A series of publicity stunts — a Satanic wedding (a journalist and his girlfriend), a Satanic funeral (a member of the U.S. Navy), and a Satanic baptism (LaVey's own 3-year-old daughter) — assured the church front-page news around the world, and then it was full speed ahead on the highway to hell.

LaVey's first book, *The Satanic Bible*, blended together various world views, including a strong dose of Nietzsche, and set the standard for future Satanic worship — selfish hedonism, a little elitism, a little humor, and a lot of black clothing. (The book still moves off shelves today, particularly around Halloween.) As the church grew, it attracted prominent celebrity members like Sammy Davis Jr., Jayne Mansfield, and Tina Louise. LaVey was the subject of magazine articles, wrote a "Letters to the Devil" newspaper column, published a few more books, and consulted for Hollywood films. A group of members split off and formed the rival Temple of Set, and San Francisco's Yellow Pages then boasted two entries under the Satanic church category.

The church weathered a so-called "Satanic Panic" in the 1980s, when it seemed every stupid heavy-metal band was writing songs about the devil, and bonehead teenagers were molesting animals and each other. The Church of Satan adamantly denied any involvement. When the hysteria passed, the 1990s brought a new group of people interested in the principles of the church, from rock poster artist The Coop to Marilyn Manson.

In 1997, the world once again was shocked by a stunt from Satan, when church priest Steven Johnson Leyba performed a controversial ritual at a birthday party for a San Francisco political strategist. The media wasn't attracted just because Leyba allowed a Satanic-looking symbol to be carved into his back, nor was it simply newsworthy that a dominatrix urinated on his open wounds. International media was most impressed that Leyba was then sodomized by a woman wearing a bottle of Jack Daniel's, after which he stood up and took a long

**Church of Satan**
P.O. Box 210082
San Francisco, CA 94121

# We Are One

**A**ny church that can claim clergy members like the Rolling Stones, the Beatles, Norman Lear, Wolfman Jack, Merle Haggard, Johnny Carson, Hugh Hefner, President Lyndon Johnson, Debbie Reynolds, and Mae West, can't be all bad. Seriously, would the Wolfman rip you off? Even though most people sign up on a lark, the Universal Life Church claims millions have received their credentials, and says it's now the largest such church in the world. The general message is one of love, and the only religion should be a conglomeration of all the other world's religions. And anyone — let's say that again — anyone can become an ordained minister.

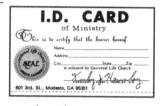

Feisty octogenarian Reverend Kirby J. Hensley began his ministerial duties way back in the 1930s, and ended up in Modesto, where he founded the church in 1958, and where it is still headquartered. The perennially upbeat Hensley still acts as Church President today, and can be found foaming off at the mouth in the newsletters. Hensley's wife assists as church secretary, and a dedicated staff prints up all the organization's literature.

If you would like to become a minister, just write your full name on a piece of paper, and mail it into the church. You'll soon receive an official certificate and membership card, free of charge, and boom — ordained for life. Call yourself Reverend, go nuts. Universal Life Church ministers are licensed to legally perform weddings, funerals, baptisms, and any other official services. Make up the service however you wish, or order the big "Universal Book," which contains examples of official services. For the truly devout, the church offers advanced degrees in Divinity, Metaphysics, Motivation, and Religious Science.

As an official minister, you are entitled to start your own tax-exempt congregation, but the church stresses very strongly that you keep detailed and accurate book-keeping records. They should know. They've beaten the IRS in court many times.

**Universal Life Church
601 3rd Street
Modesto, CA 95351
(209) 527-8111**

guzzle of the whiskey. Many prominent San Francisco citizens who were in attendance, including the mayor, immediately stated they had left the event early.

Although LaVey died in 1997, and his estate has been divided up among heirs, church members carry on his legacy of the world's scariest religion.

Photo: John Nystrom

# Wall of Sound

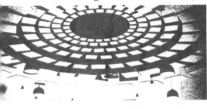

Listeners sit in concentric circles, surrounded by speakers in sloping walls, a floating floor, and a suspended ceiling. They come here to the Audium each week to hear groovy tapes of sculpted sound compositions created live by a tape performer, who directs the show through any combination of 169 speakers. This is the only theater in the world constructed specifically for sound movement. In other words, you don't need to be an audio geek, but it would probably help.

Professional musicians Stan Schaff and Doug McEachern devised this method of routing sounds through a combination of many speakers, and began pursuing their idea of a new musical vocabulary based on the exploration of sound space. They gave concerts in the early 1960s at local universities, and then in 1965 built their own theater on 4th Avenue, and presented weekly performances. By 1972 they had attracted the attention of the National Endowment for the Arts, and a grant enabled them to design and construct a special Audium theater, which opened in 1975 at its current location. They continue to give weekly public performances, and tour the college seminar circuit.

"The overriding realization that emerged from our early endeavors was that the sound was beginning to be free, to be something quite different," explained co-founder Stan Schaff in 1990. "The environment itself began to be important, and in a way became another kind of language — the way the audience sat, the lighting, the whole ambiance — all of it began to speak of a special kind of language. The space itself is a new kind of instrument; it is something to be performed, to be shaped. The sound itself becomes free to be itself in full time, in full space. It isn't visual geometry; you can't measure and divide it up in a nice, 'inches and feet' way. It's a combination of points in space, but also an interior space, too, which become somewhat tied together."

No commercial recordings exist of Audium performances. You have to show up, and you'd better make it Friday or Saturday nights at 8:30 p.m., the only time the Audium is open.

**Audium
1616 Bush Street
(415) 771-1616**

• • • • • • • • • • • • • • • • • • • • • • • • • • • • • • • • • • • • • • • • •

The Lower Haight neighborhood sports an exciting melange of black families, white-kid yuppies, junkie fools, and co-dependent dogs lashed to parking meters, staring balefully into cafes. Sooner or later, all of them will stroll into the culture off-ramp known as Naked Eye News & Video, including the dogs. An overhead monitor will be screening either a noisy Hong Kong action movie, or a live clip of Iggy Pop, rolling around in broken glass. Customers will invariably linger longer than necessary, soaking up the mad selection of videos, comics, foreign newspapers, mainstream mags, and tiny poetry zines. And then the staff will change the video to an Italian scream-queen getting disemboweled.

Riding herd over this storehouse of crazy information is owner Steve Chack, who moved from Connecticut to San Francisco in 1967 ("Why did *anybody* move to the city in

Photo: Paul Trapani

# Yuppie Poop

**W**hat the hell is fake dog poop doing in the middle of the Marina District, amidst the Thai chicken wraps and the $2,000 baby strollers? Well, because there's a demand, says the manager of House of Magic.

This store is the last of an era, the old-fashioned novelty shop, where walls and shelves are crammed with silly wigs, costumes, cheesy magic tricks, fake poop and vomit, phony boobs and bellies, and latex masks of disgraced politicians. Open since 1967, the store's employees are the same kids who once poked around the shelves in junior high school.

"We never got over the stupid shit," smiles Tony, the manager.

Tony says wigs are very popular items, because people going out to a party often need an instant costume. The older customers gravitate to things like the golf gags, but surprisingly, the younger Gap/Banana Republic yuppies are quite taken with the phony dog poop. The store has had to order more poop to keep up with the demand.

House of Magic also attracts old-school magic and ventriloquist fans, who purchase their collectibles by appointment only. But there's not much demand for items related to hypnotism — it's apparently illegal to hypnotize people for entertainment in California. The store has undergone one major change — it doesn't sell toy guns anymore. Not long ago a customer bought a gun from them, then promptly walked next door to the bank and robbed it.

Tony shakes his head. "The place was filled with FBI people."

**House of Magic**
**2025 Chestnut Street**
**(415) 346-2218**

# ······ Weirdo Info

1967?"), and watched way too many videos. His friends opened the Naked Eye store in 1987, and Chack took over the tiny storefront a few years later. With 8,000 videos, hundreds of magazines comics, and fringe zines, all the weirdo info will occasionally attract strange customers. A homeless bum dressed as a cowboy once came into the store, and when the clerk's back was turned, shoplifted a single magazine — the zine called *Pathetic Life*.

People who rent a video should look closely at their receipt. Another bonus of Naked Eye are the overeducated clerks, who have gone into the computer system and added funny little messages to the video database. Instead of the film title *Dumb and Dumber*, for instance, the receipt prints out the phrase "This Film & Its Fans."

**Naked Eye News & Video**
**533 Haight Street**
**(415) 864-2985**

# Kitsch Fit

**M**arket Street commuters glimpse the TV monitors from across the street, playing video clips of 1960s cereal commercials and Jackie O's tour of the White House. Brightly lit windows act as stained-glass icons to the secret church of the anal-retentive collector — Partridge Family lunch boxes, Pee-Wee Herman dolls, punching nuns, Oscar Meyer wiener-mobiles, Betty Boop and Bob's Big Boy statues, Lesbian Barbie, Pope condoms. If you dare to enter this store jammed to the ceiling with American schlock detritus, the effect is like being swallowed by your childhood TV set.

Owner/manager David Sinkler says kitsch is definitely indigenous to the Midwest. He grew up in Cleveland, where his parents filled the house with collectibles. After his hometown buddies all opened kitsch stores around the country — Uncle Fun in Chicago, Sister Fun in Minneapolis, and Big Fun in Cleveland — he opened San Francisco's Uncle Mame in 1994. But he travels frequently back to the Heartland to buy more stock for the store.

"People have bigger houses. They don't throw things away. Everybody had attics, and everybody had parents."

He sees a wide variety of buyers, with many tourists from Germany and Japan, but customers are usually in their 20s, curious about things they didn't grow up with. Given the fickle kitsch barometer, it's impossible to gauge exactly what the public might crave from week to week, but Sinkler is seeing a trend away from T-shirts, much like the idea of buttons has dropped off since the 1980s. Magnets and keychains remain extremely popular, especially among kids 12 to 17, who like to walk around with 20 keychains hanging from their backpacks.

So what kind of freak packrats are attracted to this stuff? Are they kindred spirits to hardcore collectors like 19th-century madman Sir Thomas Phillipps, who allowed his wife and daughters to live in squalor while he pursued his goal of owning one copy of every book in the world? Perhaps the affliction is psychological. According to retired psychoanalyst Werner Muensterberger, author of *Collecting: An Unruly Passion*, "Possessiveness, when it appears as a symptom, is always a secondary phenomenon, implying anxiety."

The only anxious people at Uncle Mame, however, are usually married men standing outside the store, waiting for their wives to finish shopping.

**Uncle Mame**
**2241 Market Street**
**(415) 626-1953**

"The overwhelming amount of visual items is scary," says Sinkler. "It's just too much for them!"

# Spellbound

Walking through the hip-n-trendy Mission District, it's impossible to overlook the Botanica Yoruba store on Valencia, which emits wafts of incense out onto the sidewalk. To the uninformed, it seems to be some sort of bizarre voodoo shop, but reasonable minds know better. Let's take the words one at a time.

*Botanica* is American Spanish, from the Spanish *botánico*, and refers to any shop that deals in herbs and charms, used especially by adherents of Santería. *Yoruba* is the African people of southwest Nigeria, numbering about 13 million, unusual among Africans in their tendency to form urban communities. Yorubans brought their Santería religion to Cuba when they were imported as slaves, and their beliefs eventually drifted to the United States. An estimated 1 million Americans now practice some form of Santería, which blends African deities (orishas) with Roman Catholic saints. Reincarnation is a major part of Santería, as is the sacrifice of animals, which the Supreme Court ruled in 1993 to be a constitutional religious practice.

Armed with this knowledge, it's easy to explain the statues inside the front door of the store, which are set up as shrines, with burning candles and pieces of cake sitting at their feet. Now it all makes sense — the shelves of votive candles, oils, bath salts, and bars of soap, all of which contain special powers to resolve life's bigger problems. According to these products, we all apparently could use some help in these five categories:

1) breaking up with someone;
2) getting together/falling in love with someone;
3) winning the lottery/bingo;
4) getting rid of evil; and
5) dominating another person.

More complex rituals take place behind a curtain in the back room, decorated with an altar and more burning incense. Common sense says you'd best not start bad-mouthing the validity of items in the store, or you'll walk out the door, and suddenly a sharp stabbing pain in your kidneys will make one side of your body go limp, and within a week you'll be in a hospital bed, sucking nutrients through a tube, with a team of doctors standing over you, shaking their heads.

If you need any help, just ask Pete or Yolanda Rivera. And yes, they take American Express.

Botanica Yoruba
998 Valencia Street
(415) 826-4967

# Freaky Funnies

I t wasn't so long ago that San Francisco and underground comics were synonymous. You couldn't leave your apartment without stepping over an underground cartoonist. At the same time hippies moved to the Bay Area in search of whatever, weirdo introverted artists also showed up, and started drawing strange new hybrids of a treasured American art form — graphic and funny depictions of drugs, sex and general debauchery that were simply too sick and wrong for the Sunday newspapers. Faced with no method of distribution, R. Crumb actually sold his comics on Haight Street out of a baby stroller. Several underground publishers started up in the Bay Area, and

via a network of head shops and music stores, comics were able to properly infect America's youth. The industry has since split up into several other companies around the country, but one hippie comics outpost remains — Last Gasp, which sports the slogan "Brain candy for the masses since April Fool's Day 1970."

From a warehouse in the Mission District, Last Gasp's distribution system circulates titles from over 500 different sources, including 2,000 comics, as well as graphic novels, magazines, marijuana cultivation guides, and all types of fetish, beatnik, hippie, occult, and conspiracy topics. The publishing arm of Last Gasp has produced over 500 titles, from *Zap* and *Weirdo* comics, to books by Robert Williams, Winston Smith, and Frank Kozik, on up to a Leonardo DiCaprio calendar, which shipped 200,000 copies.

Presided over by bearded, ponytailed Ron Turner, a hybrid of Santa Claus, ZZ Top, and Rip Van Winkle, Last Gasp acts as catalyst for San Francisco's freak culture, and throws legendary Christmas parties right in the warehouse.

Ironically, Last Gasp's first huge best-seller was comparatively mainstream — a history of the squeaky-clean TV pop band The Monkees. But most recently, the company found itself involved in a controversy on Capitol Hill over a humorous art book it published by well-known lesbian activist Tee Corinne, *The Cunt Coloring Book*. During a sweep of the San Francisco Public Library's James C. Hormel Gay and Lesbian Center, the Traditional Values Coalition discovered Corinne's book and sent it around the U.S. Senate. Their reason was not to titillate congressmen or convince women to turn lesbian. The conservative Christian watchdog group hoped to stop the appointment of James Hormel as ambassador to Luxembourg. Heir to the Hormel meat fortune, Hormel himself is gay, and because of his $500,000 donation to the library center, it was named for him. Senators apparently examined *The Cunt Coloring Book*, with its pages of female genitalia, and decided not to confirm the appointment of Hormel.

Last Gasp claims the Christian group did not purchase the book, but simply made copies of it, and this was, technically, copyright infringement.

"We considered sending the senators pink crayons," smiles Turner, "so at least they could have fun in their theft."

Last Gasp
P.O. Box 410067
San Francisco, CA 94141-0067
(415) 824-6636

# Panther Power

I f anything terrified America's white power structure of the late 1960s, it was the televised image of black men marching on the state capitol in Sacramento, wearing black leather jackets, black berets, and carrying shotguns. This was a serious wake-up call, from Oakland to the world. And along with everything else, they had a really cool logo.

Huey Newton and Bobby Seale first met as students at the Old Merritt Junior College campus. In 1967 they opened their first office at what is now 5624 Martin Luther King Jr. Way, declared the formation of the Black Panther Party for Self-Defense, and forged a Ten Point Program manifesto, which listed self-determination, demands for full employment, reparations for slavery, and decent housing and education. In 1969 the party began a free pancake breakfast program for Oakland schoolchildren. The Panthers concept quickly gained notoriety, not the least because of the founders' appeal. Seale was witty, and had been a stand-up comic. Newton was the handsome intellectual street fighter, who wrote essays about the meaning of Bob Dylan. Eldridge Cleaver authored the best-selling *Soul on Ice.* They studied revolutionary politics, and could quote from Mao Tse Tung and Malcolm X. According to David Hilliard, longtime Panthers chief of staff, the first members were sons of immigrants from the rural South, who were accustomed to dealing with white rural Southerners. When the Panthers encountered the Oakland police force, many of whom came from white rural backgrounds, it was déjà vu all over again.

By 1970, the FBI considered the Panthers Public Enemy Number One, and infiltrated the Party in order to crush it. Midnight raids were conducted, gunfire erupted, bodies turned up, friends sided against friends, and like everything else in the 1960s, the hope started to unravel. Bobby Seale and Elmer "Geronimo" Pratt were thrown in prison. Eldridge Cleaver appeared in *Rolling Stone* magazine, marketing a line of men's slacks with a built-in codpiece. The Panthers fell out of the public eye, and in 1989, Huey Newton was shot dead by an Oakland crack dealer. One irony of the Newton slaying: In court, the killer admitted that when he was a kid, he used to eat at Panthers breakfasts.

Today, members of the Black Panther Party remain visible in local and national politics. Historical tours of Panther sites in and around Oakland run on the last Saturday of every month.

Black Panther Legacy Tours
c/o Dr. Huey Newton Foundation
(510) 986-0660

# Skin to

**D**rop by any freaky sex event held in the city, and chances are the people in attendance are going to be internationally known practitioners of their craft, whether it's penis and clitoral piercings, or decorative designs cut into the flesh. The Bay Area sexual underground is by all accounts the strangest and most experimental in the country, and at one time or another, nearly all of these people have been photographed by Charles Gatewood.

Photo: Charles Gatewood

Through his Flash Productions, Gatewood claims to be the world's largest producer of tattoo and piercing documentary videos. Originally from Missouri, he studied anthropology, then worked for magazines like *Rolling Stone*, shooting portraits of Rod Stewart and William S. Burroughs. He provided an image for a popular Bob Dylan poster, and won a Leica award for a photo essay book on Wall Street. But mainstream work wasn't enough to hold his interest.

Gatewood started visiting the hot zones of America's freak culture, shooting bizarre, tweaked-out human behavior, whether it was seedy alcoholic bars, S/M clubs, tattoo conventions, or drunken transvestites stumbling down the streets at Mardi Gras. In 1988 he moved to San Francisco to document the city's underground, and what he calls "radical sex pagans." Since that time he's published several glossy photography books, and shot dozens of specialty videos, depicting everything from Bangkok piercing rituals to outlaw biker rallies, Satanic blood cuttings, and naked girls rubbing food all over themselves. His notorious portrait of a tattooed fetus still raises heartbeats of those viewing it for the first time.

The 1985 anthropological documentary *Dances Sacred and Profane* examined Gatewood's peculiar career, following him from photo shoots to art gallery lectures, and included one unsettling moment where he attempted to lie naked on a bed of nails. The following year, many of his tattoo and piercing photos appeared in the excellent *Modern Primitives* by North Beach publisher Re/Search, a book which has since become an underground classic.

Besides Gatewood, the other principal subject of both the film and the Re/Search book was an unusual and eccentric Bay Area man named Fakir Musafar. Known as the "Father of the Modern Primitive Movement," Musafar has devoted his life to studying primitive rituals and manipulating his own body.

Born in 1930 in South Dakota, Musafar began his studies early, piercing his own penis at 13, and inventing all sorts of ways to separate his consciousness from his body. But fearing nobody would understand, he kept it all secret. For years he lived a

# Win

normal life in a variety of fields, working as a demolition instructor, ballroom dancing teacher, and Silicon Valley advertising executive. All this time he continued to push his body to the extreme, from attaching clothespins to his skin, to hanging weights from his penis, wearing corsets to constrict his waist, and sticking daggers through his chest.

His first public appearance occurred in 1970, when he lay on a bed of swords for an astonished crowd at San Francisco's Ripley's Believe It or Not museum. Eight years later, he unveiled the Fakir Musafar persona at a Reno tattoo convention, taking the name from a 19th-century Sufi who stuck daggers and other things into his body. Musafar believes himself responsible for coining the "Modern Primitives" phrase, with the idea in mind of a non-tribal person who responds to primal urges and then does something with the body, in an expression of pleasure with insight.

Hardcore primitives know full well the Musafar story, but for those who might have heard a little about him, the one image that most sticks in people's brains is Gatewood's famous photo of

Photo: Charles Gatewood

Musafar re-creating the O-Kee-Pa Indian Sun Dance ceremony (first exposed to Americans via the Richard Harris film *A Man Called Horse*). Accompanied by Gatewood and *Sacred and Profane* co-directors Mark and Dan Jury, Musafar visited an isolated field in Wyoming, and with the help of a friend, hung from a tree by flesh hooks imbedded into his chest.

Musafar's company Insight Books has published *Body Play & Modern Primitives Quarterly* magazine since 1991, filling its pages with photos of "unusual people doing unusual things with their body." Body manipulation methods he helped develop are now the industry standard for safety, reliability, and eroticism. He continues teaching Fakir Body Piercing and Branding Intensives, the only courses of their kind in the world, which are licensed by the state of California. In between everything else, he lectures at colleges, and offers shamanic body rituals for individuals and groups.

So if you drop into a strange sex community performance in the Bay Area, chances are that Charles Gatewood will be sitting at the edge of the stage, camera in hand. And if it's a special occasion, Fakir Musafar may be on stage or in the crowd, wearing daggers in his chest, and a quill stuck through his nose.

# Get With the

"**W**hat if your future was a function of your creation, rather than an extension of your past?"

"What if you were committed more often and upset less?"

What if you paid hundreds of dollars for the privilege of attending weekend seminars that told you advice like the above? Don't laugh too hard. Thousands of people did, giving their money to San Francisco's Werner Erhard, father of the world's most successful and controversial New Age human potential programs. His original company, Erhard Seminars Training (est), ended in 1984, but another incarnation of his philosophies is still based here in the city, the Landmark Education Corporation.

Erhard's rise to fame began as most self-made careers start — as a product of frustration and grandiose self-worth. As the accepted media legend goes, he was born Jack Rosenberg, and lived in Philadelphia, selling encyclopedias and used cars, until one day he couldn't take it anymore. He ditched his family and bought a plane ticket to the West Coast. While on the flight, he thought up a new name for himself, choosing it out of a magazine article on West Germany. He found work in the Bay Area, and one day in 1971, while driving over the Golden Gate Bridge, he had a flash of epiphany — a series of workshops that taught people how to be more themselves and fulfill their lives. And also make Erhard some good money.

"**What if your future was a function of your creation, rather than an extension of your past?**"

The result was est, an amalgamation of Zen Buddhism, Scientology, psychotherapy, and self-motivation. Erhard watched his idea of "getting it" catch on beyond his wildest prediction. At its height, between 1971 and 1984, est classes were taught in 20 U.S. cities, signing on 50,000 new customers a year, including celebrities like John Denver, Valerie Harper, and Diana Ross. Outsiders called the enthusiastic, sparkly-eyed students "est-holes." Similar programs like Lifespring started up in its wake.

The est phenomenon quickly became another classic aspect of the 1970s Me Generation. Workshop students were not allowed to leave the room for bathroom breaks. Friends and spouses pestered those closest to them to find the money and go through the program immediately. Some businesses required their employees to take est training. People who grew up in the Bay Area remember attending "kiddie est," where dozens of small children would be gathered in a big hotel ballroom, while their parents went to est meetings upstairs.

In the 1980s, est techniques were repackaged for corporate clients, and the name was changed to The Forum.

"I am difficult to understand," Erhard told a reporter in 1988. "But I

# Program

know how to talk. I can talk like you're supposed to talk if what you want to do is to be understood. But I don't care about being understood when I'm working. I care about giving people access to

## "What if you were committed more often and upset less?"

the thing that concerns them, and not explanations or descriptive access but action access, being access."

A few years later, Erhard's life began to implode. His daughter appeared on *60 Minutes* in 1991, and accused her father of sexually molesting her, raping her sister, and choking her mother. The IRS filed over $21 million in liens against him and est. A former personal aide to Erhard declared in court that he was to kneel at the foot of Erhard's bed each morning, put his hands under the covers, and massage his employer's feet and calves. One woman, claiming Erhard's organizations turned her fiancé into a robot, started a nonprofit group devoted to providing unflattering information about him.

According to a British newspaper, Erhard sold his business for $250,000, when it was supposedly valued at $45 million. Landmark's literature says Erhard licensed his est/Forum "technology" to his former employees in 1991, who launched the Landmark

**BREAKTHROUGHS:** If we knew how to produce breakthroughs, then they would no longer be breakthroughs. Instead, what we produced would be an extension of something we knew from the past and have applied to the future. The nature of breakthroughs is that they don't fit in the past. If a breakthrough cannot be produced by knowing how, how does it happen?

company. He then left the country, and has not been publicly heard from since.

Landmark claims 44 offices worldwide, teaching courses primarily to corporate clients. Tuition ranges from the $325 basic Forum, on up to the $1,700 Wisdom Program. Erhard has no management or ownership role in Landmark, but his brother Harry Rosenberg is on the board of directors.

Landmark Forum
353 Sacramento Street #200
(415) 981-8850

# California Anti-Cuisine

E ach year tourists come to California and find themselves sitting eagerly in some fancy-pants restaurant, ogling the nouveau cuisine menus, salivating at the presentation on the plates and mentally counting exactly how much money do the kids really need to go to college, and maybe it's really worth it to blow all of the nest egg on this, the absolute last word in dining experiences. Nowhere is this trend more apparent than in the Bay Area, where the idea of California cuisine originated at Berkeley's Chez Panisse, and has spread to many other pretentious up and coming contenders. We now live in a world where newspapers and magazines give continual Abyssinian tongue baths to all the local chefs, and critics yammer on about unnecessary flavor collisions like roasted-fennel-pine-nut-squash-radicchio-caper-flan appetizers with honey-gorgonzola mayonnaise. Meanwhile, the rest of the population has a sandwich and life goes on. Normal people don't eat like this, unless you start turning tricks on the corner. Fortunately, there are other alternatives — strange, forgotten or peculiar hellhole chowhouses you have to see to believe. While you may recoil in horror at the scummy neighborhoods or sleazy customers, you must admit: they're all pretty weird.

# Sixth Street Treat

For years, Sixth Street between Market and Mission streets has been the absolute worst strip of civic blight in the city. You may be a stone's throw from City Hall, but you're also one block from pawn shops, donut emporiums, dingy bars, tattoo parlors, strip joints, and guys who deal drugs out of their artificial limbs. Pedestrians along this stretch must prepare to walk a horrendous gauntlet of homeless bums and babbling SSI drunks with bloodied heads.

But don't let this stop you from enjoying a terrific meal.

Whether you're looking for lunch, or, if you're really feeling adventurous, a meal after sunset, Tu Lan is one of the best Vietnamese places in town, and always crowded. How they keep it so excellent is baffling, considering the location. Over the years, I personally have witnessed:

1) A 2-inch-long cockroach scuttle up the wall behind a table of diners;

2) A homeless guy wander in the doorway, lean against the frame, whip out his johnson, and begin peeing right there on the floor;

3) A homeless guy walk in with scabbed legs, talking to himself and carrying a 6-foot length of tow chain around his neck.

Watching the Tu Lan staff deal with such dregs of the human race is part of the fun, because they have to encounter weirdness every single day. They never get mad, they just patiently and politely usher the bad element back out onto the street. The food gets rave reviews, especially the spring rolls. Just don't park your car within three blocks of this place.

Photo: Paul Trapani

Tu Lan
8 Sixth Street
(415) 626-0927

# Club-Kid Chow

E ach weekend come 3 a.m., a line slithers out the door of this 24-hour Church Street diner. Not just any line of hungry patrons, but an undignified menagerie of tweaked-out ravers, overdressed club kids flush with disappointment, off-duty strippers, tuckered-out prostitutes, and bar drunks under the delusion that a late-night steak and eggs dinner is the quick path to sobriety. Forget about visiting during normal-human-being daylight hours. Plan to stop in sometime between 3 to 6 a.m., because you'll want to be in the vortex, the ideal time to witness Sparky's in full plumage.

David Bowie's "Diamond Dogs" is blasting so loud, you can barely hear your waitress shouting the specials. Or is that because you're just too plumb wasted? Boy, those fluorescent lights are bright. There's an awful lot of club flyers on the counter. Does every single person have slitted eyes? Hey, does that Goth girl really have a live rat nesting in her hair? Are those handcuffs hanging off the hips of a 14-year-old boy? Are these actually French fries? Is the food the best in the city? Or is it the worst? Does it really matter? You're messed up, and it's still open.

**Sparky's**
**242 Church Street**
**(415) 621-6001**

# Basket of Brisket

E very neighborhood has its barbecue joints, but you can't beat Brother's for atmosphere. There are exactly two tables in this place, so don't think about having a seat, just come on down, get it, and get out. The parking lot is often full of folks sitting in their car enjoying a fine order of short ribs, or on a nice day, hanging

out in the sunshine, eating it off the hood. A few guys might be standing around, brown-bagging an afternoon cocktail. The staff occasionally turns up the soul station and dances to Barry White's "Never Gonna Give You Up." Many places will post awards and notices behind the counter. Brother's displays only one — a thank-you letter for catering an office party from the local AAA office.

When that brick oven starts doing its thing in the early afternoon, sending the aroma of grilled meat up and down Divisadero, the whole neighborhood knows it's just about time to get something to eat.

**Brother-In-Laws**
**705 Divisadero Street**
**(415) 771-8929**

# Send in the Chefs

**B**ecause of Clown Alley's proximity to law firms and the Financial District, jokes have circulated for years that the ideal lunch spot for San Francisco's lawyers and bankers would have to be a circus-themed establishment. Barrister Melvin Belli, who worked down the block, proudly admitted he ate here regularly.

The bizarre clown motif apparently began with the restaurant's original owner, Enrico Banducci, the North Beach raconteur also responsible for many nightspots, including the venerable Enrico's restaurant, which still bears his name. The story goes that Banducci named Clown Alley after the under-the-grandstands area where circus clowns gather before entering the ring. Banducci sold the place to a man named Al Pailhe, who eventually passed it down to his son Bill. For the next 35 years Bill Pailhe ran Clown Alley, building up a local clientele who enjoyed the good greasy burgers and garish menus with wacky astrology predictions. Claiming he was tired of doing it every day, he finally closed it up in March of 1996.

Others were determined to give it a shot. The location relaunched as Sophie's Cookhouse, then Spaghetteria, then it sat vacant again. Locals mourned the old days, as everybody seems to do in San Francisco, and every time Pailhe dropped by the neighborhood, the old customers would harass him, pining for the glory days of the beloved Clown Burgers and shakes. In the fall of 1998, Pailhe threw up his hands and reopened Clown Alley. Same address, new sign.

THE ORIGINAL
CLOWN ALLEY
NORTH BEACH

Clown Alley
42 Columbus Avenue
(415) 421-2540

# Island Feast

If you're looking to find a great bowl of poi, the last place you'd expect to go is the outer Sunset District. Rows and rows of drab identical housing shrouded in fog does not necessarily scream "tropical party on the beach!" And yet this strip along Judah Street is the focal point for Hawai'ian culture in San Francisco — the Punahele Island Grill, and across the street, the Hawai'i Store.

The Grill's menu is pretty standard, and decor is minimal South Sea Island motif, but you're not expecting to find hula dancers or a roast pig luau. It's the entertainment you're after here. A stage with loudspeakers indicates a possible karaoke scene on the weekends, but the waitress says it was slowing down, so now they just play videos. This is actually fortuitous, because it means your meal will be serenaded by loud concert footage of the late 400-pound ukulele player Israel Kamakawiwo'ole in concert. (His uke is dwarfed by his substantial heft, but Israel definitely belts it out with a lot of soul, and when he finishes, the restaurant echoes with the video's applause.) No foo-foo drinks with umbrellas. Beer and hi-balls are self-serve, available from the adjoining bar.

Stroll directly across the street to the Hawai'i Store, where you can pick up pretty much anything Hawai'ian you can imagine — frozen meat, coconut bras, cookbooks, perfumes, tiki torches, monkey pod bowls, Kona coffee, or the exact pattern of Hawai'ian shirt worn by Tom "Magnum P.I." Selleck.

**Punahele Island Grill**
**2650 Judah Street**
**(415) 759-8276**

# Burger and a Beer

The food's slightly better at the Java Hut just down the street, but let's be honest. If you're looking for fine cuisine along this stretch, there's something wrong with you in the first place. Red's Java House is worth a stop for their classic lunch special — a cheeseburger and a Bud in a bottle for three bucks. Named for its previous owner, an Irish boxing manager called "Red," this Epicurean emporium also serves donuts in the morning, with plenty of napkins. A coffee roasting machine sits in one corner, which may or may not be operational. Nobody's ever seen it turned on. Customers range from construction workers to cell-phone yuppies. If the weather's nice, everyone sits outside and guzzles their Buds, pestered by seagulls, while health nuts jog past on their lunch hour.

**Red's Java House**
**Embarcadero at Brannan Street**
**no phone**

# Gunplay and Porridge

**N**othing particularly special about this basic Chinatown restaurant, where white people go to claim an authentic Chinese cuisine experience. But in 1977, there was another item on the menu — gunfire.

In the early morning hours of September 4th, the entire place was shot up in a gang turf war. Three members of the Joe Boys gang, wearing ski masks, entered the crowded restaurant in search of the rival Wah Ching gang, who regularly hung out at the Golden Dragon. Realizing the situation, the Wah Ching guys hit the floor and pulled tables over their heads, so that when the Joe Boys opened fire, they only hit bystanders. Five people were mowed down, right in the middle of their mu shu pork, and 11 more were injured.

Many in Chinatown were enraged that two off-duty policemen were eating in the restaurant at the time, and when the shooting erupted, they did nothing but hide under tables.

A former Joe Boys member told a reporter the shooting didn't target anybody in particular, but was done as a warning to the Wah Ching and their ally, the Hop Sing Boys.

One of the Golden Dragon waiters who still works there was an eyewitness; he remembers everyone freaking out as the three gunmen fired at will into the crowded room.

"I laid down on the floor!" he says today.

Do people still ask him about it? "Too many! That was a long time ago!" He adds that all three kids were sent to prison.

The Golden Dragon is said to specialize in roast duck and Chinese porridge.

Golden Dragon
816 Washington Street
(415) 398-3920

# Enter Through the Kitchen

**S** tanding at the narrow entrance to Sam Woh, on a steep street in the heart of Chinatown, you might think you're stepping into a time warp. Guests must enter through the kitchen, where the crew hacks with cleavers at vegetables and pieces of fish. An old man hunches over a gargantuan bowl of rice, steam billowing up into his impassive face. Stairs ascend to one side, taking you up three stories of small tables and little wooden stools. An actual functioning dumbwaiter hoists up plates of food from the kitchen to the brightly lit floors.

In the 1950s, the beats came here after their poetry readings in North Beach. So the story goes, Gary Snyder taught Jack Kerouac how to use chopsticks here, and they were both thrown out for causing a disturbance. Another legend has it that one night in the 1970s, Robin Williams and Andy Kaufman acted up for the crowd. But the best reason to remember Sam Woh is the late Edsel Fong.

For decades, Fong held unofficial status as the rudest waiter in San Francisco, snapping at customers and correcting their orders as he saw fit. He was fond of forcing you to write down not only your own order, but the orders of the table next to you. Despite this treatment, he was actually just having fun, and people loved him. One entire wall was covered with Polaroid photos of Fong smiling with beautiful young female customers.

I once had the experience of attempting to read a book while having lunch at Sam Woh. Fong snatched the book out of my hands (Henry Miller's *Quiet Days in Clichy* — what can I say, I was young), said, "You don't want to read that," and slammed down a black three-ring binder: "Read this." It was his personal scrapbook, full of his many newspaper blurbs, and acting contracts for bit parts in Hollywood — most of which seemed to be in Chuck Norris movies. And then he slipped me a free egg roll.

After Fong's death from cancer a few years ago, the Sam Woh waiters tried to keep up the rudeness, but it wasn't the same, so they went back to being indifferent. The food never was very good, but it's open until 3 a.m., and they don't mind you bringing in booze. Up on a wall a single photo remains of Edsel Fong, the happiest, rudest man in the city.

Sam Woh
813 Washington Street
(415) 982-0596

# Dinner With Dick Cavett

This Chinatown restaurant is located upstairs from the street level. An elevator opens onto a black-and-white marble floor, with three different dining rooms, arranged around a big wooden pagoda. It is here that you can spend lots of money, look out the windows, and enjoy the very same view shared by Erik Estrada.

In fact, unless you've recently sold shares of a profitable high-tech firm, there's no reason to ever eat here. You don't even need to ascend the elevator. Just visit the lobby level, because the walls are filled with the oddest assortment of color 8x10 celebrities. We're talking famous glamour-pusses from that peculiar *Hollywood Squares*-level of notoriety, most from the 1950s through the 1970s:

Rick Barry (twice), topless queen Carol Doda, Jayne Mansfield spilling out of her dress, Sammy Davis, Jr., Jack Palance, Karl Malden, Jackie Chan, Erik Estrada, Lana Turner, Vincent Price, Englebert Humperdinck, Nancy Kerrigan, Mick Jagger, a scarily face-lifted Barbi Benton, Dick Cavett, and Dennis Weaver.

EMPRESS OF CHINA
ROOF GARDEN RESTAURANT

The best photo is posted at the doorway off the street. Offering that familiar Ollie-North-pardoning, this-will-not-stand, read-my-lips grimace is a framed color shot of President George Bush, and underneath it reads "Manager Jimmy Wong served Crispy Chick and Butterfly Prawns for His Pleasure."

Empress of China
838 Grant Avenue
(415) 434-1345

# Canine Shrine

**A**fter parents take their children to the San Francisco Zoo, visiting the screeching monkeys and lethargic jungle cats, the little tykes are bound to be whining about food. Something must quickly be stuffed down their gullets. In years past, families would head straight across the street from the zoo to the old Doggie Diner. The cuisine never was much to speak of, other than your basic burgers and fries, but dangling above the building is an icon of immeasurable local importance — the very last surviving dog head from the old Doggie Diner chain.

Beginning in the 1940s with one lone outpost, Doggie Diner grew into a proud and bustling syndicate of 30 all-night diners throughout the Bay Area, offering gut-bomb burgers, sausages, and chili dogs. But the changing climates of real estate and political correctness are not kind to America's greasy spoons, and eventually the Doggie Diner empire dwindled down to this lone hound with a hat, most recently known as the Carousel Diner. What once beckoned weary travelers and hungry drunks is now a final, forgotten signpost for a long reign of heartburn and indigestion.

As the diners closed up, their doggie heads disappeared. Many of the heads were confiscated by art pranksters, but the Carousel's example is the only canine head still standing. It has even been designated an official city landmark. When children ask about the doggie, adults simply gaze up at it in silence. You could attempt to explain its history and underlying significance, but the kids wouldn't understand. How could they?

**Carousel Diner**
**2750 Sloat Boulevard**
**(415) 564-6052**

# Weight-Watching in Westlake

In recent years, America has grown fond of farming its own history for entertainment. Each generation of youth will stumble upon elements of pop culture and snicker over their latest archeological dig, whether it's cigars, tiki drinks, polyester bell-bottoms, or Herb Alpert records. If meat-and-potatoes cuisine ever makes a comeback — and who's to say it won't — you'll be able to trace the trail all the way back to the source at Joe's of Westlake, a 1950s-era structure tucked down the peninsula in Daly City, just off the Great Highway.

Although they would be welcome, you won't see irony-soaked kitsch kids in this place. You will see lots of good American folks young and old, parked behind Herculean plates of food, celebrating the timeless rituals of birthdays, weddings, anniversaries, divorces, and ongoing marital affairs. Stocky, 50-something waiters navigate the crowded dining rooms like they were once star fullbacks in high school, and they probably were.

Joe's is a big plus for Weight Watchers rejects — nearly everyone here is pushing the scales with an extra 20 or so. And booze is definitely spoken here. The accepted ritual is to have a few stiff belts at the bar until your table is called. The black-vinyl lounge, with piano bar and fireplace, looks like the set from an episode of a 1970s cop show. At any moment Mannix could slide onto a stool and chat up a hooker, looking for some answers.

A live lounge act entertains Wednesdays through Sundays, and the dining room serves until midnight. It's never too late to turn back the clock and eat a piece of meat the size of your head. And when you're done, you can waddle out into the expansive parking lot, turn around for another look at that beautiful Joe's sign, and slap your big American gut. Welcome home, brother.

Joe's of Westlake
John Daly Boulevard at Lake Merced, Daly City
(650) 755-7400

# Cheap Meat

**A**long the tourist-choked strip of Powell Street off Union Square, next to the overpriced electronics stores and questionable luggage shops, one business stands out from the others. Its gaudy blinking light bulbs suggest a strip joint or casino, but in fact it's a restaurant. In the window, chunks of glistening animal flesh rotate under a heat lamp. If you're a carnivore on a budget, you've just found your Holy Grail. This is the cheapest steak dinner in San Francisco. This is Tad's, part of a national chain of Tad's, all across this great meat-eating land.

Slide your plastic tray along the aluminum shelf, and tell the nice folks behind the counter what you want. As they fling your order on the grill, notice that the decor is 1880s whorehouse, with red velvet wallpaper, askew chandeliers, and those mirrored tiles that can really "open up" the room. Every table comes stocked with a myriad of steak sauces and other bottled flavor enhancers. Pay the man, shut up, and sit down.

The meat is always gristly, but keep in mind that complimentary potato and iceberg lettuce salad. As your eyes roam the room filled with fellow steak-lovers, and you sip your Miller Genuine, you observe that most people are either eating alone, or with their plump, pale-skinned tourist families. A complete steak dinner for eight bucks. Repeat this to yourself, over and over.

Tad's
120 Powell Street
(415) 982-1718

# Tequila on the Brain

From the street, Tommy's looks to be your average Mexican restaurant. It's been around since 1965. Tortilla chips are cooking in the window. The menu stars your basic Mexican ingredients, rearranged in various combinations. And some people do stop here for the food. But most come for the tequila tasting bar. This isn't just the best collection of tequila in town, this is the largest selection of 100 percent agave tequila outside Mexico. This is Tequila Geekland.

Fetishists all know the story. The blue agave plant grows exclusively in the rich volcanic ashen soil of Mexico's highlands. After the plant reaches 150 pounds (about eight to 12 years), workers hack off the spikes, and toss the pineapple-shaped piñas into a

stone oven for a couple of days. The baked piñas are then crushed, sugars are separated from the fibers, and yeast is added to the sugars to produce a mash. This brown mash gets distilled into tequila, which is set aside to age in tanks or barrels. One hundred percent agave means this tequila is top of the line, and is not blended or mixed with any other tequila or demineralized water. In order to be labeled Reposado, a tequila must rest "in repose" between two and six months in wood, under government seal. This 100 percent agave squeezings tastes very smooth, and unlike rotgut tequila, won't turn your throat into a scalding hot steam pipe. But you do get crazy drunk.

Tommy, the owner, isn't stupid. Each year he makes trips to his homeland and brings back the best tequilas in the world for his restaurant. His tasting

# Home Fries & Baby Bottles

Once a couple of gay bars, The Dead End and The Cissy, this South of Market space was converted to a restaurant in 1972. But it's not just any chowhouse. For almost 30 years, Hamburger Mary's has stuck to its winning formula — home-style food cooked to order, home fries that make you weep, cream for coffee dispensed from baby bottles, and just to make it even more festive, a full bar and pinball machines. Dinner isn't quite the same after you've been immersed in a nutty atmosphere of loud rock and roll, and antique memorabilia that suggests Norman Rockwell meets Oscar Wilde. The staff has always been gender-bent, and until the 1980s, you could walk in and watch your burger grilled by a topless female chef.

The idea has since expanded to Mary's franchises in Maui, Sacramento, San Diego, San Jose, Portland, Seattle, and Vancouver. Gay guidebooks sniff that Mary's "is no longer predominately gay due to its proximity to 11th Street's 'Breeder Alley,'" but it's still one of the best sloppy burgers in town.

**Hamburger Mary's**
**1582 Folsom Street**
**(415) 626-5767**

Tequila Photos: Jose Cuervo

bar includes several tequilas that are no longer even made, but if you ask nicely, he'll probably have discontinued strains, like Jorongo Reposado, Distinqt Platinum, or the Porfidio Extra Aged Crock Añejo Nom 1007. They even have Chinaco Black Label, the rarest tequila in the world.

If you're a true tequila nerd, plonk down your five bucks and sign up for Tommy's Blue Agave Club, the nation's largest bunch of tequila tasting fanatics. Upon your graduation, you receive an oak-framed Tequila Master Diploma, a booklet and T-shirt, and a ceremony that involves trying half the selection of the bar. Good luck, it's been nice knowing you.

**Tommy's Mexican Restaurant**
**5939 Geary Boulevard**
**(415) 387-4747**

# Ice Cream Therapy

Y ou've just exited the Discolandia record store on 24th Street, your head reeling from high-energy Latin pop tunes. You stand on the sidewalk to consider your next move. Lowriders creep down the street, their stereos thumping through the back-seat mega-speakers. Maybe it's time to relax, unwind from all this chaos. Suddenly the answer comes. Ice cream.

Just down the street sits the St. Francis Fountain, a neighborhood fixture for over 80 years, and reportedly the birthplace of the 49ers football team. Opened way back in 1918 by James Christakes, the business is now operated by his grandson, and from the looks of things, not much has changed. They still make all their own ice cream and candy. The kids still drop by in the afternoons, modern-day Archies and Veronicas hanging out after class for a malt. Parents still bring in their children, who drool openly at the glass-enclosed display of fresh sweets. Old guys still stop and sit in a booth alone, contemplating a sundae before them.

You slide onto a stool and place your order. A girl behind the counter reaches into a beat-up stainless steel case that looks like it fell off a truck and scoops out your ice cream. Everything's going to be okay.

Photo: Sharon Selden

**St. Francis Fountain
2801 24th Street
(415) 826-4200**

# American Buffalo

A popular tourist attraction in Golden Gate Park, the herd of wild bison graze contentedly in their paddock, staring without judgment at the hordes of joggers, rollerbladers, and rental cars full of pointing tourists. Few visitors, however, observe the beasts and stop to think: "I wonder. If one were to pick out the best-looking buffalo, kill it, eviscerate the carcass, cut up the meat, and make a big pot of stew, what would the result taste like?"

Curious carnivores are in luck, because fresh buffalo stew is one of the specialties at Tommy's Joynt, the garishly painted bar/hofbrau on the corner of Van Ness and Geary. One of the few steam table places left in town, Tommy's has been around over 50 years, and dishes out the platters for both tourists and locals. Some slices of meat, a couple of side dishes, a cocktail in a short glass — all you need is a fedora and a pack of Lucky's, and you're either a private eye or a traveling salesman. Although Tommy's is a favorite retreat for the local Cacophony Society art-brat party planners, and rock stars like Metallica and Tom Petty, reservations are not accepted. Everybody has to wait in line.

**Tommy's Joynt
Geary at Van Ness Avenue
(415) 775-4216**

# Magic Mansions

This odd, singular building is the brainchild of advertising eccentric Bob Pritikin, who bought the place in 1977, when it was a run-down rooming house, and set about snazzing it up into a deliberately campy, exaggerated version of a bed-and-breakfast.

Rooms at The Mansions range from $129 to the $350 Presidential Suite, with a deck, two fireplaces, and a wine bar. Bigshot guests have included Barbra Streisand, JFK Jr., John Cleese, Robert De Niro, Carrie Fisher, and Robin Williams, all of whom have no doubt furrowed their brows over the five weird museums accompanying their stay — the Document Museum, with the actual resignation letter signed by Richard Nixon; the Magic Museum, with documents and memorabilia from magicians like Houdini and Blackstone; the Sculpture Museum, which contains works from Beniamino Bufano; the International Pig Museum, with hundreds of paintings and artifacts about pigs; and a Museum of Art and Antiques. The building also features its own ghost — the niece of the original owner, a 19th-century silver baron.

The multi-talented Pritikin doesn't just own the place. In addition to dabbling in interior design, collecting art, performing magic, and writing the book *Jesus Was an Ad Man*, Pritikin has mastered the musical saw, and can rip out renditions of "Moonlight Sawnata" and "The Last Time I Sawed Paris." Dinner is punched up with a live magic or comedy show every night, starring Bob Pritikin. The Mansions' menu is *prix fixe*, but you could be eating burnt cardboard — who cares what it tastes like? You're getting a ghost, a pig museum, *and* a guy who plays the musical saw.

**The Mansions**
**2220 Sacramento Street**
**(415) 929-9444**

# Raw Vegetable Flesh

This strange idea for a restaurant opened in San Francisco in 1995, as Raw, the Living Restaurant. At the tender age of 21, chef/owner Juliano devised a peculiar menu composed entirely of fresh uncooked vegetarian ingredients. Woody Harrelson, Demi Moore, and Robin Williams dropped by to give it some celeb legitimacy, and the nutrition subculture stood up and applauded — finally, raw food lovingly prepared, and just as overpriced as other restaurants! Juliano has now sold the business and moved on, opening other locations in Hawaii and Los Angeles, but the world's first raw restaurant continues under the name Organica.

Photo: Sharon Selden

One first notices the Middle Eastern architecture, framed nature photos, extremely loud classical music, abundant plants, a bulletin board covered in flyers, and patrons sitting in drawstring pants and extremely comfortable shoes. This could be anyplace in Berkeley, really. But then it dawns on you. There are no warm, comforting smells wafting from the kitchen. Organica doesn't have any ovens. Dishes are instead prepared in special dehydrators that don't exceed 105 degrees, after which enzymes apparently break down and the food technically isn't "live" anymore. And that won't do.

The special "living" pizzas are made of a pressed spongy crust of seeds and other mysterious things, on top of which are lumped various vegetables and fruits, with a sauce poured over it all. It's actually really tasty. The ravioli plate arrives as a burst of purples, reds and yellows, also quite tasty. Other typical dishes find their raw equivalents, from burritos to sushi, meat loaf, and angel hair pasta. The staff says their desserts are the most popular orders. About an hour after eating at Organica, your stomach may start to rumble, but this reaction is common, especially if your body is accustomed to the usual fatty, colon-clogging, artery-blocking diets of the rest of America. And if you're already vegetarian, this cuisine is bound to be better than all those damn tofu dishes served up by the other veggie restaurants.

Organica
1224 9th Avenue
(415) 665-6519

# Cosmonaut Cuisine

**T**he collection of creepy porcelain dolls is gone, as is the long bar, but the stocky man with Leonid Brezhnev eyebrows still greets you at the door with a thick Transylvanian/Russian accent: "Goot eeef-ningk!" Out in the avenues of the Richmond, this restaurant is still where Russians can duck in for an upscale meal, and on the weekends, hit the dance floor, accompanied by the one-man band on keyboards and drum machine.

The walls and ceiling are covered with 13th-century murals, depicting scenes from Russian folklore and history. In other words, lots of battles with guys on horseback. Something to look at, as you tear into your order of shashlik (marinated rack of lamb), chicken a la Kiev (boneless chicken breast), okhotnichaya kotleta (pork tenderloin with mushrooms), stuffed quail Romanoff, or blinis (crepes served with red or black caviar).

If you're not that hungry, slide into a booth for a couple of belts of the house special, a smooth concoction called Buffalo Grass vodka. Take a moment, and ponder how it happened. Russia was first in space. They made great movie villains, and provided the big Commie threat for three decades of U.S. presidents. Now they've lost the Cold War, their government's in the toilet, their leaders are either drunk or resting in a sanitarium, everything's a black market economy, and you're sitting in a piano bar restaurant in the Richmond, surrounded by crazy murals, drinking Russian booze, and watching families cut the rug. Funny how things turn out.

**Russian Renaissance Restaurant**
**5241 Geary Boulevard**
**(415) 752-8558**

# Bar Noir

It's no secret this is a town of dreamers and drunks. You often hear people say that "the bars are great." Under this polite observation is the implication that we're all just sad alcoholics, with nothing else to do except drown our sorrows in the foggy night. To be fair, there are a lot of bars here, many of them older than their patrons. And there are a lot of people drinking inside them, especially on Monday and Tuesday nights, it seems. As a city, we must play the cards we've been dealt. And when you're drinking your life away atop a 150-year-old slab of walnut, somehow it doesn't seem quite as depressing, now does it? Order another round! You're not just a pathetic pickle-head with no family to speak of, you're enjoying the rich saloon culture of a once-vital port town! The watering holes in this chapter are for the true libation spelunker, the purist who longs for a more tolerant era of booze. Most of these portals of hooch lie completely off the radar of hipness, and may not be around much longer. So step inside and belly up. Even if you're not a rumpled, apple-head-doll loser, you can at least feel what it's like to be one.

# Piano Bar Platters

**S**urrounded by tony art galleries and fancy hotels, this sports hofbrau remains a complete aberration in downtown Union Square. Stepping inside the door is like traveling back to World War II, where the atmosphere says it's V-J Day all over again — except you're not going to grab the girl next to you for a victory kiss, because she'll be a retired alcoholic in stretch pants, sitting at the piano bar, belting out an off-key version of "Tie a Yellow Ribbon." Unless you're looking for that sort of thing.

But if you're looking for walls covered in photos of long-dead baseball players, you've come to the right place. Frank J. "Lefty" O'Doul opened his namesake watering hole in 1958, after a long career as player for and then manager of the San Francisco Seals team. O'Doul helped develop the career of Joltin' Joe DiMaggio, which is probably why the I.D. card of DiMaggio's one-time squeeze Marilyn Monroe is blown up and framed above the bar.

The Lefty's crowd ranges from tourists watching TV sports, to gamblers at the bar checking their racing forms, the pie-eyed songbirds in the corner at the piano, and old folks from nearby residential hotels, sitting at tables, gumming their turkey platters.

Which cliché best describes this old-city tableau — "Runyonesque" or "Kafkaesque"? It's definitely not "Capraesque."

But drinks are cheap, and plates of meat, cut for you as you watch, are served up from steam tables with a side of cottage cheese. And some of the seniors are pretty feisty. Occasionally an old lady will get 86'd, and stand outside on the sidewalk, squabbling with police officers.

**Lefty O'Doul's
333 Geary Street
(415) 982-8900**

# Kilts and Cabers ··············

**I**n every neighborhood of the city, there are bars that align themselves with that community — i.e., Irish, Russian, African-American. Irish bars can be found in the vicinity of Irish households, for instance. Makes sense. Everything's centrally located, and it's usually a short stumble home. Citizens of Scottish heritage don't have their own neighborhood, but they can claim an authentic Scottish bar — it just happens to be in the Tenderloin District, nestled squarely in the midst of strip clubs, tranny bars, prostitutes, street junkies, and a cab company.

But all of that — well, most of it — disappears once you stroll inside the two-story

Edinburgh Castle, and gawk at the medieval wooden beams, flags hanging from the ceiling, caber clamped to the wall, and some kind of bizarre yet important rifle, dramatically lit and mounted in a frame. Since 1958, the Castle has been pouring the largest selection of scotch in the city, and serving up fresh orders of fish and chips from the shop around the corner, wrapped in the morning paper. During the '60s, San Francisco State University President I.S. Hayakawa, later to become a U.S. Senator, could be found filthy drunk here. For the last several years, the bar has also functioned as headquarters for the Scottish Cultural Arts Foundation, which has sponsored a whole slew of events, from ceilidhs (wild Scottish parties) and art gallery exhibits to literary readings, World Cup football screenings, live music, theatrical productions, '60s-mod James Bond events, and the annual Bobby Burns night, where customers can

# Phone Booth Bar

**S**ince January 1, 1998, it's been illegal to smoke in any bar within the state of California. Designed to protect employees from secondhand smoke, the law has met with mixed reactions. Has the rest of the country looked down at our Nazi-esque, politically correct ways? You bet they have. Have they erupted into big smokers' hack-laughs, stubbed their Winstons in their plates of mashed potatoes, and called us a bunch of sorry-ass pussies? Sure. Do people still smoke in bars in California? Yep. You can legally smoke in one San Francisco bar to your heart's content. That's because the owner doesn't care about smoke, and he has no employees. But you better arrive early. There are only seven seats.

A mere sliver of a tavern, The Black Horse London Deli claims the title of smallest bar on the West Coast. Owner Joe Gilmartin says the fire code allows a maximum of 15, but he's packed 33 people into the place, and even did a photo shoot with live sheep. Decorated with British and Irish posters, it's supposedly modeled after an English countryside pub. Either that or a phone booth.

The Black Horse shuts down at 11 every night, to not keep the neighbors awake, and is closed Tuesdays and Wednesdays. Despite these restrictions, it's definitely worth a visit, because you're likely to bump into colorful characters like "Sarge." A retired military man and auto parts counter person, Sarge usually stands grinning at the end of the bar, wearing an Elks Lodge cap cluttered with Elks-related pins. He also speaks like a '60s TV movie version of a hippie — "Out of sight, man!" "Far out!" — and make jokes like "You heard of a wino? I'm a beer-o!" And then 20 minutes later, he cracks the same joke. Regulars like Sarge get the option of a private drinking club, where customers punch a time card into a clock and record their actual time spent in the establishment. They receive their own mugs, and preferred privileges.

Perhaps because space is tight, the Black Horse serves only two beers, two types of cigars, and chunks of orange cheese. Although Gilmartin plays boxing videos and displays photos of legendary boxers, the crowd is very friendly. That's what happens when you leave smokers alone.

**The Black Horse London Deli**
**1514 Union Street**
**(415) 928-2414**

slurp plates of haggis, serenaded by a kilted bagpiper. Historical Edinburgh highlights include the first American stage version of the play *Trainspotting*, based on the 1993 novel by Irvine Welsh, and the night someone puked all over the caber.

Anyone can understand the Scottish stuff — the cabers, flags, sheep guts, and dusty old mugs that dangle from hooks — but what's the deal with the hundreds of gold English coins embedded in the top of the bar?

"Old empire number," explains SCAF founder/bar manager Alan Black. "Twentieth-century British monarchs look up at the patrons sitting at the bar. Very empire. Even when you're drunk we're watching."

**Edinburgh Castle**
**950 Geary Street**
**(415) 885-4074**

# Tippling in Chinatown

L i Po may have been a big-shot Chinese poet from the Tang dynasty in the 8th century, but even in this Chinatown bar that bears his name, he would have a hard time getting the bartender's attention. Since at least 1928, it's been difficult to get a drink here. But if you do manage to get someone to bring you a cocktail, settle in and check out the decor. No, not the cases of beer stacked by the front door. The enormous Chinese lamp dangling in the middle of the bar is definitely impressive, especially when accompanied by the Beatles' "Penny Lane" on the sound system. Trademark concoctions served here include what tastes like

kerosene in a glass known as Chinese rice whiskey and something called the Li Po Special, which features seven shots of booze.

Across the street from Li Po is the Buddha Lounge. It's best to bring a fun-loving crowd with you, because you won't find it here. The law isn't posted, but it's more of an unwritten rule that this place must have no more than three customers at once. As with Li Po, the friendliness is overwhelming. The restrooms are an adventure in themselves, because the bartender must buzz you downstairs through a chicken-wire door, then you walk into the basement, where the walls and floor are painted blood red. This is so that when you're killed and hacked into pieces, it's easier to hide the mess.

**Li Po**
**916 Grant Avenue**
**(415) 982-0072**

**Buddha Lounge**
**901 Grant Avenue**
**(415) 362-1792**

# Wild West Women

T his wood-paneled Bernal Heights tavern reminds you of an Old West saloon, except the women aren't dance-hall girls in garter belts, they're buffed-out gals in work boots, shooting eight-ball. The Wild Side West is the oldest women's bar in the city, and all signs point to the fact that the struggle is long over, boys, and the chicks won the war. Portraits of nude females decorate the walls, as does a display of high-heeled shoes, painful footwear from an earlier era of male-dominated repression. And there seems to be a central decor motif of old toilets with plants growing out of them. The atmosphere is mellow and friendly, but if a smart-ass gunfighter were to stroll in and start in with the cute talk, you know he'd get the business end of a pool cue. You don't have to be a lesbian cowgirl to have a drink here, but if you happen to be a lonely cow-punchin' filly, looking for a little you-know-what to warm up that sleeping bag for one, Wild Side West is definitely one watering hole worth the stop.

**Wild Side West**
**424 Cortland Avenue**
**(415) 647-3099**

# Saloon Secrets

**F**ormerly The Drift Inn, the Yong San Lounge looks drab and inconspicuous, as if to not attract attention at all. *Exactly.* The location figures prominently in the Gemstone File, the granddaddy of all conspiracy theory documents, which has both baffled and irritated paranoid nuts since the 1970s. At this bar in the Tenderloin District, CIA spooks and Watergate burglars supposedly met up and whispered secrets of unearthly importance, from the Kennedy assassinations to Howard Hughes and Ari Onassis.

The actual Gemstone File is over 1,000 handwritten pages, and portions have been floating around since the late 1960s. Its origins trace back to a San Francisco gem salesman named Bruce Roberts, who specialized in creating synthetic rubies. He apparently exchanged these phony gems for information, which introduced him to a web of intelligence spooks and political contacts, and the horrors of a world that was not at all how it seemed. JFK, Mafia, CIA, FBI, Watergate, Onassis — as the conspiracy grew more complicated, Roberts saw the dots connecting between every single world political scandal and assassination, dating back to the 1930s, and started writing it all down.

Some of this document could be true, but much of it is absolutely ludicrous. Frustrated journalists have spent years attempting to fact-check it, and it's best left as an entertaining read. In 1975, about the year the File stops, a Skeleton Key was published, which summarized and outlined the whole mess in a rough chronological order.

Among the Gemstone fun facts:

· Both J. Edgar Hoover and Senator Estes Kefauver were poisoned with a slice of apple pie, and Kefauver had a heart attack *on the floor of the Senate!*

· The day after Mary Jo Kopechne died at Chappaquiddick, Teddy Kennedy's friend's sister ran away to Norway, where she was kidnapped by Mafia and locked up *in a heroin factory!*

· And speaking of heroin, after 14 years of heavy smack use, reclusive millionaire Howard Hughes finally overdosed; as his casket was lowered into the ocean off the coast of Skorpios, Albanian frogmen were waiting under the water, and whisked the corpse away to Yugoslavia *to check dental records!*

· LBJ was slipped poisonous apple pie at his ranch, and his last words were, *"You know fellows, it really was a conspiracy"!*

While piecing together his reportage, Roberts frequented the Drift Inn. During the early '70s, federal spooks often dropped in for a beer, and listened to Roberts spout his Gemstone theories. According to Roberts, this bar was where G. Gordon Liddy first hatched his Watergate burglary plan, and the tavern was wired for sound by Arabs, Russians, Chinese, even the bartender, who was hired by Katherine Graham, publisher of the *Washington Post.*

Roberts died in 1976 of lung cancer (not apple pie, as far as we know), and the bulk of his Gemstone documents ended up with conspiracy theorist Mae Brussell. After Brussell died in 1988, her files were stashed in a secret location by KAZU-FM, the Pacific Grove radio station that aired her weekly programs.

Today the bar is a Vietnamese neighborhood spot, but who knows? Maybe that guy staring out the window is meeting his coordinate from the Saigon Secret Police, who will introduce him to the pilot who led the Clinton Administration missile attack on the Sudan, and who was once a lover of Robert Kennedy, Jr.'s former high school girlfriend, who worked in the State Department....

Yong San Lounge
(formerly The Drift Inn)
895 Bush at Taylor Street
(415) 771-1838

# Birth of the Booze

The most likely history of this potent slug to the forehead traces back to the 1860s at the Occidental Hotel, where a customer, waiting for a ferry ride across the bay to Martinez, asked bartender "Professor" Jerry Thomas for something strong enough to last the journey. Thomas whipped up a concoction of gin, bitters, vermouth, and a maraschino cherry, and named it the martini, in honor of the man's destination. The name stuck, and we lost a couple of ingredients along the way. The Financial District watering hole known as the Occidental Grill not only took its name from this hotel, it inherits a fine tradition of martini shaking as well — one bartender can pour 75 martinis a day. Martinis come in any flavor you desire, and on the walls hang sketches of "Professor" Jerry, hard at work in his laboratory. Those big glass jars stashed behind the bar? Hot peppers soaking in white tequila, waiting for a margarita with an attitude.

### The Martini

### The Irish Coffee

A plaque is bolted to the entrance of the Buena Vista Cafe at Fisherman's Wharf, officially commemorating the site as the entry point of the Irish coffee to America. This concoction of scotch whiskey and Irish creme first arrived in 1952, courtesy of the late Stanton Delaplane, Pulitzer Prize-winning columnist for the *San Francisco Chronicle*, and no stranger to a beverage himself.

Since then, millions have sipped these little beauties, because they're not even alcohol, are they? Really, they're just like coffee, just a little pick-me-up to get the motor running. Fifteen Irish coffees later, as you steady your bobbing head and squint out the large picture windows of the Buena Vista, you can admire the view of the harbor and the never-ending parade of tourists.

Photo: Sharon Sehlen

### The Mimosa

Established in 1864, Jack's Restaurant was named for the jack rabbits that once romped through nearby fields, and that eventually found their way onto the menu. Jack's became a regular stop for 19th-century writers Mark Twain and Bret Harte, followed by a parade of governors, senators, actors, film directors, and attorneys. The building's upstairs floor featured private rooms for prostitutes, or as refined society termed it, "more social" encounters. In the 1940s, two such bigshots, Alfred Hitchcock and financier Louis Lurie, were knocking back a few at Jack's (perhaps taking a break from a "more social" encounter), and they started to wonder what would happen if one were to mix champagne and orange juice. So somebody did. The color reminded them of the mimosa flower, so they christened their new libation the mimosa. Or so the story goes. Who's to say, really? They're both dead. It could have been anybody. Pick two dead famous guys and name an old restaurant, and something probably happened there. After an extensive refurbishing, Jack's reopened in 1998, the owners adding fancy chandeliers, heavy drapes, repainted gilded bas reliefs, and a 30x15-foot skylight.

**Occidental Grill**
**453 Pine Street**
**(415) 834-0484**

**Buena Vista Cafe**
**2765 Hyde Street**
**(415) 474-5044**

**Jack's Restaurant**
**615 Sacramento Street**
**(415) 421-7355**

Photo: courtesy Rich Upton

SONNY BARGER'S KICKSTARTIN' JALAPEÑO HELLFIRE SAUCE

Action aplenty with the Bay Area Tankers (page 22),
the Black Panthers (page 35), and the Hell's Angels (page 94)

Photo: courtesy Hearst Castle

Photo: Sharon Selden

Follow your
dreams, from
William
Randolph
Hearst's castle (page 166), to the
Foot Worship boutique (page 108)

Indulge yourself at the Sex Institute (page 121), and Erik Estrada's favorite Chinese restaurant (page 48)

Photo: Sharon Selden

JAKE
O'CONNELL
MY BELOVED
AND ETERNAL
FRIEND
I WILL MISS
YOU ALWAYS
25 DEC 1976
25 FEB 1988

The infamous
Laughing Sal
(page 124), and
pets that push
daisies (page 176)

MOTHER OF
CIVIL RIGHTS
IN CALIFORNIA
SHE SUPPORTED THE
WESTERN TERMINUS OF THE
UNDERGROUND RAILWAY FOR
FUGITIVE SLAVES 1850-1865. THIS
LEGENDARY PIONEER ONCE
LIVED ON THIS SITE
AND PLANTED THESE
SIX TREES

PLACED BY THE SAN FRANCISCO
AFRICAN AMERICAN HISTORICAL
AND CULTURAL
SOCIETY

MARY ELLEN PLEASANT MEMORIAL PARK

1814 1904

Madams that ran
the town, from
Mammy Pleasant
(page 111) to
Sally Stanford
(page 112)

Photo: courtesy Tattoo Art Museum

Museums of the peculiar, including tattoo art (page 142) and Dashiell Hammett (page 140)

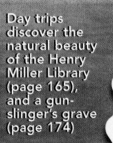

Photo: courtesy Henry Miller Library

Day trips discover the natural beauty of the Henry Miller Library (page 165), and a gunslinger's grave (page 174)

EARP

WYATT BERRY STAPP
1848 ~ 1929

JOSEPHINE SARAH MARCUS
1861 ~ 1944

"...That nothing's so sacred as honor,
and nothing so loyal as love!"

Driving people to the brink, the first Gold Rush nugget (page 135) and X-rated cakes (page 120)

Photo: Anthony Pidgeon

Photo: courtesy Paxton Gate

FATHER OF LSD

Pure

ALBERT HOFMANN

An explosion
of emotion,
with stuffed
mice (page
172) and the
museum of
blotter acid
(page 128)

Photo: Clarissa Horowitz

Photo: courtesy Ripley's Museum

Big treasures are often small, from Pez
dispensers (page 126) to shrunken heads (page 130)

Best Wishes
Ann Calvello

Ὁ ἉΓΙΟϹ    ΙΩ ΑΝ HC

Let us sing all songs
to God. Let us pursue
Him in the right-
eous path. Yes it is
true; "Seek, and ye
shall find."

St. John Will·I·AM Coltrane

Spirituality
can be found
anywhere,
including
roller derby
(page 79) and
the church of
John Coltrane
(page 26)

Photo: courtesy The Sharper Image

JEAN
JENNINGS
as "Belle"

JOHNNY
HOLMES
as "Father
Clement"

Mitchell Brothers'

*Autobiography of a Flea*

...as told by the
smallest voyeur
of them all.

First steps in new
directions, with
The Sharper Image
(page 16) and a
porn film about
an invisible insect
(page 106)

End of the road, whether it's toy poop (page 31) or tree-stump cremation urns (page 192)

Back to basics
at Sam Woh
restaurant
(page 47),
and toilet
guitars (page 18)

Photo: courtesy Charlie Deal

Patty Hearst's first arrest (page 91) and Lenny Bruce's last performance (page 90)

Photo: courtesy DPF

SANTA CRUZ
SURFING MUSEUM

Image: courtesy S. Clay Wilson

Party down with the
adult diaper club
(page 100), the surfing museum
(page 164) and the straight bar once
known as Dick's (page 67)

# Drink Just Like Grampa

On the first floor of 450 Post Street is Farallon, one of the most expensive and exclusive restaurants in the city. One floor above Farallon is the Kensington Park Hotel, some of the most expensive and exclusive accommodations in the city. But just one more floor up dwells the landlord of the building — the oldest active Elks Lodge in the United States. And within this apple-pie slice of America's Heartland, overlooking the busy Union Square traffic, sits its most popular feature, the bar.

Established in 1868 by East Coast stage performers who wanted their own hangout, the Elks organization expanded to California and opened San Francisco's B.P.O.E. Lodge No. 3 in 1876. Since then, the city's finest examples of citizenry — i.e., alcoholic, back-slapping businessmen — have taken the sacred Elks oath of membership, underneath the carved wooden ceiling of the grand meeting room.

Members of Lodge No. 3 take great pride in their sacred den of Elkness. The athletic facilities, from the weight rooms to the swimming pool, sauna, a couple of dusty handball courts, and billiard tables, are given great importance. Hallways are lined with snapshots of recent spaghetti feeds, and taxidermied elk heads lurk above the rooms. If an Elk can boast of nothing else, it's American pride. Flags are everywhere. Old Glory. Stars and Stripes. Long may she wave. A framed photo of the nation's very first Flag Day hangs in the dining room. Held in San Francisco's Golden Gate Park, this august ceremony was presided over by President Truman, who was an Elk, goddammit.

Vintage pin courtesy: Lon D. Marrs, Depression-era mayor of Amarillo, Texas

But mainly, people congregate here because of the bar. It's not particularly special in terms of decor (a big-screen TV) or food (nightly dinner specials like "country-style ribs"). The view out to Post Street is nice. But it's camaraderie that's most important.

When you're an Elk, you're here to booze it up and yuk it up. Even on an off night, the bartender slurs his words, and the guys sitting on barstools have at least two drinks in front of them at once. Insiders swear they've seen most members totally shit-faced at one function or another — completely word-slurring, red-eyed, pig-drunk, including the women. Alcohol not only breaks down inhibitions, it can increase the entertainment value of an octogenarian with hearing aids tripping over the leg of his chair.

Despite all this alcohol hoisted in the name of hearty brotherhood, the club is vehemently anti-drugs. They even go out of their way to print up brochures explaining how you can tell if your child is on drugs. Unfortunately, not only does this stance sound completely hypocritical, the assumptions are absurd:

- "Is the child not doing chores, late coming home, not cutting grass?"
- "Has the child switched clothes styles, refused to talk about new friends, or become very interested in rock music and concerts?"
- "Does the child show a loss of ability to blush?"
- "Does the child forget who vomited in family car?"
- "Does the child forget to replace the liquor stolen from parents' cabinet?"

(Taking drugs is one thing, but Christ, don't steal our booze!)

But let's not get too critical of the Elks. They need all the help they can get. If you want to go here for a drink, there is one catch. You either need to arrive accompanied by a member, or quickly join the organization.

San Francisco Elks Lodge No. 3
450 Post Street, 3rd floor
(415) 421-5230

# The Curse of the Owl

People don't just stop by C. Bobby's Owl Tree bar for the jukebox, despite its intoxicating fury of Journey, Roger Miller, and Tom Jones. They don't just come here for the complimentary bowls of Rice Chex party mix, or to rinse the taste of the Tenderloin trick out of their mouths. They come here for the owls. Since the place opened in the 1970s, owls have been perched everywhere you look. Painted owls, stuffed owls, owl figurines and statues, owls owls owls. According to a bartender, Bobby, the owner, just likes owls.

Another, much more interesting and conspiratorial reason for the owls sits right across the street. Kitty-corner from the Owl Tree, a brick fortress covered in ivy stands guard. The Bohemian Club is the most-feared private club in the world. Founded in 1872 by Bay Area

journalists, poets, and actual bohemians, who staged theatrical shows for their own amusement, the Bohemian Club has now grown to become an exclusive group of white male politicians, industrialists, and power moguls.

The Bohemian Club's symbol is the owl. It makes sense, because owls live in the woods, and the Bohos own their own redwood forest. Every summer at the secret Bohemian Grove north of San Francisco, titans and dignitaries let their hair down, drink themselves silly, and pee in the trees. The grove is broken up into separate camps, and members put on little plays and musicals, often dressing up like women — *just like actual bohemians!* Rumors circulate that hookers are shipped into the compound in limos.

The Bohemian slogan "Weaving spiders come not here" is obviously designed to dispel the notion that just because George Bush, Henry Kissinger, and George Shultz might party (and pee) together, they would discuss which country to bomb, or which world leader should be squeezed with economic sanctions. How absurd. These people don't have time for such nonsense. They're too busy staging Shakespeare in drag!

Drop by the Owl Tree and gaze across the street at the Bohemian Club. While one is a sleazy bar and the other is an exclusive citadel, both are decorated exactly the same — owls everywhere.

**Owl Tree**
**601 Post Street**
**(415) 776-9344**

# Beers and Blues

Built in 1861, The Saloon bills itself as the oldest bar in San Francisco, surviving the 1906 fire, as the story goes, via a bucket brigade of panicked citizens. This rickety wooden structure is not just old, it looks as though the next quake could wiggle it right off the lot and send it sliding down Columbus Avenue. But this would never happen, because The Saloon is permanently glued to its foundation with over 100 years' worth of special tavern adhesive — a fermented, hardened paste of cigarette butts, crusted alcohol, bum piss, and broken guitar strings. An odd mixture of people comes here to listen to the live blues bands, from weathered locals with speed-freak faces to puzzled tourists in pastel warm-up suits.

Other blues bars are further up Grant Street, but this is by far the oldest and the stickiest.

**The Saloon**
**1232 Grant Avenue**
**(415) 989-7666**

Photo: Paul Trapani

# Dick's for Drinks

Courtesy: S. Clay Wilson

**Dick's Bar
290 Sanchez at 16th Street**

**E**ven though this bar no longer exists, it should be remembered for three reasons. First, it was for years one of the few straight bars in the primarily gay Castro District. If you were a hetero feeling oppressed, you could seek sanctuary from all the gay culture. Or if you were gay and felt like stepping into a hetero time warp, you could peek in the window and see what the poor straights were up to.

Second, Dick's was a big hangout for drug dealers. In the early 1970s, a man in a business suit sat at the bar in the afternoons and sold polished wooden boxes of LSD. One hundred bucks bought you 40,000 hits of clear gelatin "windowpane," a total of 1 million micrograms.

And third, Dick's functioned as the unofficial business office and mailing address for legendary underground cartoonist S. Clay Wilson, who lives a few doors down the block. As Wilson's "Checkered Demon" comic character cruised through panel after panel of unbelievable debauchery, his publishers were instructed to mail his commission and royalty checks directly to the bar.

After years of being boarded up, the space has reopened as the Daimaru Sushi restaurant. No drugs, no demons, no sexuality whatsoever.

# Jewish and Irish?

**O**ut of the teeming hordes of Jewish/Irish sports bars in the Bay Area, this facility is no doubt the finest. The owner opened up in 1977, first naming his business Greenberg's, then adding the "O" to make it sound more like a neighborhood bar. Irish envy, or savvy marketing? Every St. Patrick's Day, O'Greenberg's puts out the appropriate spread — corned beef and bagels, served on tables hewn from great slabs of wood. At any moment a character from *The Ginger Man* by J.P. Donleavy is going to stumble in and pound his fist for a pint.

The tavern has also been a convenient and necessary watering hole for mortuary students from the funeral home across the street. According to one student, who was at the time clearly defying the rules by sitting there on a barstool, the school warns its pupils to avoid hanging out at the bar, because after a few cocktails, the apprentice undertakers have been known to loosen the jaw and spin grisly tales of the inner workings of their biz. So remember, the next time you stop into O'Greenberg's for a pop, and the guy next to you starts waxing eloquent about body fluid drainage, or how much the human liver actually weighs, or what a headless torso looks like after being munched on by garfish and snapping turtles, just keep in mind, as you're trying not to lose your lunch, that he's actually fudging the rules.

**O'Greenberg's
1600 Dolores Street
(415) 550-9192**

# Tiki for Your Thoughts

S tarted in 1939 by a merchant marine named Sam, who wanted to recreate a bit of the South Pacific, Trad'r Sam sits plunked out in the fog of the Richmond District. Since that time, the joint's had just three owners total, and more than likely the same furniture. Its dirty booths are woven out of cane, each named after a different island chain. Beyond this, the tiki theme evaporates in a decor of neon liquor signs and pinball machines. This half-assed attempt at tiki makes it all the more charming and authentic.

Behind the horseshoe bar are TV monitors, very thoughtfully angled so even the most fucked-up guy in a dress can still watch sports without having to lift his head from the bar. The drink menu is long and confusing, and doesn't list any of the ingredients, but you know they're all rum, so don't bother speculating on the subtle differences between a Tahitian Deep Purple and a Surfer on Acid. They're all insanely strong and filled with hunks of fruit. If you're feeling creative, like maybe you'd rather have the Deep Purple colored blue instead of purple, the bartender will make whatever you want. Just don't come here on the weekends. Avoid the young-white-people crowds and stop in on a Tuesday, to catch the cross-dressers and the occasional fistfight.

**Trad'r Sam**
**6150 Geary Boulevard**
**(415) 221-0773**

# Here, Fishie Fishie

Y ou wouldn't think this swank establishment would belong anywhere near this tawdry book, but Bimbo's 365 Club is the only bar in town with a live chick mermaid swimming in a giant fishbowl, and even in this day and age, that's still worth something. No, she's not the "Bimbo," and no, the place isn't named for a stupid girl. It's actually Italian for "little boy." The boy, in this case, being Agostino Giuntoli.

At age 19, Giuntoli left Tuscany, Italy and sailed to America. He worked in San Francisco as a janitor and cook, and the nickname "Bimbo" came from a boss who couldn't pronounce his name. Unfazed by his new moniker, Giuntoli found a partner and opened the 365 Club at 365 Market Street, and a city weary of the Depression stopped in to whoop it up. Celebs traveled across the country and elbowed in to see the shows, sip gin from coffee cups, and ogle the chorus girls, one of whom, Rita Cansino, graduated to the movies and changed her name to Rita Hayworth. Customers marveled at the optical illusion of Dolfina, The Girl in the Fishbowl, who seemed to be swimming buck naked in the fish tank behind the bar. When Giuntoli moved his club to its present location on Columbus Avenue in 1951, newspapers described the new Bimbo's as full of "jugglers, dance teams, stand-up comics, crooners, chantootsies, Stage Door Johns, a proper band in proper uniforms."

Photo: Sharon Selden

This grand tradition of mobster elegance continues today thanks to current owners Gino and Michael Cerchiai, the founder's grandsons. The club hosts corporate parties, private events, and live music shows, from Chris Isaak and Jewel to the Brian Setzer Orchestra and Combustible Edison. A full kitchen whips up classic Italian fare and serves it on candle-lit tables. The wine room still features a shotgun leaning up against the wall from the old days, but gin now comes in a respectable martini glass. The main bar, also known as The Continental Lounge, remains home to the world-famous "Girl in the Fishbowl." For a quick $125, your party can feature its very own naked swimming chick.

**Bimbo's 365 Club**
**1025 Columbus Avenue**
**(415) 474-0365**

# Ricky's Retreat

You'll find Ricky O's only after the third try, but what a find — the sole bar in Japantown that isn't either karaoke or part of an overpriced tourist restaurant. Ricky Oda opened his joint in 1991, and will win you over with his friendliness. Few know that he's only in his mid-30s, and has already lost one leg and a lung to cancer. The atmosphere feels very familial. For example, Ricky's mother, Kanako — who ran one of the first stores in Japantown, back when the center opened in 1968 — can occasionally still be found filling in for her son.

Ricky O's also feels like family because you're essentially dropping by someone's house. The front door is lined with blinking Christmas lights. The TV is old enough to have rabbit ears. The bar seems to have more baseball trophies than bottles of booze. Tables are cluttered with newspapers and other junk, and someone is usually eating take-out in the corner.

Saturday nights are best, when the bar tunes into the *Iron Chef* TV program, a bizarre Japanese cooking game show that airs in only four U.S. markets. The hyper-dramatic *Iron Chef* has a Bay Area cult following, but watching the show here at Ricky's, surrounded by Japanese restaurants and sitting in a Japanese bar, you feel you're getting something more than snickering white kids partying in someone's living room.

Essentially, *Iron Chef* pits a challenging chef against one of the show's three "house chefs," in a frenetic contest to cook a five-course gourmet meal in one hour. Assisted by professionals, competitors utilize the best-stocked kitchen you've ever seen. A chuckling host, looking like the bastard child of Yanni and Chuck Woolery, keeps the action moving, and a panel of four celebrity judges grades the final results.

The phone will ring at Ricky's during the program, as regulars check in to make sure the bar is watching. A recent visit for this book finds the challenger to be Ron Siegel, a young chef from San Francisco's Charles Nob Hill restaurant. Yanni/Woolery unveils the secret ingredient that both contestants must include in their meals, and it's — lobsters! The two chefs then battle it out for the next 60 minutes, furiously chopping, boiling, rolling, trimming, taking pans in and out of ovens, with cameras peering over their shoulders, and shots editing faster than any MTV video. Ricky's customers debate each dish as it materializes on-screen. At the end of the duel, the gladiators are sweaty and nervous. The judges sample the lobster dishes. Suddenly, Siegel is announced to be the unanimous winner — the first time any American has ever defeated the champion.

"It was a very emotional time," says Siegel in a post-competition interview. No kidding!

Ricky O's opens for business at 5 p.m.

Ricky O's
22 Peace Plaza
Tasamak Building, Japan Center
Post at Buchanan Streets
(415) 921-8928

# Gay Bars!

You might think San Francisco became the nation's homosexual mecca during the 1970s, but gay bars have actually been around since the Gold Rush. One of the classic 20th-century joints was The Black Cat (710 Montgomery near Columbus), a "bohemian" bar that opened in 1933 and grew more gay through the decades. In 1950 the owner took the state ABC board to court and won the right for gay bars to exist in California. Sunday afternoons the Cat hosted "drag operas," with ditties like, "Just when you think you've found a man / You find him cruising the Emporium can." The Cat closed in 1963, but the name lives on via a swank jazz joint on Broadway.

Another post-war scene developed on the Embarcadero, where bars catered to straight sailors and merchant marines who were looking for something more. (These buildings have now been renovated into fitness clubs and ultra-expensive restaurants.)

The Castro and Polk Street both have gay bar histories, but South of Market was the first and definitely the most notorious. In 1962, Sonny Liston beat Floyd Patterson for the world heavyweight championship. While fists flew in the boxing ring, in South of Market's gay scene, fists were headed for a different destination entirely. The Why Not and The Toolbox bars ushered in a new breed of gay bar and bathhouse. Guys dressed up like bikers and cops, S/M was consensual, and the walls were coated with Crisco. Guys peed on each other, and tripped on acid while dangling from slings. The Folsom district became known as the Miracle Mile, and until the mayor closed down much of the action in the 1980s, it was the wildest thing going in town.

Some businesses have changed hands, but most of the hangouts no longer exist. Exact dates are sketchy for the Handball Express at 975 Harrison, which emphasized fisting, and The Cauldron at 953 Natoma, which required all patrons to be naked except for boots. The Ambush (1973-1986) at 1351 Harrison marketed its own line of poppers, and has been described as smelling "like a strange mixture of battery acid and vegetable shortening." The Boot Camp at 1010 Bryant gave out free Kentucky Fried Chicken on Sunday afternoons.

A look at the South of Market area today constitutes a walk down Memory Lane for gays who survived AIDS. The DNA Lounge live music club, 375 11th, was once a leather bar called Chaps. The V/SF dance club, 287 11th, was once The Covered Wagon (early-mid 1970s), The Leatherneck (mid-late 1970s), Dirty Sally's (late 1970s), The Stables (late 1970s), Drummer Key Club (early 1980s), and The Oasis. The 1015 Folsom dance club was once The Tubs, the Folsom Street Baths, Big Town, and eventually The Sutro, San Francisco's only bisexual bathhouse, which closed in 1984 with a two-day party, where customers burned safe-sex pamphlets in the street. The Globe Youth Hostel and Jack's Bar at 1147 Folsom was once site of the Folsom Street Barracks,

four stories of unimaginable gay fantasy insanity — drugs freely available at the door, 100 candle-lit rooms of bunk beds, leather slings, darkened toilets, free Crisco — before getting destroyed in a 1976 fire, which leveled an entire block. An Episcopal mission and outreach center now stands on 8th and Howard, former home of The Club Baths, which served 800 customers at once. Called the pinnacle of the bathhouse scene, it closed in 1984. Restaurant and jazz music club 330 Ritch once was home to the Ritch Street Baths, 330 Ritch Street, which featured a Jacuzzi, and was affiliated with the national Club Baths chain. A laundromat at 164 8th marks the former site of The Trench, where every Tuesday was "Uncut Nite" — if your penis was verified by the bartender as being uncircumcised, he rang a big ship's bell and you received a free shot of schnapps. The Powerhouse, 1347 Folsom, is still a leather bar, and was once the following bars: In Between (1971-1972), Cow Palace Saloon (1972), No-Name Bar (1973-1976), The Bolt (1977-1978), and The Brig (1979-1985).

953 NATOMA

The Paradise Lounge music club, 1501 Folsom, once was FeBe's, one of the first gay biker bars in the nation. On one wall of the venue hangs a memento from the era, a Michelangelo's David statue modified to look like a gay biker with a big package. Stop in and toast it.

### Gay Bar Survivors

If not the oldest continuous gay bar in the city, The Stud is right up there, opening in the late 1960s at 1535 Folsom between 11th and 12th (present location of The Holy Cow dance club). A popular gay stoner hangout, The Stud gained a reputation as San Francisco's quintessential alternative gay bar. Patrons of the era speak of it with almost

spiritual reverence, and with good reason. The business operated for a time as an ordained chapel of the Universal Life Church, holding "services" after the 2 a.m. closing time so that the bar could remain open into the early morning hours. In 1987, owners moved it to its present location at 9th and Folsom, where the walls are lined with vintage muscle-boy photos and posters for the original Stud. For years it boasted a pinball machine called "You Go, Girl." These days it hosts the weirdest gender-twisted evening in town, known as "Trannyshack."

Another old-school gay bar, The EndUp opened in 1973, taking its name because it was the last bar before the freeway exit. Throughout the '70s, it was the hangout of clean-cut college boys, and hosted the San Francisco "Mr. Groovy Guy" Contest. Scenes involving jockey shorts in the book *Tales of the City* were set here. These days The EndUp is less gay and more tweaker, and most lively on Sundays at 6 a.m., when powderheads feel the need to stop grinding their teeth and have a cocktail to wind down before putting on the shades for the drive home.

HANDBALL express

**The Stud**
**399 9th Street**
**(415) 252-7883**

**The EndUp**
**401 6th Street**
**(415) 357-0827**

# Life's a Drag

**A** man dressed in women's clothing may be a staple of British humor, but here in America, we take our drag more seriously, and if it's done right, even consider it high art. Genesis for much of the nation's drag-queen aesthetic was Finocchio's in North Beach, its enormous neon blinking sign hovering over the Broadway strip. At this shrine to old-school dress-up, guys were putting on wigs and falsies for most of a century, belting out show tunes for the tourists.

The club's name came from an Italian immigrant named Joseph Finocchio, who guarded the door to his father's North Beach nightclub during Prohibition. While working there, he got the idea for a live show of transvestites, who would entertain, serve drinks and josh around with the primarily male clientele. In 1936 Finocchio's opened as the city's first tranny club. Local police objected, but Finocchio convinced them he would run the place straight — no mingling with the customers. For the next 50 years, Finocchio's grew into an essential stop for tourists, residents, and military personnel, returning home from overseas and hungry for a woman, even if she turned out to be a guy in a wig, singing Shirley Bassey songs.

"When I first started," Finocchio once told reporters, "there was a lack of understanding, but now people realize it is entirely different from what they were thinking. People accept our show more as pure entertainment than they did in the past. They see it as an artistry rather than a perversion."

Finocchio died in 1986 after 88 full years, and his family continued to operate the business until a tear-filled closing night in 1999.

But perhaps you're looking for something a bit more up-tempo, more inventive and less traditional. Prefer your lady-boys with a Latin flavor? Head on down to the Esta Noche bar in the Mission District, just off the notorious one-stop-shopping underground pharmacy known as the 16th Street BART station. Drag shows begin nightly at 11, which gives you plenty of time to walk down the street, meet your crack dealer and smoke yourself into a berserk fool. On weekends, you might want to stop in before 9 p.m. to avoid the cover charge, but that means you'll be pretty shit-faced when the show starts. Which might be a good thing.

No drag-bar tour is complete without a pass through the colorful Tenderloin District, and that means the Motherlode. Look for the entrance ablaze in colorful rainbow flags.

# Time to Rumble

**R**ows of sun-bleached homes line the hills of Daly City, and in their midst, a watering hole that should be registered as a historical landmark. Stepping inside the Silver Moon Saloon is like paying a pilgrimage to the shrine of Bay Area boxing. Every square inch of the place is plastered with old gloves, fight posters, and photos of famous and not-so-famous boxers. A pair of infant's boxing mitts hangs off the cash register. For boxing fans, the Silver Moon brings back memories of the good old days — sparring at the "Bucket of Blood" ring down in the Mission, or crowding into the weekly fights at the Civic Auditorium, across from City Hall. People once wore tuxedos for an evening of civilized bloodshed, and the mayor was cutting deals at ringside. Now that boxing has become more of a television-dominated sport, few local venues have survived in the Bay Area.

Photo: Paul Trapani

Once a month a group of retired boxers called the Roundhouse Boys meet here in the afternoon for a cold-cuts buffet and way, way too many cocktails. These guys are the real deal. Cars pull up, and pug-nosed fighters hobble their sore and arthritic bodies into the bar to swap stories with some guy they punched out 40 years ago. Each meeting ostensibly culminates with the group honoring a new boxer into their hall of fame, but mostly, it's about booze and bullshit. A gravel-voiced boxing manager named Tommy might even explain to a newcomer the real secret of training a fighter:

"No fuckin' pussy. Thirty days, minimum."

The white-haired tough guy makes a slicing motion with his hand.

"MIN-I-MUM!"

**Silver Moon Saloon**
**212 School Street, Daly City**
**(650) 756-9377**

Photos: Paul Trapani

Once inside, wait for your eyes to adjust to the dim lighting, and observe that every woman is a man, but not every man is aware of this fact. Motherlode trannies are among the best put together in town. Customers can sip a beer and watch the lip-synch show, set up on a stage decorated with a fainting sofa (or is it for swooning?). More adventurous guys will escort their favorite performer into a back area, because obviously it's difficult to whisper sweet nothings over the noise of the bar.

**Finocchio's**
**506 Broadway Street**

**Motherlode**
**1002 Post Street**
**(415) 928-6006**

**Esta Noche**
**3079 16th Street**
**(415) 861-5757**

# The Fame Game

A quick glance at any local newspaper will tell you that San Francisco has little in the way of celebrities. Nick Cage, Sharon Stone, a couple of athletes, a few quirky citizens here and there. Unlike other cities, folks will spot a celebrity walking down the street, and purposefully act as though they're just another human being, because that's the cool Northern California way to act. Famous people don't hang around the Bay Area unless they're seeking anonymity. The city is not an industry hotbed of the fame-producing entertainment machine. So then why even have a chapter about celebrities? A couple of reasons. One, whenever famous people come to visit, they invariably do something really stupid and get their name in the news. Which automatically earns a mention in this book. And two, even though you rarely spot any celebrities, San Francisco resolutely insists on tooting its own horn as a metropolis that is bristling with exciting stars. If you crave a metropolis overflowing with famous faces, then go check out Los Angeles. But if you like your celebs dropping dead or getting arrested, or pressing their B-list pawprints into cement, then read on!

# Fun Nuns

One of the first confirmed, only-in-San-Francisco sights I can remember, upon moving to the city in the early 1980s, was of a Catholic nun walking along California Street, in front of the Grace Cathedral church on Nob Hill, in the middle of the afternoon. Something about the nun was off-kilter, even vaguely disturbing. Although she was clothed in habit and robe, she seemed different than your everyday, plain-Jane nun. She wore colorful Converse sneakers. Her face was smothered in thick white pancake makeup and garish eye mascara, accented by a full mustache and beard. Obviously this was a special kind of nun.

Photo: Paul Trapani

To describe the Sisters of Perpetual Indulgence as drag-queen Catholic nuns is a nice shortcut, but they would rather be called "social activists/philanthropists/spiritualists/drag artists." For over 20 years they have acted as good-will ambassadors for the city, appearing at all sorts of functions and benefits, doing everything from handing out condoms on campuses, to dispensing holy communion wafers and tequila at the annual Burning Man art event in the desert. Like most local oddities, they came from someplace else.

According to Sister Phyllis Stein the Fragrant, the Sisters began in 1976 in Cedar Rapids, Iowa, when a group of men with theatrical ambitions borrowed some old habits from Roman Catholic nuns to stage a version of *The Sound of Music*. Three years later, the same costumes somehow drifted across the country and ended up in the Castro District. The Museum of San Francisco officially records the Sisters' origin as April 14, 1979. Their first known public appearance consisted of three guys wandering through the city in full habits, one of them carrying a machine gun and smoking a cigar, with the stroll ending up at a nude beach. They surfaced again with a memorable pompon routine at a softball game, and staged their first fundraiser as a bingo/disco benefit for gay Cuban refugees.

They worked on behalf of activists. Some were actual nurses, and did their part to promote AIDS awareness. As the makeup grew more garish, and the habits more outlandish, members personalized themselves with funny names: Sister Florence Nightmare, Sister Roz Erection, Sister Missionary Position. In 1982, Sister Boom Boom ran for city supervisor, listing her occupation as "Nun of the above." She received over 23,000 votes. A 1987 appearance during the Pope's visit to San Francisco placed the Sisters on the official papal list of heretics.

The Sisters' organization has grown and expanded to over 20 convents worldwide, with international headquarters remaining here in the city. Their ceremony of induction is, of course, quite elaborate. To become a member you must first apply, and then you become a Novice, which means you can only appear in public in a white veil. After six months, the Order votes to make the Novice a Fully Professed Member. A vow is taken, promising to "promulgate universal joy and to expiate stigmatic guilt." And then you may wear the full nun's habit, and accessorize it with wild makeup, Converse sneakers, or whatever.

Sisters of
Perpetual Indulgence
http://thesisters.org

# Fans Incorporated

**A**ccording to Fan Asylum's company literature, Tim McQuaid "attended his first rock concert and became so fascinated by the powerful force of the live performance and the strong connection between the performer and the audience that he was soon attending any and every concert he could. He became a major fan of all music, captivated by the near religious experience created by great artists and their loyal fans."

Such passion for rock and roll would naturally propel him to work in the San Francisco management office for the mega-rock band Journey. McQuaid ended up taking over Journey's fan club, and within a year took its enrollment from 800 members to over 20,000. Discovering his natural talent for this sort of thing, he branched off from the Journey empire in 1984, hired three employees, and launched his own fan club management company. Fan Asylum has since expanded to a worldwide operation, with offices in Tokyo and London. Working from a South of Market warehouse, McQuaid and his crew manage and coordinate fan clubs for the biggest names in the biz, from Aerosmith and Primus to Melissa Etheridge, Boyz II Men, Bush, Megadeth, Janet Jackson, Lenny Kravitz, Whitney Houston, and Sheryl Crow. Who knew?

The fan industry has come a long way from mailing out autographed photos of David Cassidy. Fan Asylum produces web sites and quarterly newsletters for its clients, doling out career news, photos, contests, and merchandise. They set up telephone hotlines for eager beavers to call in and receive the latest news and recorded messages from the stars, and will even organize special travel packages, so fans can jet across the country and sit in even closer proximity to their super-ultra-fave celebrity.

"Whether you're a fan or the management for an artist looking for these services," they boast, "Fan Asylum has the experience and know-how to bring you incredible fan clubs and experiences!"

**Fan Asylum**
**1250 Folsom Street**
**(415) 865-2727**

# Puppet on Patrol

The art of ventriloquism traces all the way back to ancient Greece, but most of us know "vents" from television and nightclub acts like Edgar Bergen and Charlie McCarthy, Willie Tyler and Lester, or Ronn Lucas. That is, until the 1990s, when San Francisco embraced the nation's most unusual crime-fighting duo — SFPD Officer Bob Geary and Brendan O'Smarty

A member of the police force since 1963, Geary never planned to carry a hand-manipulated dummy while on duty. As a kid, he played with a Howdy Doody string puppet, but set the doll down, he says, when he reached puberty. He completely forgot about the land of make-believe until 1991, when the Police Department created a CPOP (Community Police on Patrol) division, to emphasize "creative and ingenious methods for handling beat situations." Geary thought about what he could contribute, and the answer came to him — a partner that was a ventriloquist puppet, dressed in a miniature hat and uniform.

Courtesy: Bob Geary

A friend suggested he name it Smarty, because "he's no dummy," but when the puppet arrived in the mail to Geary's home, he unpacked it and thought, "This is a very significant piece of artwork — I can't just call him Smarty." He therefore gave him the lofty name Brendan, and added the O to make him Irish.

"I didn't want to hurt the guy's feelings," he explains.

But the innocent world of puppetry is not without controversy. When the public discovered a cop was walking his beat with a vaudeville dummy, police officials feared a backlash and asked Geary to get rid of it. The general population loved O'Smarty, however, so something had to be done. In November 1993, voters noticed Proposition BB at the bottom of their election ballot: "Shall it be the policy of the people of San Francisco to allow Police Officer Bob Geary to decide when he may use his puppet Brendan O'Smarty while on duty? [YES/NO]" The measure passed 51 to 49 percent, and hit the national press. In typical San Francisco fashion, someone complained that it was extending an Irish stereotype. There was more. Geary says putting O'Smarty on the ballot cost him $11,465, and so he wrote it off on his taxes. The IRS didn't agree, and took him to federal tax court, where the issue remains undecided.

In the meantime, Geary and O'Smarty enjoy their only-in-San-Francisco reputation. Professional acts approach the two at ventriloquist conventions for autographs. A member of both AFTRA and SAG actors' unions, Geary has done some hand modeling, and once co-starred with Don Johnson and Meredith Baxter in a 1981 TV movie, *The Two Lives of Carol Letner*. A major motion picture studio has retained an option for Geary and O'Smarty, but they are under contract not to discuss it. Geary does allow that the few scripts that have come his way were terrible, and featured Brendan using foul language. The two are still waiting for the proper roles.

When not walking a beat in North Beach, or driving a radio car, the crime-fighting duo visit hospitals and senior citizen organizations, and participate in anti-drug programs. The neighborhood chamber of commerce even asked if O'Smarty could be their mascot. Geary replied, "I don't think he would mind it at all."

**Bob Geary and Brendan O'Smarty**
**San Francisco Police Department**
**North Beach**

# Hell on Wheels

s there any good reason why a little man on skates would circle a banked wooden track and hurl himself at top speed directly into a clump of much taller and heavier men? Better yet, is there a reason why you were staying home on a Sunday afternoon, watching it on TV? Let's face it, there's never been any good reason to do either, unless you've got the flu, or are rotting on your deathbed in a hospital.

But if you're seriously in search of a quality roller derby experience that takes you back to the glory days, it's all located right here in the Bay Area.

Among the stars is Ann "Banana Nose" Calvello, a part-time supermarket clerk who has been skating professionally for six decades. Costumed in mismatched skates, with a deeply suntanned face, and hair dyed in multiple colors, this 68-year-old still enjoys kidney-punching, chair-swinging, and rail-flipping with the best of them.

(One imagines an entire evening of track competition starring Calvello's resurrected peers, but the sheer magnitude of such a combination — Red Erdman, Elmer "Elbows" Anderson, Midge "Tuffy" Brashun, Earlene "747" Brown, Don "Jughead" Lewis, Betty "Tiny Mite" McTague, Joanie "Blonde Bomber" Weston — is too exhausting an idea even for aficionados.)

Roller derby has entertained the masses in one form or another since the 1930s, when brothers Leo and Oscar Seltzer conceptualized the idea of a skating contest on a Chicago restaurant tablecloth. After some modifications to the sport, the two moved their brain-storm to Southern California in 1950. By 1958 the base of operations had relocated to Northern California.

Roller derby peaked in the 1960s, when several national companies toured simultaneously, and millions witnessed the spectacle via television. It was said that Bay Area performances actually outdrew the Oakland Raiders. But in 1973, the year after Raquel Welch appeared in *Kansas City Bomber*, the circuit was shut down, leaving roller derby relegated to occasional revivals and benefits.

Courtesy: Liz Pike

Bay Area diehards are determined to launch a new International Roller Derby League, staging occasional benefits in San Francisco and outlying communities. Organization in the IRDL is loose. Whoever wants to put on a uniform — or who can drive into the city — can skate. Teams are often assembled for one evening, and players rotate among teams.

After 60 years, roller derby rules still mean nothing. Whistles blow and action stops after every single lap, leaving the track strewn with crumpled, groaning bodies. While frenzied patrons yell encouragement, their children kick the seats in sugar-induced fits. Everybody should go at least once.

**International Roller Derby League**
**(408) 292-7783**

# Star-Studded

Too often, San Francisco gets compared with Los Angeles, and among the many conclusions drawn is that the Bay Area just doesn't measure up in terms of legitimate celebrity star power. This is a flat-out lie. Hollywood Boulevard may flaunt its sidewalk of stars, but we can gloat over our *three* different sets of celebrity sidewalks. Don't kid yourself, Tinseltown. The action is happening up north.

For instance, you're walking down Seventh Street South of Market. Perhaps you're strolling to the City Clinic for a free AIDS test, or you've just been released from the local jail. Suddenly, the names and handprints of the world's biggest stars materialize below your feet on the sidewalk — Wolfman Jack, Hervé Villechaize, Cliff Robertson, James Doohan and George Takai from *Star Trek*.

Overwhelmed, you stop to regain your bearings. In front of this filthy, stained stretch of concrete sits a warehouse for City Tow. Could it be that you're a few steps away from the magic of the movies? Well, maybe in another decade. Once upon a time this building was the home of San Francisco Studios, Northern California's answer to the Hollywood machine. When the studio opened, hopes ran high that the industry was going to relocate up from Los Angeles and make its films here at San Francisco Studios. Unfortunately, the industry didn't agree, and within a few years the building stood vacant, rented occasionally for post-production work. But even today, as the city's tow company conducts its business, outside its doors linger the handprints of cinema's grandest luminaries.

Or perhaps you find yourself on Geary, amidst the bustle of Union Square, where tourists tromp by eating slices of pizza, and vanilla-scented hookers compete for corner space with piss-soaked street beggars. Up ahead in the distance, scrawled in the few cement squares in front of the Hotel Diva, a name looks vaguely familiar. You investigate further. My God, it's true! The handprints of Keith Carradine, star of the Will Rogers musical! And next to him, Joel Grey! And Cher! And Lily Tomlin! Not a huge collection of names, but all have appeared

# Sidewalks

at the nearby Geary theaters, and all are legitimate bigshot stars.

Now, let's say you're walking through Civic Center, admiring the magnificent remodeled dome of City Hall. In front of you looms the austere Bill Graham Civic Auditorium, a solid 7,000-seat venue that has hosted boxing matches, the 1920 Democratic National Convention, the Hookers' Balls, as well as concerts by U2, John Denver, Prince, and the Rolling Stones. In 1992, the building was renamed for the late rock promoter Bill Graham, who died in a helicopter accident.

And again, rising up from the grey sidewalk like five Phoenixes from the ashes are yet more remnants of legendary stars, their uneven bas-relief portraits encircled by the words "Bay Area Music Awards," i.e., the Bammies awards, sponsored by now-defunct *BAM* magazine (which renamed them the California Music Awards). But you don't care what the awards are called, because these are bigshot stars! Promoter Bill Graham! Metallica, transplanted from L.A.! Hometown hippie relics like Jerry Garcia, Jefferson Airplane, Carlos Santana, and Janis Joplin, who lived in San Francisco for a whopping three years! And bluesman John Lee Hooker, who recorded his first hit records in the 1940s while living in Detroit! Man oh man!

(A final sighting as we go to press — a celebrity sidewalk of exactly one set of handprints exists in front of the Fugazi Theater on Green Street, home of the long-running goofball musical, Beach Blanket Babylon. The lone, inexplicable, pathetic tribute? Socialite Charlotte Swig Shultz.)

Maybe Hollywood doesn't have anything to worry about after all.

Photos: Sharon Selden

City Tow sidewalk
7th Street between Folsom and Harrison

Hotel Diva sidewalk
440 Geary Street

Bill Graham Civic Auditorium
99 Grove Street

# Punkers Eat Their Own

Run by a volunteer staff of punkers, Berkeley's Gilman Street music club is best known as the birthplace for the bands Green Day and Rancid. A basketball court at one end allows kids to shoot hoops while listening to bands. Gilman is also known for another incident. On a spring evening in 1994, members of the Bay Area punk rock community turned on their icon, Dead Kennedys singer Jello Biafra, and beat the crap out of him.

Like many creative artists in San Francisco, Jello Biafra, aka Eric Boucher, grew up someplace else. In his case, Boulder, Colorado. He moved to the city, and formed the seminal Bay Area band the Dead Kennedys, which poisoning the minds of youth with anthems like "California Uber Alles" and "Nazi Punks Fuck Off." His often abrasive political views were most easily digested whenever he added a dash of devilish humor. In 1979 he ran for mayor of San Francisco, on a platform requiring Financial District businessmen to wear clown suits to work. His campaign slogan was, "There's always room for Jello."

He founded the Alternative Tentacles punk rock record label, and appeared in courtrooms twice over charges of obscene album cover artwork. After the Dead Kennedys broke up in the late 1980s, he kept busy in the music business, signing bands, doing spoken-word appearances, and making more records.

On May 4, 1994, Biafra was hanging out at Gilman Street, watching a show by the Fixtures when, according to Biafra, a slam dancer crashed through the crowd, landed on Biafra's leg, and broke it.

According to Biafra, he asked the slam dancer for an I.D., and the kid laughed at him, saying, "Well, you're such a rich rock star, you can deal with it yourself."

The confrontation quickly turned into an argument — imagine, in a crowded rock club packed with angry punks! — and according to Biafra, the slam dancer pushed him to the floor and his friends jumped in. Five or six kids punched and kicked Biafra, yelling, "Sell-out rock star! Kick him!"

One of Biafra's legs was broken, and he sustained extensive damage to the ligaments of one knee as well as a superficial head wound.

On the bright side, the club is all-ages.

**Jello Biafra attack**
**924 Gilman Street**
**924 Gilman Street, Berkeley**
**(510) 525-9926**

# Opium or Non?

**M**arketing is a tricky business. Although the Mark Twain Hotel on Union Square has been purchased and renamed by the Ramada Inn chain, evidence of the old regime is everywhere. The hotel brochure prattles on about Mark Twain. The bar proudly features Mark Twain's books, and the adjoining restaurant is named Huckleberry Finn's. But it's all a big lie. A hotel manager freely admits that although Samuel Clemens once lived in San Francisco, he never actually stayed here, nor does he have any connection at all to the building. The hotel was most likely so designated because the former owner's brother was named Mark, and at the time it seemed like a good marketing gimmick. Fortunately, an even better gimmick was discovered in the hotel's history.

In January 1949, Billie Holiday played a gig in the city, staying in Room 203 of the Mark Twain Hotel. As was her custom, much of her spare time was spent stoned out of her gourd. On January 22, police arrested her and her husband/manager, John Levy for possession of a pipe and a "stick" of opium, her second drug bust in two years. Newspapers slapped the scandal on the front pages, and described the stick as being worth "less than $50." Both were released on $500 bail. During the trial, Holiday's attorney apparently turned on Levy and blamed him for everything, and the jury found her not guilty.

Fifty years later, Ramada staff have commemorated this little dance with the cops, and now advertise Room 203 as the Billie Holiday Suite. A nifty plaque hangs outside the entrance, and the walls boast framed news clippings and a pleasant color portrait of Holiday. When Holiday fans call in advance to reserve the room, the Ramada graciously charges no additional "opium celebrity" fee above the regular rate.

# Caught in the Can

**A**mong many thieves and charlatans to frequent the Bay Area was bank robber Babyface Nelson, who apparently liked the area so much he even dyed his hair to avoid locl authorities. One of his hangouts still stands today — the San Francisco Brewing Company in North Beach, the last operating Barbary Coast saloon. The solid mahogany bar caters mostly to tourists, serving 20 types of domestic and imported beers on tap, along with several brewed by the owner right there on the premises. Whoever ran the place back in the old days definitely sucked up to the underworld. Boxer Jack Dempsey worked as a bouncer at the front door. Babyface Nelson sipped a few beers here, and one day he picked either the wrong bar or the wrong day. Authorities found him in the basement, hiding in what is now the women's room.

**Babyface Nelson capture**
**S.F. Brewing Company**
**155 Columbus Avenue**
**(415) 434-3344**

# Chet Baker Punched Out

**S**ausalito's Trident nightclub opened originally in 1961, owned by Frank Werber, manager of the Kingston Trio. The location was perfect — right on the wharf, with an excellent view of San Francisco and the Golden Gate Bridge. During the '60s it evolved into a redwood-and-ferns restaurant, with colorful hand-lettered menus and young waitresses wearing see-through blouses. A few different versions circulate about what exactly happened to jazz trumpeter Chet Baker here in the parking lot back in 1968. One is that after buying some heroin, Baker was caught in a stairway and accosted by a man. Baker pretended to have a gun in his pocket, and the man left. The next day, five guys pounced on Baker, dragged him out into the parking lot, and whaled away on him. Another version is that Baker had screwed someone over on a drug deal, and the five guys were sent to mess him up, so they concentrated on his mouth because that was his livelihood. Regardless of which story is true, Baker's two front teeth were no more, but as he says in the Bruce Weber documentary *Let's Get Lost*, he had already been missing one for years. Baker died in 1986 after falling out of a window in Amsterdam.

**Chet Baker mugging**
**Horizons (formerly the Trident)**
**558 Bridgeway, Sausalito**
**(415) 331-3232**

# Scary Real Estate

**E**verybody has heard of Lombard Street, the so-called "crookedest street in the world." Every single day, tourists run to Lombard like lemmings, drive their rental cars down the winding turns, and at the bottom, stop and furiously take photos of other tourists doing the same thing. But amidst all this excitement, there is melancholy. Virtually nobody stops to check out the haunted house of socialite Pat Montandon.

During the 1960s, the city proclaimed this young frisky blonde its newest "It girl." She hosted a movie program on KGO television, and was known around the party circuit. A few drinks, a few laughs, a few men (from Frank Sinatra to attorney Melvin Belli, whom she married in a Shinto wedding ceremony in Japan, a coupling that lasted all of 13 days). She lived in a groovy apartment with a view, and people referred to her as San Francisco's "Queen of the Jet Set."

But one night at a party, Montandon made a fatal mistake. She forgot to get someone a drink.

That someone was a palm reader, who apparently was so offended at her faux pas that he then placed a curse upon her. For the next several years, Montandon claimed her life was a living hell. Her house was haunted, plagued by supernatural forces beyond control. Room temperatures fluctuated. Her dog developed a mysterious sore that wouldn't heal. Neighbors smeared obscenities in the building's foyer. A big house party attended by Ted Kennedy was interrupted by a fire. Another fire broke out and killed her secretary. She did some investigating, and found that since the building was constructed in 1909, five couples who lived there had gotten divorced, and several people had died in the apartments, three by suicide.

Photo: Sharon Selden

The curse didn't stop at her home. *TV Guide* ran a cover headline that implied Montandon was a prostitute, and she was forced to file a libel suit. She was bumped from being a guest on Merv Griffin's talk show by the boyfriend of the model Twiggy. One missed drink had turned into a bad hair day times a thousand.

Freaked out by this string of bad luck, she turned to the solace of writing, in hopes of exorcising the forces of evil from her life. *The Intruders* was published in 1974, detailing her many horrors in a white-knuckled gush of emotion, a brilliant melding of self-involved paranoia and B-list showbiz glitz. Her experiences weren't nearly as exciting as other supernatural cases of the day, but she was considered a socialite, and let's face it, their lives are a little more important than yours or mine.

Montandon recovered sufficiently to move into another home, which she named the Enchanted House. In 1990 she opened a peculiar shop in the Marriott Hotel, Pat Montandon's Perestroika Store, which sold Russia-themed fur hats, vases, and $750 dresses made from army blankets. She then wrote a chatty, first-person society column for the *San Francisco Examiner*. To this day, her old house still sits on Lombard, radiating memories of deadly fires, and dogs with sores that won't heal.

**Montandon Haunted House
1000 Lombard Street**

# Manson Family Values

Technically, Charles Manson was a nobody during the year he lived in San Francisco. The world had yet to hear about acid-crazed hippie chicks with Buck knives, and the big Helter Skelter race war fought with dune buggies. Bored youth had yet to wear Charles Manson T-shirts and listen to Manson tribute CDs. You could argue that, as with many who relocate to the Bay Area, Charlie finally learned who he was. Perhaps for the first time, he looked within himself and listened to his inner psycho-child, and understood his life mission in the grand cosmos. Whatever happened inside his head, it certainly wasn't the first time somebody had to leave town to get famous.

After years of cooling his heels in jails and reformatories, this freelance car thief/pimp/Scientologist/musician landed in Berkeley in March 1967, panhandling on Telegraph Avenue and playing guitar at the Sather Gate entrance to the campus. As Manson later told a reporter, one day a street kid handed him a flower, and told him about the Haight-Ashbury district across the bay, full of free love, music, and drugs. Manson took his advice, and clocked in some quality time dropping acid, sleeping in Golden Gate Park, bagging chicks, and listening *to a lot of Beatles records.* Other people circulated around him, mostly girls, and the communal group shared a flat on Cole Street, just off Haight. Goo goo ga joob, man.

Photo: Paul Trapani

But the Summer of Love vibe was growing bad, Manson would later say. The scene was coming down fast. People were ripping each other off. To get away from the madness, Charlie gathered his followers together — Susan Atkins, Squeaky Fromme, and Patricia Krenwinkle among them — packed everyone up in a school bus, and took them on their own magical mystery tour for a year and a half. They ended up in Southern California, hanging out with Dennis Wilson, living at Spahn Ranch, and we all know the hilarity that ensued at the Tate and LaBianca residences in 1969.

Manson was convicted of orchestrating the murders, and from his prison cell watched a cult status grow up around him — bootlegs of his music, videos of his appearances on talk shows, his face plastered on clothing and posters. Comedians like Sam Kinison performed routines about the murders. Musician Trent Reznor built a studio named Le Pig, threw wild parties, and recorded the Nine Inch Nails album *Downward Spiral*, all in the same house where Sharon Tate was stabbed to death. Manson's web site, maintained by longtime Family member Sandra Good, posts his artwork and music, and keeps fans abreast of what he's up to. He's had 10 parole hearings since 1978, and is due for the next one in 2002.

Manson's former flat in the Upper Haight is a pleasant Victorian, and is frequently photographed by tourists.

**Manson Family home
636 Cole Street**

# Busted Flat in Baton Rouge

It's too easy to dismiss Janis Joplin as a Southern Comfort-guzzling speed freak who made her own jewelry from chicken bones, sang like she was going to throw up a lung, and OD'd on heroin before her last album was released. She did more than that. She also paid rent within the San Francisco city limits.

Raised in the oil refinery seaport of Port Arthur, Texas, she spent some time singing in Austin cafes and bars, then moved to the Bay Area in 1966 and hooked up with Big Brother & the Holding Company, the house band at the Avalon Ballroom (now the Regency II movie theater on Sutter and Van Ness). In early 1967, she moved into a one-bedroom apartment, living there during the Summer of Love and her performance with Big Brother at the Monterey Pop Festival, before getting evicted for owning a dog. She recorded with a few more bands, did the Ed Sullivan show, and on October 4, 1970, scored a good batch of heroin and overdosed in her room at the Landmark Hotel in Los Angeles. Jimi Hendrix had already cashed in two weeks earlier, and Jim Morrison retired from life within the year, but they never established residency here, so enough about them. Joplin was cremated upon her death, and her ashes were scattered along the Marin County coastline.

Janis Joplin home
122 Lyon Street

# Reefer Ballet

photo: Anthony Pidgeon

Born to a poor peasant family, Rudolf Nureyev defected from the Soviet Union during a Kirov Ballet performance in 1961, and paired up for a long partnership with British Royal Ballet's acclaimed ballerina Margot Fonteyn. He liked to party, and mingled easily with the rich and famous. Some said he was the greatest male dancer in the world. Eventually he branched out into TV and film, and conducting and choreographing. He last performed in public in 1992, and died of AIDS a year later. But before he left this mortal coil, he blew a little reefer in San Francisco.

On July 11, 1967, police responded to a complaint of a noisy party at an address just off Haight Street. They entered the party, saw people were smoking pot, and started to make arrests. A man swung down into the room from a window and announced to the police, "It isn't a party until I'm here." Or words to that effect. It was Nureyev, who happened to be performing in the city. Police searched the premises further, and found Dame Margot Fonteyn hiding on the roof, wearing a white mink fur. Eighteen were arrested, including the assistant manager of the Seattle Opera, and 12 "marijuana cigarettes" were confiscated. Charges were later dropped, and that evening, 200 hippies danced in front of the Opera House on Van Ness Avenue, where Nureyev and Fonteyn were appearing.

Rudolf Nureyev pot bust
42 Belvedere Street

# Jefferson Airplane Hangar

Photo: Anthony Pidgeon

**B**uilt at the turn of the century for a lumber baron, this four-story mansion, with its mahogany banister staircase, somehow ended up into the hands of the newly successful Jefferson "Feed Your Head" Airplane. The band painted the exterior all black, and in 1968 moved their instruments, business offices, personal belongings, and drugs into the house. Administrative staff enjoyed a clear view out the windows of stoned kids stumbling through Golden Gate Park. Long-winded *Rolling Stone* reporters dropped by for long-winded interviews, and the parties commenced. The cover photo of Airplane's album *Bless Its Pointed Little Head* was taken at one bash in 1968, and the mansion hosted another legendary party on New Year's Eve 1979, after the Blues Brothers played their final show in the city.

The band dissolved and re-formed a million times, always managing to crawl back into the headlines, especially singer Grace Slick. She was once stopped at the gates of the White House with Abbie Hoffman, attempting to dose President Nixon with LSD. As a celebrity judge for a local nightclub version of "The Gong Show," she showed up stinking drunk, yelled at everybody, broke a couple of microphones, and was dragged offstage to cheers from the audience. (That evening she was stopped for erratic driving, mouthed off to the Highway Patrol, and ended up spending the night in jail.) And in 1994, police responded to a report of domestic abuse at her Tiburon home, and arrested her for leveling a shotgun at the officers.

In the mid-1980s, Airplane guitarist/song-writer Paul Kantner put the mansion up for sale. The party was finally over, but the building's address is forever immortalized as the title of one of the band's greatest-hits collections.

Jefferson Airplane home
2400 Fulton Street

SAN FRANCISCO ● 88 ● BIZARRO

# Winters Wigs Out

Photo: Sharon Selden

**A** favorite city landmark, the *Balclutha* sailing ship was built in Scotland in 1883, and sailed the Cape Horn route for many years, bringing European goods to the West Coast and taking California grains back home. After the turn of the century, it served as a lumber ship, and an Alaskan salmon cannery. And at the dawn of the 1960s, it was in the news again, when a crazy comedian climbed the rigging and refused to come down.

Originally from Springfield, Ohio, Jonathan Winters became a popular nightclub draw and frequent television guest. His act contained few punchlines and no jokes, but audiences found it hilarious to watch him pick up a prop and invent a character on the spot. His instinctual free-form style left a big impression on future comedians like Robin Williams.

In 1959, following a series of shows at the Hungry I in North Beach, Winters startled the audience by abruptly getting serious. In the middle of his act, he suddenly went off on a rant about Alcoholics Anonymous, and when his cigarette lighter didn't work, he burst into tears. He then ran out of the club, dashed several blocks down to Fisherman's Wharf, and climbed up the rigging of the *Balclutha*. Police arrived and attempted to talk him down, but Winters hollered, "I'm the man in the moon!" The wild-eyed comedian was handcuffed and taken away to S.F. General Hospital, where he spent the night in a psychiatric ward isolation cell.

Over the ensuing decades, Winters has appeared in many films and TV shows, painted and written books, and has spoken out freely about his bouts with mental illness. The *Balclutha* has also served as a Hollywood movie prop.

Jonathan Winters freak-out
Balclutha
Fisherman's Wharf

# Criminal Tribute

**W** e may consider O.J. Simpson the subject of the most famous murder trial in history, but not so long ago his hometown neighborhood thought him a hero, and commissioned a mural that honored this kid from the projects who rose to the top of the heap.

In the Potrero District, kids hung out on the courts, and like many of them, Simpson joined a street gang. By age 13, he was a member of the Persian Warriors. A gifted athlete, he played football for Galileo High School (which retired his jersey), won the Heisman Trophy while at USC, then turned pro and set several NFL records with

Photo: Anthony Pidgeon

the Buffalo Bills before closing out his career back in San Francisco with the 49ers. And then he retired to Southern California — Brentwood, bloody knife, Bronco on the freeway, racist cops, opportunistic attorneys, greedy book authors, etc. Although eventually found liable in a wrongful death decision for $33.5 million, O.J. still earns a good living from protected assets. Perhaps he could kick a few bucks down to the Potrero Hill Rec Center. The mural could use a touch-up.

O.J. Simpson mural
Potrero Hill Recreation Center
17th Street and Arkansas

# Lenny's Lament

Jazz/beat comic Lenny Bruce wasn't always revolutionary. He started off as a nice, funny guy who served in the Army, and entered the entertainment world via the sleazy burlesque circuit. But he was already different than the others. He told stories by jumping in and out of different character voices, and made jokes about previously taboo subjects like religion, sex, drugs, and the Cold War. The country wasn't quite prepared to hear him, but fortunately, liberal-minded San Francisco was. Not only did he first make headlines in North Beach, at the end of his life it was one of the few areas that still allowed him onstage.

His first major nightclub show was in 1958 at a North Beach lesbian bar called Ann's 440 (440 Broadway), where critic Ralph Gleason caught the show and gave Bruce a rave review. He appeared on television, and released several albums, including a live recording at Carnegie Hall. One album cover depicted him smiling, reclining on a picnic blanket in a graveyard.

But darn it, he kept going on about religion and sex, and using naughty language. As thanks for his satirical commentary, the country repeatedly prosecuted him for obscenity. Bruce became a Freedom of Speech icon throughout his trials, supported by dozens of writers, critics, and celebrities, from theologian Reinhold Niebuhr and psychologist Theodor Reik, to Richard Burton, Liz Taylor, Woody Allen, Bob Dylan, Paul Newman, Susan Sontag, Lionel Trilling, and Rudy Vallee. He was a cultural hero, and yet America didn't know what to do with him. Faced with expensive attorney bills, he ended up defending himself in the courtroom, and his nightclub act included more and more of his legal battles.

On March 29, 1965, while staying in the Swiss American Hotel (534 Broadway), a naked Bruce fell out the second-story window into the parking lot, landing on his feet and breaking both ankles. He was taken to the hospital, and whatever he was saying was enough to make attendants tape his mouth shut. Newspapers reported that "The 38-year-old comedian put on a performance so sick that doctors slapped a bandage muzzle over his mouth."

Later that year he collaborated with San Francisco filmmaker John Magnuson to document his live act for use as evidence in court. Shot at the Basin Street West (Broadway and New Montgomery), the unedited result was released as *The Lenny Bruce Performance Film*, and was, according to Magnuson, his last regular club gig. His last-ever performance would be across town at the Fillmore concert hall (Geary and Fillmore), on a double bill with Frank Zappa and the Mothers of Invention. The following year he was discovered on his Los Angeles bathroom floor, dead of a heroin overdose. Promoter Phil Spector claimed the cause of death was actually "an overdose of police." Four years later, a New York State Court of Appeals reversed his obscenity conviction — too little, too late.

# Rich-Girl Robber

I t's not easy to be born into affluence, especially if you're the granddaughter of William Randolph Hearst, and you attended the best private schools and vacationed at San Simeon. You'd have to become a radical terrorist to feel like you're really participating in life.

On February 4, 1974, two black men and a white woman kidnapped a 19-year-old Patricia Hearst from her apartment in Berkeley (all that money, and she still ended up at UC?). They beat up her boyfriend Steven Weed, and fled. Law enforcement agencies hunted for weeks, to no avail. She was considered a victim — kidnapped by black militants! — but a few months later, a group robbed a Hibernia Bank in San Francisco. Security cameras revealed images of a woman who looked an awful lot like little Patty, wearing a black beret and cradling a semiautomatic rifle. The image of the rich heiress-turned-militant thug ran on covers of *Time* and *Newsweek*, and was seen around the world. Her

Photo: Paul Trapani

kidnappers announced they were the Symbionese Liberation Army, and their leader was Donald "General Field Marshall Cinque" DeFreeze, who did time for armed robbery and was once a police informant.

Patty released taped statements to the media that ridiculed American capitalism. She changed her name to Tania, and called her father a "corporate liar." Even though he was a "liar," Daddy still forked over a $2 million ransom, in the form of charity to California's poor people. Trucks pulled into ghetto neighborhoods and dispensed cases of food.

Hearst stayed with the SLA for a year, shuttling between safe houses in the Bay Area. And then, on May 17, 1974, the dream of an international SLA cabal that would free the world from all oppression was crushed. Over 500 armed police and SWAT teams surrounded a bungalow in South Central Los Angeles, where Cinque and five others were holed up. After a two-hour shoot-out, the house suddenly burst into flames, burning all the inhabitants beyond recognition. Hearst was arrested a year later at 625 Morse Street in San Francisco (just southwest of the Crocker-Amazon playground).

Her trial could qualify as a circus. A news photo showed her wearing a T-shirt that said "Pardon Me," but the judge was adamant that the rich girl had to tick off some time in the joint. She was sentenced to seven years for armed robbery, but served only eight months before being released. She returned to prison in 1978, and after 22 months, President Carter signed an order releasing her. How often does that happen to bank robbers? She married her bodyguard, Bernard Shaw, and at her wedding, the maid of honor was Trish Robin, daughter of the owner of the same Hibernia Bank.

Patty Hearst wrote a book, *Every Secret Thing*, which is available at the gift shop of Hearst Castle, and in recent years has enjoyed a new career as a star of John Waters movies.

**Patty Hearst abduction site**
2603 Benvenue Avenue #4, Berkeley

**Patty Hearst bank robbery**
Hibernia Bank
(now Hollywood Video)
1450 Noriega at 22nd Avenue

**Patty Hearst capture site**
625 Morse Avenue

# The Goofy Gettys!

In a sense, you could call the Getty home a duplex — except with this duplex, the two buildings connected are Pacific Heights mansions. In 1992, Gordon Getty threw down $3.75 million for the mansion next door, to make room for a swimming pool and a few other things. When the family owns its own Boeing 727 (nicknamed "The Jetty"), you can do things like that.

If your name is Getty, it isn't necessary to have a job. J. Paul Getty busted his ass in the oil fields many years ago to ensure that the kids wouldn't starve (Gordon is the fourth of five sons). The old man made an awful lot of money, and at one point even wrote a book called *How to Be Rich*. But with such horrendous amounts of wealth inevitably comes nutty behavior. In what apparently was a botched attempt at a hoax, Gordon's nephew Jean Paul Getty III claimed to be kidnapped by Italian Red Brigades, who supposedly cut off his ear and demanded $1 million ransom. J. Paul Getty Jr. renounced his U.S. citizenship and moved to England. In 1967, Gordon sued his own father for $5 million in dividends held in trust. It must have been a good move, because by 1983, *Forbes* listed Gordon as the richest man in America, citing his net worth at $2.2 billion. The following year, Gordon engineered a high-profile merger of Getty Oil and Texaco, and the deal was so prosperous that the Getty family went to court to argue over who would get what. The squabble resulted in a division of the family trust into six parts; the Getty name is attached to many diverse interests including the slick Getty museum in Los Angeles.

But none of this financial stuff matters much to the San Francisco Gettys. They would rather be musicians.

Gordon fancies himself a classical composer, and outward signs indicate a lifestyle typical of many musicians. He often appears in public somewhat rumpled, necktie poorly tied, and for years drove a beat-up car, parking it in front of the mansions. And as often occurs in the careers of musicians, intent is misunderstood and reviews are mixed. In 1985 the San Francisco Symphony, to which Getty is a major donor, debuted his 12-minute cantata of his own opera, *Plump Jack. San Francisco Chronicle* critic Robert Commanday observed, "If you or I had written this, it wouldn't have gone beyond the living room."

Gordon's work has been heard very infrequently since then, but no matter. There is another generation of Getty blessed with the muse of song. Under the pseudonym Spats Ransom, Gordon's son Peter writes and records with his own rock band, The Virgin/Whore Complex. Material varies from personal rich-kid reflections to music accompaniment for the letters written to police by the notorious Zodiac Killer. As with his father, Peter Getty has learned the importance of distributing one's music. He runs his own indie record label, the extremely well-financed Emperor Norton Records. And another tip learned from Dad — his band refuses to perform live.

Gordon's wife, Ann, keeps visible in society affairs, and another of their sons, Billy Getty, invests in various businesses, including a restaurant and a wine shop. But by and large, the San Francisco Gettys are a fairly calm bunch. They have yet to snap and do something really insane, but when they do, we'll all be waiting for it.

# House of Romance

**D**riving through Pacific Heights, it's tempting to play the guessing game. Who are the eccentrics living in these old mansions? Are the owners even still alive? Or are their corpses lying undiscovered, rotting away in a four-poster bed surrounded by dusty heir-looms, like a scene from a William Faulkner short story? One of these gargantuan residences, the 55-room Spreckels Mansion, occupies nearly a full block of Washington Street, bordered by Jackson, Gough, and Octavia streets. Built in 1913 for the family of sugar magnate Claus Spreckels, it's now the humble abode of romance novelist Danielle Steel, perhaps the city's wealthiest woman. Since 1990 Steel has sat inside this estate at a manual typewriter, cranking out books that sell millions and drive critics insane.

Since publication of her first book, *Going Home*, back in 1973, , Steel has seen nearly 40 of her books published, selling over 200 million copies total, with several made-for-TV movies thrown in just for fun. She shakes down the reading public for an estimated $25 million a year, all without ever doing a book tour. Pick any of her novels, and you can finish it in a weekend, chewing up and digesting her trademark hooks — divorce, affairs, unexpected death, infertility, prolonged illness, miscarriage, usually with a happy ending. But while she's been crafting juicy soap opera fiction, San Francisco has been watching another non-fiction plot unfold — her own life. The much-recounted mythical tale of the world's best-selling romance novelist spins out with as just much drama and chaos as one of her stories. Culled together from her biography and newspaper articles, it goes something like this:

Born the only child of a German father and Portuguese mother, Steel overcame childhood polio and cancer, and graduated from New York's Lycee Francais at 15. She was lonely, and traveled frequently. At 18 she launched into a string of marriages, hitching up to Husband #1, banker Claude-Eric Lazard. One daughter later she got divorced, and at 25 found work in a department store, then in public relations. While conducting research on conscientious objectors, she visited a prison and met Husband #2, bank robber and convicted rapist Danny Zugelder. While pregnant with Zugelder's child, she answered the door one day and met William Toth, then working for a moving company. She divorced Zugelder and, expecting a child in two weeks, took Toth as Husband #3, a burglar and recovering heroin addict. She then divorced Toth and upgraded in the spousal department to Husband #4, shipping executive John Traina. After yet another divorce, Silicon Valley venture capitalist Tom Perkins stepped up to the plate in 1998 and became Husband #5.

But while the man problem appeared abated, gossip still circulated about her appetite for estate jewelry and vintage cars, and the party one night at the Getty mansion when her beeper went off, she stepped outside, a limo pulled up on cue with her baby, and she proceeded to breast-feed the child.

Her life continues to attract high drama. A disgruntled former employee unsuccessfully sued Steel in 1994, alleging emotional abuse. Not long thereafter, she filed suit against an unauthorized biographer, attempting to stop the use of a court document about her teenage son Nick. He ended up fronting a Berkeley punk rock band, but plagued by a history of mental problems, the poor kid died of a heroin overdose. His mother financed local punk benefits in his honor, and then wrote a book about him.

Constructed of white Utah limestone, Steel's home once appeared onscreen as a nightclub in the 1957 Sinatra film *Pal Joey*.

**Danielle Steel mansion
2080 Washington Street at Octavia**

# Screaming Night Hogs

I t's a familiar San Francisco story: A young writer moves to the city, can't get published, and ends up broke, hungry and frustrated, standing in line for a job he knows he will hate. In the case of Hunter Thompson, who was trying to support a wife and baby, help came in the form of the Hell's Angels motorcycle club.

*The Nation* first published a Thompson article about California's outlaw biker gangs, and the exposure led him to sign a book deal on the Hell's Angels. He and his family spent the next year living in a first-floor apartment on Parnassas in the Upper Haight, hanging out with the baddest bikers of all time. Harleys pulled up to the house at 2 a.m., and Angels stayed up with Thompson, smoking dope and listening to Bob Dylan records at top volume. In 1966 Random House published *The Hell's Angels: The Strange and Terrible Saga of Outlaw Motorcycle Clubs*, and Thompson never went hungry again.

He was the first to chronicle their history, beginning with the fighter pilots who roared their bikes around the Hollister area, still tweaked from World War II. He explained the photos from the infamous Hollister biker rally that were staged by photographers, to make the place look even more lurid and dangerous. He mentioned Marlon Brando's 1954 film *The Wild One*, based on the same incident, which every biker knew by heart.

He revealed that the Angels opened their first chapter in San Bernardino, which they called San Berdoo, and how they devised the infamous colors and skull logo. Another chapter opened in Oakland, which became the world headquarters, and they named a tough, charismatic kid named Ralph "Sonny" Barger as their president and supreme leader.

Thompson ended his book with a description of the Angels beating him up and breaking his nose. They later said that he exaggerated what happened, and that they just shoved him around a little. But they had to admit that he was the first to introduce them to the outside world. Soon, everybody wanted a piece of America's last true outlaws. The club consulted on cheesy Hollywood biker films (*Hell's Angels on Wheels* featured Jack Nicholson in the role of an Angels prospect named "Poet"). Angels tripped with Ken Kesey and the Merry Pranksters, and provided security for rock concerts throughout the 1960s, including the ill-fated Altamont show (see Chapter VIII, "The Grim Reaper Revue").

Angels were targeted by police and feds for years, who believed the club to be the biggest organized crime syndicate in the world — prostitution, racketeering, and production and distribution of methamphetamine, nick-named "crank" because bikers transported bags of the stuff hidden within the crankcases of their engines. Cops were continually busting Angels throughout the U.S., and the group grew tired of other people getting their story wrong. Beginning in the early 1970s, they started work on their own documentary film. Production stalled, and the film *Hell's Angels Forever* took three directors before finally getting released in 1983. This would be the Angels' explanation of their philosophy, which was summed up as: "The greatest pleasure in life is doing what people say you cannot do, and doing it with the people that you love." The film included footage of a concert by Willie Nelson, Bo Diddley, and Jerry Garcia, who gave his observations about the Angels:

"If I see a guy that weighs 400 pounds, and he's got on leather, and big sharp metal things, man, and swastikas, and things, I know for *sure* that I don't wanna fuck with that guy, man. You know what I mean? And that's cool, because that's telling me who he is, you know what I mean? And I have the choice of, I'm either gonna go in there and make

**Hunter Thompson home
318 Parnassas Street**

# Deadquarters

**A**ny true Deadhead already knows this address, the Haight-Ashbury home of the ultimate hippie band. The Grateful Dead only lived here for two years, from 1966 to 1968, but that's enough time to establish the origins of a 30-year mythology of drugs, brown rice, and spacey out-of-tune songs that lasted 45 minutes.

The Dead lived here in a loose-knit hippie community, sharing the women and wine, and quickly found their Victorian house to be a regular stop on the Gray Line "Hippie Hop" bus tour, which drove tourists through the heart of the 1960s youth problem. Gigs were spontaneous in those days. The band once played a free show in the Panhandle park on two hours' notice, stretching an extension cord across Fell Street to provide power. In October 1967, police conducted a drug raid on the house, finding a small amount of pot, and arresting band members Bob Weir and Pigpen, along with some hangers-on (Jerry Garcia and his girlfriend were apparently out shopping at the time). Before the Dead moved to Marin in 1968, they parked a flatbed truck on Haight Street and played a free gig as a goodbye to the neighborhood, hippies twirl-dancing in accompaniment.

On their visits to the Upper Haight to buy Dead T-shirts and stickers, people still stop by the house and take photos. But if you're any sort of true Deadhead at all, you'll gently touch the palms of your hands against the building, and absorb the psychic energy.

**Grateful Dead house
710 Ashbury Street**

a fool of myself, or else I'm gonna to be very cool. If that's what's happening, I'll be cool. But shit, is that out front or what, you know?"

But the myth has spawned its own folklore. One test to join the club, some said, was if you could build a Harley from the ground up. An Angel may have sold bike design patents to Harley-Davidson. When Los Angeles hosted the Summer Olympics, the torch was supposedly carried by a Hell's Angel. More recently, New York chapter president Chuck Zito punched out actor Jean-Claude Van Damme in front of a Manhattan strip club.

Hell's Angels aren't so much in the news these days. The club has built up its ranks by absorbing other biker clubs. Barger served some prison time for racketeering, and went back to running a Harley repair shop in the Bay Area. In the past few years he has lent his name to various products, from bottled water to jalapeño sauce, ceramic sculptures, and a partnership with Corbin motorcycle seats, publicizing a three-wheeled electric car named the Sparrow. The Angels organization is beginning to market more products, including phone cards, Kona coffee, and a line of biker leathers. The international headquarters is still in Oakland, and members remain an unmistakable presence around the Bay Area. If you are dead serious, you'll know where to find them.

After revisiting San Francisco to write a column for Hearst's 1980s *Examiner,* Hunter Thompson returned home to Woody Creek, Colorado.

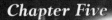

Chapter Five

# Show Me Yours First

In case you've been sleeping under a rock, San Francisco is one of the planet's most sexually liberated cities. In the past three decades, this naturally tolerant environment has introduced the world to topless and bottomless dancing, gay clubs that rivalled Rome, and the modern primitives, fetish and S/M scenes. Much like modern art, there's nothing wrong with outrageous sex, as long as you justify your actions. In this town, you can fuck a fire hydrant, as long as you have a newsletter. But if you can't explain that uncontrollable urge to fall to your knees at the sight of a dog's anus, and begin howling and furiously licking your own hands, well then, San Francisco doesn't need you. You're one sick bastard — probably from the Midwest — and should be locked up for observation at a state university. But if you were, say, the editor of *Pawlick* magazine (or www.pawlick.com), acting out the symbiotic relationship between bestiality and self-love in a consensual field experiment, that's okay. Everyone would simply recognize you as the Dog-Butt Guy. You would be flown to sex-positive events across the globe, and all of Finland will speak of your exciting work here in the Bay Area. This chapter represents but a fraction of the totality of the local sex world, so if you don't see something here, just be patient, and it will soon surface. Even better, start your own newsletter.

# 24-Hour Porn!

Your first introduction to this oasis of smut is the wall of glossy porn-star photos — *signed by the real girls!* — famous fannies like Nici Sterling, Nina Hartley, Tiffany Minx, and Julie Ashton (also proud endorser of the Julie Ashton "Ultra-Realistic Pussy and Ass," and the Julie Ashton "Ultra Harness Vac-U-Lock™ System"). Besides attracting the best and brightest the jizz biz has to offer, this emporium constitutes the absolute cutting edge in porn, and it's extra special, because it's open 24 hours.

Let's be honest, who hasn't had that 3 a.m. craving for the latest issue of *Black Tail, 50+, Give Us Your Jizz,* or *Shaved and Depraved*? Hey, we've all felt a 4:30 a.m. hankering for John Stagliano's Buttmaster butt probe, complete with the little handle. Now granted, the early morning crowd perhaps isn't as zesty as the white-collar guys running in for a lunchtime yank, and are probably the sole purchasers of *Lonely* magazine, but the convenience just can't be denied. It's our American right to look at dirty pictures, and we shouldn't be bound by the constraints of conventional retail hours.

Owners of Frenchy's understand the value of variety. Their video selection offers enthusiasts a wide range of categories: orgy/gang bang, gonzo, amateur, bisexual, busty, special interests (designated by an icon of a shoe), anal, all-sex, gay, Asian, interracial, or the classics. Every square inch of wall and floor space is devoted to porn products, items you know you need but just never believed existed, like the Mini-Intruder Kit. Or the Soap on a Rope, "the sudsy butt plug." Need your penis pumped? Take your pick of the Commando Pump, the Stallion Pump, or the Fireman Pump, "for that big hard hose." And when everything's intruded, soaped, and pumped up, it's time to get busy with the Piña Colada Whipped Creme. Yes, the industry really has thought of everyone.

You don't even need to walk in the door to enjoy a taste of Frenchy's. Just drive by the marquee sign, which regularly rotates its wacky slogans. Immediately after the 7.1 earthquake in the middle of the 1989 World Series, the shop's sign proclaimed: "Earthquake sale, save on vibrating sex toys."

**Frenchy's**
**1020 Geary Street**
**(415) 776-5940**

# Budget Lust

Not only is admission free at this female-owned North Beach peep show, once inside the door, even the biggest penny-pinching perv will notice the Lusty Lady is the best strip-club bargain in town. For a mere quarter — half of a Snickers bar, really — a window will rise, and a naked young woman will hoist up some portion of her anatomy to your sweaty, waiting face. Even when you throw in metered parking (assuming you can find a space in North Beach), you've still got a complete date with a nude girl for under a dollar.

But this discount has come at a price for the employees. After years of titillation for two bits, dancers started noticing that customers were sneaking in cameras and filming the action through the peep show's one-way windows. Talk about cheap! The girls complained to management, but nothing happened. So they got organized and approached the Local 790 chapter of the Service Employees International Union. After much negotiation, and a National Labor Relations Board union election, in

Photo: Paul Trapani

April 1997, the Lusty Lady became the first strip club in the country to unionize all its employees. The theater now provides benefits for dancers, cashiers, security, and yes, even the janitors who mop out the booths. So as you step into a booth for your 25-cent tete-à-tete, remember that even though the girl behind the glass probably doesn't have it on her person at the moment, she's still carrying a union card.

**Lusty Lady Theatre**
**1033 Kearny Street**
**(415) 391-3991**

# Adult Diapers

**S**ome years ago, when I was editing a magazine in San Francisco, a staff member brought into the office a newsletter he had discovered in the wastebasket at a local Kinko's copy outlet. The newsletter's masthead proclaimed it to be the official publication of the Diaper Pail Fraternity, a mail-order organization devoted to infantilism, located across the Golden Gate Bridge in the sleepy town of Mill Valley. Paging through the DPF's diaper-related stories and videos, and ads for adult diapers and "rhumba panties," it became apparent that this is not just a handful of folks living in a cave somewhere. A whole bunch

of people are into this stuff. In fact, an international network of giant babies meets and greets every day through the DPF, the epicenter of which is right here in the Bay Area — the top of the adult diaper heap!

Since 1980 the Diaper Pail Fraternity (aka "The Happiness Club") has brought joy to over 12,000 people with a hankering for dressing up like babies and messing themselves. The group recognizes all sexual and ethnic preferences and persuasions, with only one condition — you gotta love diapers.

Regular DPF-sponsored field trips allow giggling members to go shopping, ride the cable cars, change each other's soiled die-dies and roll around in playpens. Parties will often find people going into rooms to dress up in diapers and play like babies. They insist that children are not the focus, however, and if you have the patience to squint and read through their insanely single-spaced, fine-print newsletters and web pages, their literature confirms that this is an adults-only environment.

A DPF Roster helps people meet each other through free coded listings. Upcoming parties all over the world are announced. Adult babysitting services are offered. A secret Baby-Club internet site lets the more adventurous do their thing. Grateful letters pour in from all corners of the earth.

"I have told my wife all about DPF and in fact she has already started to write some members," gushes one happy baby. "She is also great when it comes to keeping me well diapered and deciding when or if I need a change."

A special alphabetical coding system alerts readers to all the baby-related products you can buy: Videos of babies running amok in their cribs. Comics that feature a hero named — what else? —

Images Courtesy: DPF

"Diaperman." Books devoted to infantilism case histories. Diaper-themed novelettes like *Elliott the Diaper Boy Part II* or *Leslie Goes to the Movies*. A handy 27-page *Enema Report*. Fully illustrated publications include *Big Sissy Babies Magazine* and *Modern Mommy Magazine*, for women whose husbands or boyfriends want to wear diapers and sit in cribs. Hypnotic audiotapes are categorized into nine levels, culminating in Level 1, "Baby Will Always Wet and Mess," where a repeated keyword will make the listener "helplessly wet and mess" their diapers.

And once you've read up on everything and feel up to speed, it's time to play dress-up. DPF offers hundreds of big-person rhumba panties, bibs, baby dresses with matching bonnets, rompers, sailor suits, crawlers, sleepers, onesies, pacifiers, nipples to fit onto bottles, bed pads, and mattress covers, for those inevitable accidents.

But most importantly, they sell diapers, in every shape, size and model. After approaching children's diaper manufacturers, DPF has had them create adult-sized custom jobs, in the exact same designs as those for infants, with the diaper detailing replicated down to the last plastic liner and refastenable tape. (You could probably get them pin-striped if you'd like.) The emphasis is vivid and always focused on the image and sensation of big, soft, fluffy cotton, something that will feel comfortable up against, say, a 65-year-old grampa butt with pimples. For each diaper advertised, the copy always includes the phrase, "this is the softest diaper in the world."

The ranks of the DPF are always growing, says Tommy, the group's director. The interest is such a closeted impulse, Tommy continues, that when someone realizes there are others like him or herself, they're often ecstatic to discover that such an organization exists. So if you're looking for your true inner baby, visit the secret world of the DPF to satisfy all those adult diaper needs. Lie down on your back, kick your legs and cry — you deserve it!

**DPF
Suite 127, 38 Miller Avenue
Mill Valley CA 94941**

# Breasts Across

June of 1964. The 400-pound manager of the Condor Club, Davey Rosenberg, was at the home of his boss, Gino Del Prete. Both men were looking at the front page of the morning's *San Francisco Chronicle*, which featured a photo of a 4-year-old girl wearing a new topless swimsuit by Los Angeles designer Rudi Gernreich. Business was so-so at their North Beach bar — a little jazz, a go-go girl dancing on top of a piano. They needed a good publicity idea. Rosenberg gestured to the newspaper, turned to his employer, and said:

"You want to know how to pack the place?"

"No 4-year-olds," responded Del Prete.

Rosenberg bought two Gernreich suits from the I. Magnin

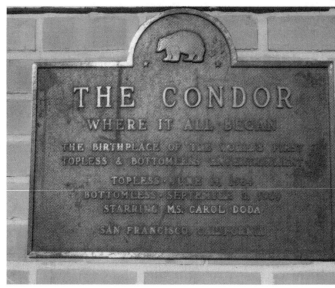

department store, and that night a Condor waitress named Carol Doda danced bare-breasted atop the piano. Unfortunately, the city's media focused instead on President Johnson's campaign tour, but a local disc jockey talked up the stunt, and the next night men swarmed North Beach to see the first topless dance club in America. Within 48 hours, the neighboring bars also went topless, and at one point, 28 clubs along the Broadway strip were advertising bare-breasted dancers.

Photo: North Beach Chamber of Commerce

Each night, the Condor's white grand piano lowered from the ceiling, and a topless woman gyrated away for the crowds. Many women became stars at the club, but Doda stood apart from the rest, especially once she took on a series of silicone injections, which expanded her chest from 34 to 44 inches. The country went nuts. Her breasts were set in wet cement in front of the club. The *U.S.S. Kittyhawk* aircraft carrier named her Pinup Girl of the Year. She starred in theatrical revues

# America

and films, and even received a Business Person of the Year award from Harvard University. Along with international fame came the inevitable backlash. Reverends wrote her disapproving letters. Restaurants refused to serve her.

But Doda kept dancing, and for 23 years reigned as the Queen of Topless. She eventually retired to pursue other interests, hosting movies on a San Jose TV station called "The Perfect 36," fronting a rock band called Carol Doda and Her Lucky Stiffs, and has ended up an entrepreneur, operating her own lingerie shop in the yuppie Marina District.

In the early 1980s, the Condor again made news when a dancer and her beefy security-guard boyfriend engaged in sex atop the grand piano. Unfortunately, the hydraulic elevating mechanism became jammed — some later theorized it was the guy's pointed-toe boots that accidentally hit a switch — and the piano rose to the ceiling and crushed the man to death. The woman was pinned underneath him for several hours until help arrived.

The original Condor soon closed for good, and a few years later reopened as a sports bar, decorated with neon beer signs and memorabilia from the topless era. Attached to the ceiling is the very same killer piano. What was once the biggest topless attraction in the world now advertises the biggest TV in San Francisco.

Photo: Sharon Selden

The Condor Club
300 Columbus Avenue
(415) 781-8222

Carol Doda Champagne & Lace
Lingerie Boutique
1850 Union Street
(415) 776-6900

# Swinging in Oakland

**A**irline commuters arriving in the Bay Area have their choice of airport destinations, either San Francisco or Oakland. But in the case of Oakland, landing in the East Bay boasts an extra feature. A short drive down the road from the airport is the Edgewater West, the world's last surviving full-time swinger hotel. Because the idea of swinging and couple-swapping seems like such a 1970s concept, you might think the Edgewater to be some sort of functioning relic from the sexual revolution. Don't worry, it is.

Admission is $25 for couples, $40 for single men, and $80 or $90 to check into a room for the night. All the rooms have sliding glass doors, which face an enclosed courtyard of palm trees, hot tubs, and a non-alcohol lounge/strip bar. Wild cats scurry across the grass, freaked out at all the people. There are few house rules, but one is that if guests leave their curtains open, this is an invitation for other folks to watch, and if the door is open, everything is fair game.

Guests stroll the grounds for hours, peeking in windows and eyeing each other for possibilities. Women may be plump, wearing flouncy lingerie, and there's a good possibility the men might be middle-aged, wearing jockstraps and windbreakers.

Although porn films are shot here, the most typical sight is not wild swinging, but 10 guys crowded in front of a room, peeking through the curtains. At one point a man will turn away, breathe booze into your face, and grumble, "She ain't even showin' any tit!"

Edgewater West
10 Hegenberger Road, Oakland
(510) 632-6262

# CIA's LSD Brothel

T he CIA's 1953 mind-control program called MKULTRA was intended to plunder the outer reaches of the human brain. Among the agency's plans were experiments with a new chemical compound nicknamed LSD, which had been discovered in the 1940s, and was being considered as a possible spy weapon. The drug was hideously potent. A suitcase full of the stuff could trip the skulls of every man, woman, and child in the United States. The CIA monitored all amounts that were manufactured, and began testing their new discovery. As research was conducted at universities (including the Stanford Research Institute, where Ken Kesey first dosed), MKULTRA leaders took LSD and analyzed each other, with mixed results. One agency employee ran crazed through Washington, D.C., until co-workers found him trembling underneath a fountain. At one federal hospital in Kentucky, seven student volunteers were kept zonked on LSD for 77 days in a row.

And at one point, the government wondered what it would be like if unsuspecting San Franciscans were given LSD while having sex with hookers.

In 1955 MKULTRA asked swashbuckling narcotics agent and former San Francisco journalist George White to set up a "safe house" in the city. More safe houses were established in other cities, but this one would focus on sex. The experimental program was cheekily code-named Operation Midnight Climax. The bald, portly White, a legendary boozehound who could finish a bottle of gin in one sitting, was handed the assignment to become the world's first psychedelic pimp.

White set up his harlot hostel atop fashionable Telegraph Hill, with picture windows that offered an outstanding view of Alcatraz. He furnished the pad in hipster Bachelor Boudoir — Toulouse-Lautrec posters, photos of manacled women in black stockings. A young Berkeley electronics student wired the place with microphones disguised as electrical wall outlets.

The United States government paid prostitutes $100 a night for their efforts in furthering the research project, and as a bonus, the women received chits that helped them avoid arrest. (According to *Acid Dreams* by Martin Lee, the project received full cooperation by the San Francisco Police Department.)

White watched the antics from behind a two-way mirror, perched atop a toilet, sipping at a pitcher of martinis. His reports enthusiastically described a parade of unwitting guys, attempting to comprehend the world's oldest profession while soaring on acid. Experiments were conducted on many different types of men — high and low society, Native Americans, and foreigners, including those who had similar backgrounds to foreign leaders, such as Fidel Castro. The study was as much about prostitution as it was the effects of LSD.

Further examination of the safe house idea left the government with the notion that feeding acid to unwitting test subjects was, oh, maybe *completely insane* (or as they put it, "distasteful and unethical"). Several subjects became ill for hours or days, and one was hospitalized. The safe house shut down in 1965, after a decade of CIA-financed acid orgies, and a year before acid was made illegal. Years later, White wrote to a colleague: "I was a very minor missionary, actually a heretic, but I toiled wholeheartedly in the vineyards because it was fun, fun, fun."

**Operation Midnight Climax
225 Chestnut Street**

# Palace

The concrete building on the corner of Polk and O'Farrell streets isn't just your everyday porn theater covered in wildlife murals, with Japanese tourist buses idling out front. Since 1969 this has been home to the Mitchell Brothers porn empire. Although it's now only one brother these days (Jim shot and killed Artie in 1993), its reputation remains as the most notorious and innovative sex emporium in the nation.

Design & Photography HEFFERNAN

Images Courtesy: O'Farrell Theatre

Back in the hippie '60s, Jim and Artie Mitchell were just a couple of S.F. State film students, who found easy money was available in making 8mm porn loops. After filming hundreds of shorts, in 1972 they premiered their first feature, *Behind the Green Door*, starring an unknown actress named Marilyn Chambers. Coincidentally, another Chambers project was just being released to the market — her face, photographed two years earlier for an Ivory soap box cover, holding up a cherubic infant. The brothers immediately knew how to market their new film: "She's 99 44/100 percent pure!" *Behind the Green Door* grossed an estimated $50 million before going to videocassette, and remains one of the most recognizable X-rated films in history.

The Mitchells frequently ended up in courtrooms and newspaper headlines throughout the '70s, and at one time ran a chain of 11 movie theaters throughout the state. When the industry shifted to video, they converted their O'Farrell film studio into a live theater, and brainstormed new and

# O'Porn

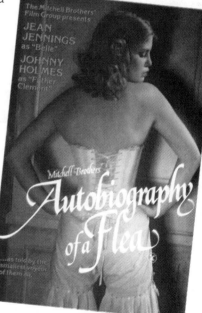

exciting gimmicks like the Ultra Room (windowless peep show booths), Kopenhagen Live (two girls, a darkened room with flashlights), and New York Live (classic burlesque seating with full lap-dancing).

Over the years, the Mitchells have attracted many rapscallions with like minds. Hunter S. Thompson worked for a time as the theater's night manager. Cartoonist R. Crumb stopped by to render some original drawings on the walls. The theater has featured a who's who of ecdysiasts, including Tempest Storm, Blaze Starr, Nina Hartley, Marilyn Chambers, Jeanna Fine, and Divine Brown. One bizarre act, a vaginal freak show named Honeysuckle Divine, taught herself to perform tricks with her privates, from blowing a party horn to discharging objects like ping-pong balls, baby powder and Jergen's lotion.

If you want to stop by and see what all the fuss is about, as you enter, take a right and check out the display room of memorabilia, including a original box of Ivory soap, signed by Marilyn Chambers.

Mitchell Brothers' O'Farrell Theatre
895 O'Farrell Street
(415) 776-6686

# Feets Don't Fail Me

To best understand the appeal of a shoe shop catering to the fetish crowd, readers are urged to consult the short story "Humiliated in Albuquerque," by Slave Shoelicker:

> "Beg," she said. "Beg to kiss my foot."
>
> I had to do it. I needed to kiss her glorious foot. My whole body was consumed with that single desire.
>
> "Kay, may I please..." I began, but Kay extended her leg and put her foot on the tip of my rock hard penis, pushing down. I moaned in pleasure as Kay said:
>
> "On your knees."
>
> I sank to my knees before her. How shameful I must have appeared. I looked into her eyes and Kay could see the pleading look written on my face. She knew I would do anything to kiss her stinky feet.
>
> "Please, Kay, I beg you. Let me kiss your feet. I'll do anything you want if you let me kiss them."
>
> "You are a worthless swine," she said. "Tell me you would rather kiss the toe cheese off my foot than your fiancé's face."
>
> "Kay, your foot is magnificent," I said, giving up all self respect. "It is far more beautiful than my fiancé. Your foot is all my heart desires. I would give Carla up in a moment for the chance to kiss the toe cheese off your foot. I beg you, please let me kiss your foot."
>
> Kay was nearly hysterical.
>
> "Beg like a dog."
>
> I put my hands under my chin and panted like a dog hopeful of getting a choice bone. Kay was stripping every ounce of pride I had left.
>
> "Kiss it, dog," she said.
>
> I bent down to her foot. The smell hit me before I reached it. It was the sweetest fragrance I'd ever known. I was lost in a state of euphoric bliss. I kissed her foot with all the passion I was able to summon. The acrid taste caused my mouth to water as if the most succulent meal had been placed before me. I began to lick her foot, drooling all over it and savoring each and every moment.
>
> Kay slid her foot past me and I started kissing my way up her perfect legs. I worshipped her with more feeling and sincerity than the slaves of ancient Egypt worshipped Cleopatra...

Photo: Sharon Selden

**Foot Worship**
**1214 Sutter Street**
**(415) 921-FOOT**

It all becomes a little more clear, doesn't it? Resurrected from the closing of the infamous Amazone S/M dungeon in Berkeley, the Foot Worship store is a decidedly more above-ground venture, and counts strippers, dominatrixes, and prostitutes among its regular customers. The shop stocks a full line of fetish footware, and also custom-makes shoes, no matter how bizarre the request. You don't have to be a sex-industry person to saunter in and stroke Foot Worship's selection of thigh-high PVC boots, or leather pumps with insane 8-inch stiletto heels. You can be an average person with a normal job. But it's a lot more fun if you *really love feet*.

# Corsets for Men!

**W**hen the Romantasy sex store was located in the white-bread yuppie Marina District, says owner Ann Grogan, their most popular items were things like handcuffs. When they moved to their Market Street location, their biggest sales became corsets. They soon went exclusively mail-order, and now claim the largest collection of qualified custom-made corsets in the world — a mind-boggling variety, from pink leather to faux fur, feathers, and San Francisco 49er patterns. More corset-related products include scarves, pins, earrings, address books, magnets, soaps, all with little images of corsets.

You're probably thinking, "Well, sure, this is more corsets than God really needs." But what about if some non-cross-dressing guy wanted to wear a corset — and still look like a guy doing it? Hence, there is the "Corvest."

Created by local corset designer Dorothy Jones, the Corvest is supposedly the first combination corset and vest constructed for men. Prices

Photo Courtesy: Romantasy

range from $395 off the rack, to $495 for a custom job. Originally the Corvest was designed for a middle-aged hubby with a paunch, who wanted to squeeze into a tux to go out on the town, but it turns out many Romantasy customers are in their 20s. Lots of Corvest owners work in sales, law firms, and computers. Grogan says that 40 percent are straight and married, and wear the thing under their business clothes. Some let their wives know, others keep it a secret. Some wear it for medical reasons, for others it's vanity — it's said to reduce the waistline by three inches. One trial lawyer reports that when he wears the Corvest in the courtroom he "feels like Sir Galihad!"

If your closet is already full of too damn many corsets, or you're a sex-toy-obsessed white-bread yuppie, check out the rest of the catalog's sexual goodies, like the Vibra-Sponge, a vibrator covered with foam. It won't make you feel like Sir Galihad, but you can take a bath with it.

**Romantasy**
**2912 Diamond Street, Suite 239**
**San Francisco, CA 94131**
**(415) 585-0760**

# Web Smut

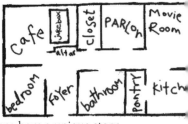

The Bianca's Smut Shack online web community amounts to a cyberspace gossip and chat lounge, with the occasional live meet-and-greet event. There isn't much sex, but then again we're talking about the online world, and as we must keep reminding ourselves over and over again, *you can't have sex with a computer.* But the site does have a unique story.

In 1994, a few digigeeks, toiling deep inside the bowels of *Wired* magazine, decided to start up their own web site of smut. Entranced by a mysterious female friend named Bianca, they named it Bianca's Smut Shack, promising to never reveal her identity.

The "Core Trolls," as they preferred to call themselves, watched as their tiny little shack of smut kept growing and growing, until someone counted up how many people were visiting each day, and the total was more than all of *Wired* magazine's official web sites put together. Apparently the people out there in Web World are less interested in dispatches from the Java applet wars, or the complexities of a new-media CEO jostling for market share of the emerging overseas microprocessor market, and would rather scroll through online flirting by young people with hip eyeglasses. Who knew?

The Bianca empire continued to grow, until tragedy struck in 1997, when the Radio Shack company — a division of the Tandy Corporation — filed a trademark infringement suit against them, insisting they drop the "Shack" part of their name because it was too confusing to hardcore Radio Shack customers (i.e., people who buy batteries). A Bianca defense campaign yielded thousands of readers e-mailing in their support. After some lawyering on both sides, Radio Shack quietly backed off, and Bianca lives on. (For those of you who are curious about possibly having actual sex with an actual person, see the rest of this chapter, or better yet, shut off your computer and get out of the house.)

**Bianca's Smut Shac**
**www.bianca.com**

# Celluloid Sleaze

During the Golden Age of Porn, in the late '60s and early '70s, you could stroll into an actual movie theater, sit down, and enjoy the simple pleasure of actors with pimply red faces and dirty feet having greasy sex up there on the silver screen. But today's technology has robbed the industry of its tawdry, realistic beginnings, and everything's now on video and on the Internet. Here in the city that pioneered porn films, one lone outpost of celluloid smut remains. The Tenderloin scuzz-pit known as the Mini Adult Theater will transport you back in time to a genre in its infancy, and is your best porn bargain in the city. Five bucks gets you three 16mm films, playing on a wall in rotation, changing Tuesdays and Saturdays. And a whole lot more.

You'll also get the man in the baseball cap, pacing up and down the aisle, saying, "Male or female, man, come on!" A stream of people may wander in and out of the restroom, avoiding eye contact. Your experience may include the rattling of bottles, the acrid stench of pot and crack, or a woman behind you yelling, "Well, take it out of your pants, muthafucker!" No doubt about it, this is true porn connoisseur territory — especially if you happen to be looking for some crack, a rotten-tooth blowjob, or a warm place to sleep for a couple of days.

**Mini Adult Theater**
**Golden Gate at Jones Street**
**no phone**

# Witchy Woman

**M**ary Ellen "Mammy" Pleasant left quite a legacy upon her death in 1904. She helped lots of slaves escape their servitude. She convinced the state Supreme Court to allow blacks on the San Francisco trolley cars. She ended up being worth an estimated $30 million. And if the stories are to be believed, she was also a spell-casting voodoo priestess who ran whorehouses and killed people. California always did attract overachievers.

Mary Ellen Pleasant moved to the city in 1852, when it was six men for every woman, and the citizenry ran amok through 700 bars and gambling houses. The illegitimate daughter of a slave woman and the white son of a Virginia governor, she already had lived a hell of a life, sneaking onto plantations and rescuing slaves via the Underground Railroad, and studying voodoo rituals in New Orleans. And now she was going to stir things up in San Francisco.

Upon arriving, she worked as a cook, then began accumulating businesses and real estate properties. This mysterious woman cut an unforgettable persona, with one brown and one blue eye, always appearing in public dressed in black silk. She easily attached herself to the city's power elite, and grew so influential people referred to her as the "Black City Hall." As prostitution was all the rage at the time, with some whores entertaining up to 50 guys a night, Pleasant jumped into the brothel business, and hustled blackmail scams on her wealthy johns. Either the prominent white men paid hush money and married their little soiled doves, or they would face a public scandal.

Photo: Anthony Pidgeon

Pleasant built a 30-room house at 1661 Octavia Street, which locals called the House of Mystery. Rumors spread of its secret passageways, weird orgies, and murders, and if you walked by, you might hear strange noises drifting from the windows. One of the more bizarre legends has it that one night Pleasant brought a container of wine up to the room of a bedridden banker friend. A scream was heard, followed by sounds of a body crashing through a balustrade. Servants discovered the man lying on the floor twitching in death, and Pleasant kneeling over him, tugging at his brains through a hole in his skull.

Who could forget such tales? Nobody, apparently. The African-American Museum at Fort Mason features a permanent collection of Pleasant memorabilia. Local scholar/performer Susheel Bibbs presents lectures and biographical enactments about Mary Ellen Pleasant, and the San Francisco Art Commission Gallery tours the country with a traveling exhibit of Pleasant's life. On the approximate site of the House of Mystery now stands a modern Pregnancy Counseling Center, shaded from the sun by Pleasant's original eucalyptus trees. Embedded in the sidewalk out front is a marker dedicated to Mary Ellen Pleasant, voodoo queen, madam, and mother of civil rights in California.

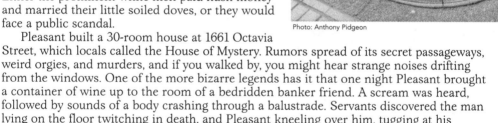

**Mary Ellen Pleasant sidewalk marker
1695 Octavia Street**

# Madam Mayor

Few in San Francisco are old enough to remember Sally Stanford these days. But around World War II, everyone knew her name. This little madam with the big nose was the city's #1 businesswoman, and operated the most exclusive bordello in the country. She hobnobbed with the rich and famous, and was eventually elected mayor of Sausalito.

She started off as Mabel Janice Busby, and by the end of her life in 1982, could have signed her legal name as Mabel Marcia Busby Goodan Fansier Bayhaam Spagnoli Rapp Gump Kenna. But she only had a few of these names back in the 1930s, when she arrived in San Francisco, after three marriages and a prison term. She took the name Stanford, the story goes, from the annual football rivalry between Stanford University and the University of California.

She began running brothels at least as far back as 1938, in locations on Bush, Taylor, Franklin, and Vallejo streets, and her reputation quickly spread. During one vice squad operation, which busted brothels all over town, a headline proclaimed: "Sally Wasn't There."

Her most famous cathouse operated from 1943 to 1949, in a lavish mansion at 1144 Pine, built originally by a millionaire for his chocolate heiress mistress. Local columnist Herb Caen dubbed it "The Sally Stanford School of Advanced Social Studies." Vice cops called it "The Fortress," because it was impossible to penetrate. Guests were ushered in through an iron gate by a doorman, and walked up a winding staircase to a Pompeian Court, a 138x50-foot room containing a multi-colored fountain, fireplace, and sunken marble tub, all underneath a high glass ceiling. Beautiful young women waited for customers in rooms with hidden passages and sliding panels. Stanford ran other operations throughout the city, but this was Skank Central.

WHAT IS
Home without a Mother

San Francisco police spent years trying to infiltrate The Fortress. One sergeant even applied for disability, brought on by years of stress trying to put Sally Stanford in jail. In 1949 the business was finally busted for good. When District Attorney Edmund "Pat" Brown, later state governor and father of Jerry Brown, was shown the little black book of clients — everyone from shahs and princes to Hollywood cocksmen, politicians, and United Nations dignitaries — he announced he would not make the names public. Customers all over the world let out sighs of relief.

Stanford retired and moved across the bay to Sausalito. In 1950 she opened a restaurant on the site of a former bootlegger hangout, and named it The Valhalla. She married, briefly, into the Gump family, and in 1962 ran for city council, under the slogans "Live and Let Live," and "Keep Sausalito Sausalito." The town was mortified at the idea of this squat woman with a bird on her shoulder governing them — *she used to run a whorehouse!* After seven attempts, Stanford was finally elected to the city council in 1972, and four years later became mayor of the city.

The Fortress was torn down long ago to make room for condos, but The Valhalla lives forever on the walls of what is now the Chart House restaurant. Walk into the bar, turn left, and check out the display of photographs, certificates, and a framed collection of women's handbags. Staff of the Chart House say that old Stanford pals (and customers) still wander in occasionally to have a drink, and admire the memorabilia of Sally Stanford, the madam mayor.

# No Circumcision Now!

Several medical studies say the foreskin is considered an essential part of the penis, whether the penis is involved in masturbation, intercourse, or just your basic utilitarian erection. The foreskin is more than just penile skin, it's specialized tissue, with many sensitive nerves, and is "uniquely endowed with stretch receptors."

So if the foreskin is such a nifty, feel-good part of the body, why hack it off a little baby?

That's the same question NOHARMM asks. The San Francisco-based National Organization to Halt the Abuse and Routine Mutilation of Males (subtitled "Men Organized Against Infant Circumcision in Defense of Children's Rights") is devoted to eradicating this practice. And once you read through their literature, and wince at the scary medical photos of what they call "genital violations," you begin to wonder — well, you wonder a lot of things. Why do we still perform circumcisions? Was it really that painful? Have I been scarred for life? And why are they so obsessed about this?

Traditionally, circumcision has been either a religious ceremony in the Jewish and Muslim faiths, or a standard prevention against infectious diseases. A hundred years ago, it was even thought to curtail masturbation. These days, the trim job is primarily a North American phenomenon, and is virtually unheard of in Europe.

NOHARMM says that up to 96 percent of babies born in the U.S. and Canada receive no anesthesia during the procedure. A 1997 study of male circumcision, as reported by CNN, found that the operation was so traumatic to infants, doctors ended the study early, rather than subject any more babies to the ordeal. NOHARMM and other opponents of circumcision say this procedure is not only painful and unnecessary, it's a gross infringement of civil rights and human dignity, and amounts to criminal assault. Female circumcision is apparently even more horrific.

To help spread the word, and save the foreskins and labias of the world, NOHARMM has developed and sells something called the Genital Integrity Ribbon, which symbolizes the ritual abuse of normal, healthy children. A brochure describes this ribbon:

"The colors blue and pink remind us that genital mutilations transcend gender. Although each side is a different color, they are two sides of the same ribbon. Male and female circumcision are also different, but they share many important similarities and are two sides of the same issue — children's rights. The 'crossed legs' of this special ribbon are a metaphor for the position used by many non-consenting infants and children to protect themselves from their perpetrators. At the top of these legs, the ribbon's loop forms a hole. The hole represents the missing genital parts and the emptiness felt by many individuals after they overcome lifelong cultural indoctrination and realize the gravity of their loss. The rust-red color of the words 'Genital Integrity' remind us of the dried blood of children that stains the collective hands of humanity."

Let's take a lesson from the healthy, skin-flapping genitalia of Europe. The foreskin and labia must live and breathe free. Long live the stretch receptors.

NOHARMM
P.O. Box 460795
San Francisco, CA 94146-0795

# Scat Scratch Fever

**O**ccasionally, sex can appear more routine than we'd care to admit. We've all been in the middle of making the beast with two backs, and suddenly a thought crosses your mind that what you're doing is kind of boring. (No reflection on your expert technique, of course.) But can you imagine being so jaded that any sexual activity seems listless and dull unless there's a lesbian dwarf getting fisted? If you're one of these special people who craves some true sexual adventure, it's time to visit North Beach Video & Movie.

No magazines or live peep-show dancers here. This is the lair of the porn-video purist. Imagine the weirdest sex act/bodily function combination possible with the human body, and then imagine the performers grunting in thick German accents. That's what we're talking here. Videos cost $100 each to buy, or $20 to watch it there. Available titles range from *Caca Privé* and *Amateur Anal Fistfuckers* Volumes 1 through 5, to the lesbian-fisting *Perverse Dwarf*, the extensive Redboard spanking series, and a bunch of videos with kinky Polaroids taped to the boxes. In the back of the store are cheap wooden booths, where amplified screams and whipping sounds drift up and over the cubicle walls. Perverts or sexual astronauts? It all depends on your perspective.

**North Beach Video & Movie
1034 Kearny Street
(415) 391-1073**

# S/M B&B

Images Courtesy: House of Differences

**T**humb through any upscale travel magazine, and you'll find an article about San Francisco that suggests a bed and breakfast as a perfect, quaint alternative to the big luxury hotels. Throughout the city, these little inns dazzle guests with their homey ambiance and fresh morning pastries. But out on a hill overlooking the Pacific Ocean sits a different kind of B&B. Elizabeth, the owner, says she doesn't do breakfast. To her, B&B stands for "Bed and Bondage."

In this four-story, former Prohibition hideout, Elizabeth has built her House of Differences. Where bootleggers once stashed illicit hooch, you can now reserve a weekend to get your ass whupped and your nipples pinched. Capacity is five couples, in rooms equipped with mirrors and bondage equipment. The truly kinky will salivate over the 750-square-foot Main Dungeon, with its suspended St. Catherine's Wheel, medical exam table, bondage and spanking benches, leather slings, and, for the supremely naughty traveler, a punishment cage.

Differences hosts special events, workshops, and seminars each month, from an erotic art gallery and basic safety lessons to something called "Potluck Playtime." Experts drop in to give presentations on subjects like caning, wax, piercing, and branding. Each Friday is a regular party, and occasionally Elizabeth will organize a "Gourmet Weekend," where a guest chef prepares a special meal to complement your disciplinary sessions.

**House of Differences
(415) 585-9662**

# Catfighting

The sun has nearly receded into the Pacific Ocean as you stroll out of the Presidio movie theater. You and your date have just seen a pleasant if uninspiring mainstream motion picture, and now it's time for a little entertainment sorbet to cleanse the palate — rinse out the schmaltz, if you will. Because you've read this book, you know exactly what to do. You keep walking down Chestnut Street, dodging the designer baby strollers and joggers with Ivy League sweatshirts, to Famous Sports Videos III. Not only is this store the third in a national chain of five outlets, it's one-stop Marina District shopping for female wrestling videos.

The shop itself opens up into a slender space, the walls lined with video boxes on football, weightlifting, golf, and martial arts, accompanied by soft classical music playing. Fairly innocent. As you keep walking through, the next room is stocked with female bodybuilding videos.

Vaguely sexual, but not really. Just a bunch of buffed gals doing what they do best. But the third room, hidden behind a set of swinging doors, reveals the hornet's nest: Rows and rows and rows of specialty fetish female wrestling, boxing, fighting, face-sitting videos, priced up to $60 apiece. These aren't fly-by-night companies, either. These are catfighting names you can trust, like Violent Video, L. Scott Sales, Leather and Lace, California Wildcats, Joan Wise, and Steel Kittens.

What video title will it be tonight? *Blow Job Boxing II (The Humiliation)*? *Bullwhip Bertha* looks inviting. Or how about *Sit on Mitch's Head*? Perhaps *Rhode Island Tag Team*, or *Hirsute Lovers*? There's no business like *Toe Biz*.

The box copy for *Cheek to Cheek* breathlessly advertises its contents:

"Featuring 4 girls in FACE SITTING Combat. Tied and Humiliated. Faces Smothered by the BARE ASSES of their opponents. Great wrestling combined with long and intense Face Sitting. This all NUDE Erotic Face Sitting Wrestling video is a must for all face sitting fans!"

And if you'd rather read than watch, a magazine rack offers plastic-wrapped editions of *Claws, German Mat Club, Catspats, Catfighting Cunts, Mane Liners, Ripe Buns,* or the self-explanatory *Battling Bitches.*

Fetishes of every persuasion are available here — fighting, shoe licking, face

# Videos!

sitting, hot oil, hairy girls, big boob girls, buffed girls, Asian girls, or girls with perfectly muscled legs and/or butts. Lots of mixed-gender combat, but one requirement of the genre, of course, is that the guys always lose. Some videos carry labels that admit their contents are specific performance scenarios customized for a wealthy client, then videotaped and resold. In other words, keep in mind *it isn't really happening just for you.*

Several people in the industry agree there has been a noticeable surge of interest in this stuff, but nobody really knows why. Perhaps because the genre strikes an odd sexual balance in today's political climate: Women are always depicted as the obvious stronger sex, and often end up pulverizing a hapless guy into submission. Perhaps the combination of athletics and fetish seems to coincide with the proliferation of TV sports programming. Perhaps we've always recognized the inherent appeal of a catfight, from Raquel Welch's cave brawl in *One Million Years B.C.* to the exercise-yard scraps of women-in-prison movies.

A fan explains the appeal of a woman sitting on his face:

"I developed a fetish for it in the live sense. It's an overwhelming kind of physical experience, and so it's easy to get into the vicarious watching on videos after having developed a taste for it. I've been into S/M and dominance and so forth, and it's just a natural form of dominance. Because there's nothing more dominant, when you think about it, than sitting on somebody's face."

One man's face-sit is another man's fishnets, in the increasingly above-ground world of fetish. We used to consider five-inch heels on a par with the devil, but now you can buy them at fashion boutiques. As long as nobody gets hurt in a catfight, who are we to judge?

Photos: Brawling Spitfires

# Gay Sex Is Back

**B**ack in the 1970s, the Castro District gained a reputation as the gay mecca of the United States. Thousands made the pilgrimage to San Francisco, and stayed for the party. Halloween once attracted 100,000 people dancing in the streets. But take a walk through the neighborhood these days, and you're more likely to see couples eating yogurt, or people standing in line at the Castro Theater for a Preston Sturges retrospective. So where's it happening? Nothing is ever going to shut down the predatory male impulse. Where are all the gay guys getting laid?

Well, nowadays one has to do a little more research. Like call up the Blow Buddies hotline.

The private club known as Blow Buddies occurs each week in a secret warehouse location, and admission is by membership only. (A membership I.D. card will also get you into the sister clubs Underwear Buddies, Leather Buddies, and Golden Shower Buddies.) Organizers are not interested in tourists looking for entertainment, but hey, if you're 21 or older and have ripped abs, they'll probably let you in. Just be aware of the dress code. Leather, Levi's, jockstraps, and uniforms are encouraged, but absolutely no sweaters, dress shirts, slacks, shiny disco clothes, coats, or zip-up sweatshirts. And no cologne or fragrance of any kind. At Blow Buddies, it's man musk only.

Once you're inside, go hog-wild over their facilities, which include mirrors, a jail cell, glory holes, "service stalls," and complimentary rubbers. The owners boast of "providing our community with a physically safe, HOT environment to meat-up!" But they're not going to hold your hand. You're a responsible adult. Bring your own handcuffs and sex toys.

Blow Buddies
(415) 863-HEAD

# Spankin' Good Time

**M**ost areas of the country, if you were to go out on the town to a swingers' sex club, get clothespins stuck all over your chest, spank a stranger's ass until it turns red, and watch a big naked woman get fisted while suspended from a sling — you might have to hunt around a bit for the location. Not a problem in the South of Market area, where the city's collective libido has manifested into an insanely popular, any-gender-goes sexual Disneyland called the Power Exchange.

Photo: Paul Trapani

Opened a few years ago by swingers Mike and Marie Powers, the Power Exchange claims to be the "largest sex club in the world," and cranks it up seven nights a week. This Magic Kingdom of Carnality is actually divided into two clubs, the Mainstation, for gay and bisexual men, and the Substation, for swingers, voyeurs, tourists, suburbanites, heteros, lesbians, gays, bisexuals, transgenders, and those who quite honestly aren't sure what sex they are. Condoms, lubes, gloves, Saran Wrap, and other safe-sex necessities are provided, but drugs and alcohol aren't allowed. What is allowed, is pretty much anything sexual you can possibly imagine. Want to put on some panties and get spanked by a dominatrix for two hours straight? Someone will be able to help you. Interested in watching your wife get groped by strangers? Not a problem. Or maybe you'd like to get your nipples buzzed by a man dressed like Robin Hood, holding a bug-zapper-like contraption? It's all here in abundance.

The club often throws special parties, balls, slave auctions, and "Bulge" underwear galas, and first-timers might check out the Power Exchange Boutique for clothing, toys, and other frisky goodies. When you get tuckered out from all the frolicking, stop in at the 1950s retro juice bar for some refreshments. Admission prices get confusing, so it's best to call ahead for information.

**Power Exchange**
**74 Otis Street**
**(415) 487-9944**

# X-Rated Cakes

**W**ant to liven up that office going-away party but you don't know exactly what to bring? Stuck with throwing a birthday bash and there's no time to plan anything? Sometimes, all a pleasant social occasion really needs is a nice frosted cake shaped like a pink pair of tits. Nothing says *Celebrate good times come on!* like an enormous chocolate phallus, splayed across the pan like a beached trout. Yes,

Photo: Anthony Pidgeon

the Cake Gallery will also whip up normal cakes, but it's those wacky sex cakes that everybody knows and loves. With regular frequency — well, regular for San Francisco, anyway — the store's staff lovingly handcrafts their pastry miracles in the shapes of everyone's favorite body parts. Your heart's absolutely set on a cake decorated with a hairy naked gay man in an S/M sling? Have no fear. The bakers won't even blink. They'll probably ask you which type of S/M sling you prefer.

**The Cake Gallery
290 9th Street
(415) 861-2253**

# Whip It Good

**L**eather jockstraps, catsuits, corsets, studded bras, bull-whips, wrist restraints — ah, it all seems so easy to obtain these days. We forget there was a time when you had to order this stuff in secret, or otherwise you were a *pervert.* Imagine! Ever since 1983, when Kathy Andrew opened her Stormy Leather shop South of Market, fetish fans have confidently walked in the door to satisfy their specific attire needs. This female-owned store has now grown to a team of seamstresses, who produce pretty much everything you need to yank your chain. Stormy Leather now claims to be the best stocked fetish store in the country. If they don't have what you need, they will design and make it for you, as they have done for dominatrixes, submissives, and celebrities like Roseanne and En Vogue. Because sadomasochism never sleeps, Stormy Leather is open every day of the week. Look for the giant half-open zipper hanging above the door.

**Stormy Leather
1158 Howard Street
(415) 626-1672**

# School for Sex

**T**his storefront may look quiet and unassuming, but behind the door on Franklin Street sits the world's largest archive of erotica and sexual materials. This is the Institute for the Advanced Study of Human Sexuality, where students can attend classes and workshops, and earn advanced degrees in sexological training. And it's been going for over 30 years.

In the mid-1960s, Methodist minister Ted McIlvenna watched the city's gay population getting beaten up by cops, and vowed to do something. In conjunction with Glide Memorial Church, he started up the National Sex Forum program, with the goal of protecting homosexuals from harassment. The idea grew into the study of sexuality in general, as the NSF held classes, shot instructional films, and amassed great quantities of erotic art. An International Museum of Erotic Art opened at Union Square in 1968, with visitors gawking at three stories of sexual art and artifacts, but the concept was too much, even for San Francisco. Mixed reactions led to the museum's closing, and in 1970 McIlvenna combined everything into the present Institute.

This peculiar organization now attracts sexually curious individuals from all over the world, from prostitutes and strippers to journalists and researchers, who drop by to study the materials. People like Robert De Niro have been seen poring through the archives, doing background for projects.

Warehouses all over the city now store the Institute's vast collection of porn films, sex toys, literature, and artwork, culled from various sources. But the educational aspect receives the most emphasis. The Institute offers many degrees in sexology, from Master of Human Sexuality to Doctor of Education, Doctor of Human Sexuality, or Doctor of Philosophy. All student applications for acceptance into the Institute must contain the usual résumé, letter of intent, recommendations, and a current photograph.

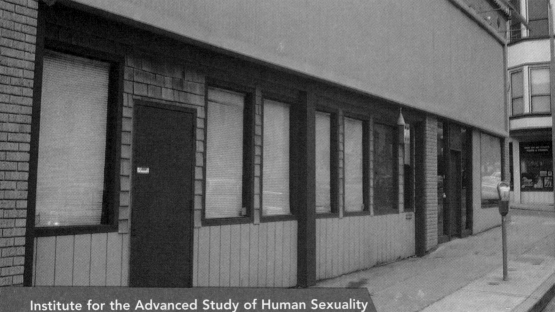

Institute for the Advanced Study of Human Sexuality
1523 Franklin Street
(415) 928-1133

# Chapter Six

# Behind the Velvet Rope

Photo: Sharon Selden

**P**erhaps it's the sheer geographical distance from the Whitney in Manhattan, or the Getty collection in Los Angeles, but Bay Area museum curators seem to gravitate towards a more offbeat aesthetic. Our local archivists ignore the impenetrable art-babble analysis, and get right to the heart of it — really weird collections of tattoos, sheets of blotter acid, and vibrators. Some of the museums in this chapter are a traditional presentation of peculiar subjects, such as Ripley's, or the exhibits at the San Francisco airport. Others result from the efforts of a scholar with a passion so strong it propels them to spend large amounts of money and years of their time collecting objects not usually found in museums — say, a room full of Pez dispensers. As you check out the following pages, keep in mind that all of these repositories are world-reknowned in their respective fields.

# Musée Mécanique

L et's say you're stumbling through the tourist trap known as the Cliff House, where Geary Boulevard meets the ocean. You've already survived the gift shop, and taken in the mixed message of Christmas ornaments shaped like Halloween figures. You've eaten the bland food, and looked at all the old photos on the walls. But what you don't know is that just a few steps away, for a couple of coins, you can cause a man to be hanged to death.

In the basement of the Cliff House, beyond the stupid trinkets and boring restaurants, sits the Musée Mécanique, a room of 140 antique arcade games. In the midst of this collection, reportedly the world's largest, entertainment is limited only by the change in your pocket:

Photo: Sharon Selden

Force a sailor with a chipped nose named Jolly Jack to giggle hysterically! Play mechanical baseball with an actual bat and ball! Coerce a group of dangling puppets to wiggle at "The Ole Barn Dance!" Inspect an adult peep booth to "see what the belly dancer does on her day off!"

These contraptions were once installed at the Playland at the Beach, a two-story beach amusement park that opened in 1914. (A few blocks away at the intersection of Cabrillo and La Playa streets, tourist info placards detail the park's colorful history.) In the days before Nintendo and PlayStation, Playland was where wayward youth wasted their time and money. After the park closed in 1972 to make room for condominiums, the devices were moved to the Cliff House and put back into service the same year as the Musée Mécanique.

Upon entering, the first thing you'll see is a glass enclosure, inside of which is Laughing Sal, a hideous five-foot mechanized doll that greeted Playland visitors for 32 years. For two quarters, Sal will erupt into maniacal laughter, her plump body will bob back and forth, and her paddle-like hands will flail up and down. It's really grotesque. You can't imagine anyone inventing such a thing. But it's actually quite fun, because when Sal cranks up, small children stop their shrieking and stare in silent horror, and as we all know, anything that shuts up the kids should be preserved as long as possible.

As you meander through the room, consider that many of these

# Viva Vibrators

As far as female-owned sexuality stores go, Eve's Garden in Manhattan was there first in 1974, but you can't keep a good woman down.

The concept soon migrated to the West Coast, and three years later, Good Vibrations opened its doors in San Francisco's Mission District. A combination retail and mail-order business of the finest in vibrating sex goodies, Good Vibes included an extra bonus with the shop — a Vibrator Museum.

This assemblage of antique electrical stress-relieving devices is guaranteed to intrigue any woman who's ever said hello to the Hitachi Magic Wand, if you know what I mean. These primitive contraptions, made of metal with those cloth-covered

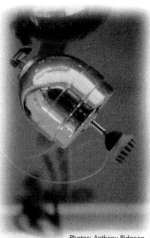

Photos: Anthony Pidgeon

cords, look as though they're about to shoot sparks and fry some labia. Examining the specimens, and assessing their inherent danger, you can't help but realize we really have evolved as a species.

After inspecting these goods from yesteryear, visitors invariably stroll over to the latest in 20th-century pleasure-giving devices — the Wall O'Dildos, where a woman's best friend comes in every color in the rainbow, and the shape of every animal in the kingdom, from sleek porpoises to wiggling woodland creatures and a giant pulsating pink plastic tongue.

Good Vibrations' only two retail stores are here and in Berkeley, but their humming sensations can be felt via Internet and the U.S. Mail around the world.

**Vibrator Museum
Good Vibrations
1210 Valencia Street
(800) 883-8423**

Photo: Sharon Selden    Photo: Anthony Pidgeon    Photo: Sharon Selden

machines are over 100 years old, and when they break down, Musée staff manufacture replacement parts right on the premises.

Your best entertainment value, however, is to stick with Laughing Sal. Linger in her vicinity, and when a pre-schooler wanders within range, quickly pump 50 cents into her slot and watch the wee one lose his little mind. And at that moment, you'll realize the intent behind the inventors of Laughing Sal.

**Musée Mécanique
Basement of the Cliff House
1090 Point Lobos Avenue at the ocean
(415) 386-1170**

# Pez

Y ou say there's no relationship between computers and Pez? You truly believe that a workstation lined with colorful children's candy dispensers is just simple coincidence? Let's examine this relationship more closely. Most of the visitors to Burlingame's Museum of Pez work in the computer industry. They visit the establishment by driving in the direction of Silicon Valley, and pulling into the parking lot of a computer store. In the back room of the Computer Spectrum shop awaits the world's largest display devoted to Pez, "America's favorite candy dispenser."

(In other words, yeah, there probably is a symbiotic relationship between computers and Pez, but nobody really wants to take it any further than that.)

Images Courtesy: Burlingame Museum of Pez Memorabilia

Not only is this museum crammed with Pez dispensers of all kinds, there are also Pez calendars, mouse pads, caps, sweatshirts, silk neckties, flashlights, and special dispenser stands so you can proudly display your archive in a clear and organized manner. The museum commissions and sells special designs as well, such as miniature helmets of your favorite NFL and NHL teams.

You're probably saying to yourself, *So what's the deal?*

Several years ago, Computer Spectrum owner Gary Doss was waiting in the nine-items-or-less supermarket line, when his wife Nancy spotted a Woodstock Pez and wanted to buy it. Unfortunately, the item would have put them over the limit and they would have had to move to another checkout line. Doss returned later, but the Woodstock dispenser was already gone. He bought a Snoopy instead, and those of you who are Pez collectors might take a moment here to nod in recognition of such sacrifice. His wife accepted the Snoopy anyway, displayed it on her office desk, and customers started bringing them more dispensers. Computer Spectrum soon had to open a back room of the store to accommodate the growing collection.

Today, Gary Doss estimates his collection is worth around $30,000. The museum features over 350 different models, including the first Pez dispenser ever made, as well as every version ever issued of Santa Claus and Mickey Mouse. On the walls are autographed dispensers from Lynda Carter (for the Wonder Woman Pez) and Jim Davis (for the Garfield Pez).

The peppermint-flavored candies first appeared in 1927, and were sold in little tin boxes and marketed to adults as an aid for quitting smoking. (The name Pez is actually an abbreviation for *Pfefferminz*, the German word for peppermint.) During World War II, the company started selling plastic dispensers, but they weren't very popular because they looked too much like a typical cigarette lighter. Then someone at the company came up with the idea of selling to kids. The plastic heads first appeared in the early 1950s. And, of course, the world was altered forever.

Today, all Pez dispensers are made in Austria, and the candy comes from a factory in

# People

Connecticut, where the president of the company is referred to as "The Pezident."

Most Pez are sold in drug stores and supermarkets to children, but we can blame the Baby Boomers for creating a market for Pez collectibles. Because the Boomers want to retain a piece of their childhood, the world now sees Pez conventions, Pez web sites, and old Pez dispensers selling for insane prices. A Mary Poppins, for instance, goes for about $1,300, which is an awful lot of Bonnie Raitt CDs.

Along with inflated prices and treasured rarities comes the tidbits of Pez folklore:

There is a vicious dispute over whether the first modern Pez dispenser was Mickey Mouse, Casper, or Popeye. The company once made a Bullwinkle Pez, but never made a Rocky. A Tweety Bird dispenser was featured in a *Seinfeld* episode. A special Elvis Pezley model was created for the movie *The Client* but never sold commercially. The only two Pez characters based on real people were Betsy Ross and aniel Boone. The most popular Pez character is Winnie the Pooh. The company's most requested Pez dispenser is any *Simpsons* character.

The most expensive Pez dispenser was similar to a Mr. Potato Head, essentially a blank canvas upon which the owner could add little parts and build his own customized face.

Unfortunately, all those little eyebrows, noses, mouths, ears, and eyes could be seen as hazardous. If one five-year-old swallowed a small plastic ear, turned blue, and choked to death, for instance, the company could be buried in lawsuits. The do-it-yourself Pez face was discontinued, and today sells for at least $5,000.

Much of the museum's collection is sold individually, from Fozzie Bear and the Tasmanian Devil ($2 each), to Robin Hood and Tarzan ($8 each), Road Runner ($20), Dumbo ($30), and the Maharaja (priced at a candy-choking $75).

Some are sold in sets: The set of five Smurf characters goes for a mere $35; the *Jungle Book* set of four (Mowgli, Baloo, King Louis, and 'Lil Bad Wolf) rings in at $70 for the lot. The set of four Nintendo game characters (Super Mario, Yoshi, Koopa Troopa and Diddy Kong) is only $32. The battery-operated animated "Candy Hander" statues of Marvin the Martian and Wile E. Coyote — of course we all remember, where the character swivels and dispenses Pez at the push of a button — are just $10 apiece.

Doss says that he sees Pez-heads from all over the world, but if you can't afford a $2,000-dollar airline ticket to visit the museum of your candy-coated dreams, you can at least log onto their www.burlingamepezmuseum.com web site and view the latest additions for yourself. Admission is free, and the shop's closed Sundays and Mondays.

Burlingame Museum of Pez Memorabilia
214 California Drive, Burlingame
(415) 347-2301

# Framed

According to DEA internal documents, the San Francisco Bay Area supplies the world with the majority of its LSD, and has done so for decades. You're probably thinking, Well, yeah, no surprise there, but shouldn't there be a repository for pristine examples of this notorious export? Fortunately, there is. In the heart of the Mission District sits a Victorian house whose walls are lined with framed examples of blotter paper LSD. It is the only museum of blotter acid artwork in the world. Curator Mark McLoud prefers to call it the "Institute of Illegal Images."

Images Courtesy: Mark McLoud

The images in question are standard-size sheets of absorbent paper, perforated into 1,000 1/4-inch squares (25x40), with acid potency ranging from 500 micrograms on down to 50-mike "disco hits." Designs vary from Mr. Natural and Grateful Dead patterns to Ozzy Osbourne, Alice in Wonderland, Mickey Mouse, and *Simpsons* characters.

Now before you drive on down to the Mission in your stinky communal Winnebago, salivating at the thought of gobbling a bunch of drugs and running naked through Golden Gate Park, remember that the paper in this museum isn't "hot." These samples have either never been dipped, or the chemical compounds have long since been neutralized by exposure to light.

McLoud grew up in Argentina in a wealthy family, and served as an altar boy at his church in Buenos Aires. As he helped press bread into wafers for the priests, he soon realized there was nothing inherently powerful or spiritual in the bread at all; the congregation was getting cheated by the priest.

McLoud moved to California as a child, and attended a boarding school. One day, a visiting narcotics officer gave an anti-drug talk to the students. McLoud stared at the officer's collection of bundles, syringes, and pipes, and the impression lasted. By 1975 he had given up his coin collection

# Epiphanies

for something better: The cool blotter acid designs he saw —
and gobbled — on the streets.

His collection debuted with an exhibit at the San Francisco
Art Institute in 1987, and has since traveled to galleries all
over the world. People who visit the shows gravitate naturally
to the designs that first scorched their minds, says McLoud,
and will stand for long periods of time in front of the sacred
squares, recalling that initial psychedelic blast that blew
open the doors of perception.

The archive began innocently enough, with sheets
McLoud purchased for
personal use. Whatever
he didn't munch he
saved for posterity in the
refrigerator. As news of his
collection spread through
the acid community,
grizzled trippers began
donating neutralized
samples of their private
stashes. These days
artists approach him and
ask to contribute images,
even though the sheets will
never see a psychoactive
chemical.

He finds his collection
appeals to everyone from
'60s french fries on down
to those initiates who
hung on for one white-
knuckled ride and vowed
never again. Essentially,
acid is one subject that has
personal meaning for everyone, even if you've never
twirled to a 20-minute
Grateful Dead song.

"I've never found anything on this planet with such meaning,"
says McLoud. "It's the one substance on earth where it teaches
you how to lose. I feel like the Pope signing wafers!"

If you're seriously interested in a visit, stop by the coffee
shop in McLoud's neighborhood and ask around. They know
how to find him.

Blotter Acid Museum
c/o Martha Brothers Coffee Shop
2475 Mission Street

# Believe It or Not

The concept of the "Ripley's Believe It or Not" cartoon may appear tame in today's Information Age, where we receive junk e-mails every day that seem much weirder than any comic panel. This museum is included here because in the case of Ripley, you have to keep in mind the following:

1) He was a product of the Bay Area, having grown up in nearby Santa Rosa;
2) He actually did travel the world collecting his information, i.e., he did the work; and
3) *He did it all without a modem!*

After an injury cut short his professional baseball career, Robert Ripley drifted back into his first love, drawing cartoons. He illustrated sports stories for the *San Francisco Chronicle*, then moved on to the sports department of the *New York Globe*. One slow news day in 1918, desperate to meet a deadline, he sketched a group of unusual athletes, including A. Forrester, who ran 100 yards in 14 seconds — backwards. Above the art-

work Ripley added the headline, "Champs and Chumps." His editor loved it, and added one change: He renamed the cartoon "Believe It or Not!"

Ripley's feature proved so popular that William Randolph Hearst signed him up for a syndication deal at $100,000 per year. Ripley now had the do-re-mi to travel the world and hunt down the bizarre and unexplained. Weirdo info became a cottage industry — at its height, his cartoon appeared in over 300 newspapers worldwide and was translated into 17 languages, and for a time, he hosted a radio program and series of film shorts.

All over the planet, readers perused the little Ripley's cartoon and scratched their heads over illustrated factoids like, "Petrified apple 75 years old" or "Long-tailed shrews: The smallest living mammals breathe *800 times a minute.*"

Ripley tromped through 198 countries during his life — always impeccably dressed in pith helmet and two-toned shoes — and brought back boatloads of oddities. The first large exhibit of Ripley's artifacts opened as the "Odditorium" at the Chicago World's Fair in 1933. Other cities soon followed, and today a Ripley's Museum can be found in many major metropolitan areas, usually within proximity of tourist infestation.

This San Francisco version is like many others in that much of the "oddities" seem benign by today's harsh standards of popular culture. Kids are growing up memorizing facts about serial killers and hunting down dental surgery photos to put on the cover of their band's CD. A stuffed, two-headed calf standing in a little diorama probably isn't going to turn many heads.

In fact, as you stroll the museum, trying to block out the noise of screaming children (and watching employees follow behind with a bottle of Windex to wipe away the residue), Ripley's stuff can seem pretty cheesy. From Pixie, the knife-eating dog, to Mortado the human water fountain, and a collection of things found inside a cow's

# Hallowed Hot Pants

Built on the approximate location of the camera shop of politician Harvey Milk, later murdered at City Hall, Harvey's is more than a shrine to a leader of the gay community. It's the Hard Rock of fabulousness. The walls and ceiling are covered with celebrity stuff from gay culture. Why, it's actual clothing worn by Liberace and Elton John! Items from the closets of The Sisters of Perpetual Indulgence! Signed memorabilia from Divine and Pussy Tourette! Crass fawning over gay celebrities no doubt disgusts just as many gays as the Hard Rock annoys music fans (hey look everybody, it's another guitar signed by somebody from The Damned!), but the drinks are strong and the music is always loud. And another free bonus — watching the Castro neighborhood sidewalk traffic through the picture windows.

Harvey's
500 Castro Street
(415) 431-4278

stomach, you think maybe it's best left to the kiddies, tweaking out on sugar.

With our heightened sense of political correctness drilled into us over the years, Ripley's treatment of other cultures can sometimes seem callous, but what saves his ass are the videos that play on monitors throughout the museum. In these flickering black-and-white images, we see Ripley joshing with African natives, and you realize he did have a genuine rapport with the people he exploited for entertainment. He might have laughed at their strange custom of wearing giant rings in their lips, but they were laughing right back at this odd, bucktoothed man in shorts and leather spats, grinning like a fool.

Specific to this museum on the Wharf is a display of artifacts from the 1989 Loma Prieta earthquake, including a car smashed by the collapse of the I-80 freeway, and a good luck troll, which has since been attached to the underside of the Bay Bridge.

Ripley died of a heart attack in 1949, at the relatively young age of 55, but the cartoon and museums continue churning out the wacky trivia factoids, and presenting statues of really fat people and paintings made of toast. North of San Francisco, in his hometown of Santa Rosa, a church building memorializes their oddball native son — *constructed entirely out of a single giant redwood tree!*

Ripley's Believe It or Not Museum
Fisherman's Wharf
(415) 771-6188

# Blimp HQ

Every weekday, young goateed nerds rip up and down Highway 101, commuting to and from Silicon Valley. But while these young millionaires are adjusting the CD volume, they have little idea that those giant hangars visible from the freeway were once home to the largest dirigible in the world, and the biggest dirigible fleet in the United States.

Tucked away on the west side of Hangar One is the Moffett Field Museum and gift shop. Managed and staffed by volunteer blimp freaks, the museum displays historical photographs, models, and memorabilia of the balloons, blimps, dirigibles, and people who made up the LTA (lighter than air) era at Moffett Field. At one time, blimps were hot hot hot.

In 1933, Hangar One greeted the arrival of the world's largest dirigible, the *U.S.S.*

Images Courtesy: Moffett Field Historical Society

*Macon.* On that day, Bay Area schools and banks closed, and a victory parade of cars inched along the Peninsula, accompanied by fire whistles and sirens.

A 785-foot-long behemoth, the *Macon* was nearly twice as large as Germany's famous *Graf Zeppelin*, and hummed along at a top speed of 87 miles per hour. Somebody had the common sense to fill the *Macon* with helium rather than hydrogen, which was the bane of the *Hindenburg's* deadly explosion in 1937, killing 36 people. (One bright spot in the *Hindenburg* tragedy: The news photo later ended up on the cover of Led Zeppelin's first album.)

The *Macon* offered accommodations for 100 officers and crew, and carried five Sparrowhawk fighter planes in its belly. The airplanes were lowered and released through a T-shaped hole in the blimp's underside. Retrieving them was something else. Like a performing air stunt, the pilots, known as the "Men on the Flying Trapeze," had to equal their speed to that of the ship and catch the trapeze with a hook at the top of the plane. The harness would then be attached to the fuselage, and the aircraft would be raised.

The *Macon* endured much early criticism, particularly after its first mission, when it was shot down twice during a mock battle. To prove itself worthy of a $2.5 million price tag, the *Macon* left Moffett Field in July 1934 in an attempt to locate the cruiser *Houston* that was carrying President Roosevelt en route to Honolulu. After traveling 3,500 miles, the *Macon* not only found the *Houston*, it descended out of the clouds and gave birth to a plane that dumped bundles of yesterday's San Francisco newspaper onto the president of the United States.

Less than a year later, the *Macon* left on its 45th flight to participate in maneuvers off Southern California. Repairs had not been completed to two of its tail fins. Storm winds south of Monterey drove the biggest aircraft in history straight into the ocean, killing two of its crew of 83. The wreckage was never found, and for years dirigible fanatics squabbled about what really happened.

# Artifacts of Concourse B

Your plane touches down at San Francisco's airport, and as you walk off the ramp, you know instantly you're not in just any old airport terminal. No posters of mountain vistas, no ads for eyewear or insurance companies. At SFO, it's usually something like a neatly labeled, glass-enclosed exhibit of antique pencil sharpeners on display. Depending on your mood or how long your flight was delayed, you don't know whether to laugh or yell, "What the fuck is this?" You continue walking to get your luggage, and in every corridor you keep seeing more displays of pencil sharpeners, antique staplers, and other desk accessories. Relax. You haven't gone insane. It's just the airport sprucing things up. Next month it might be vintage Hawai'ian shirts or martini shakers or merry-go-round animals or roller skates from a Nebraska skating museum. The airport manages 17 such galleries throughout the building, and hires curators to survey travelers and solicit feedback on what they'd like to see next. Exhibit space is so popular the galleries are booked up two years in advance. If you live here, every time you return home from a trip it's like a little surprise waiting for you.

**San Francisco Airport Galleries**
**SFO Airport**

● ● ● ● ● ● ● ● ● ● ● ● ● ● ● ● ● ● ● ● ● ●

In 1989, the daughter of *Macon* skipper Herbert V. Wiley discovered a restaurant in Moss Landing that had on display a piece of metal the owners claimed came from the *Macon*. A recovery team tracked down the fisherman who had pulled up the two-foot piece of metal in his nets, and he pointed out the location. A Navy deep-sea submersible craft was dispatched, and 1,450 feet below the surface discovered the twisted remains. The mystery was solved, and dirigible fans worldwide could finally get some sleep.

After the *Macon* crash, the dirigible program ended at Moffett Field, and the base became a training center for the Army Air Corps, instructing the likes of actor James Stewart. After World War II, the facility reverted to a NASA station, and a Navy outpost for the P-3 "Orion Hunter" anti-submarine patrol aircraft. After the Clinton Administration closed Moffett in 1994, it became home for the NASA/Ames Research Center and Lockheed Martin Missiles and Space Co. Inc.

**Moffett Field Historical Society Museum**
**Hangar One, Moffett Field**
**(650) 603-9827**

# Eyes on You

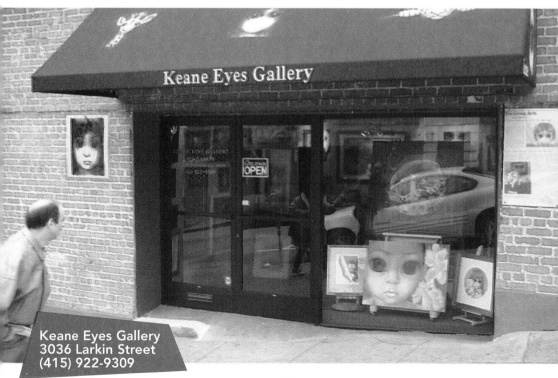

In the 1960s, the big-eyed waifs of the brazenly self-promoting Walter Keane were the biggest selling art in the world. After meeting at an art show in Sausalito in the 1950s, Walter and Margaret Keane teamed up and produced hundreds of big-eyed paintings, and they opened galleries in both San Francisco and Manhattan. Media taste-makers like Jack Parr and Earl Wilson praised the paintings, some of which sold for as much as $100,000. Celebrities like Joan Crawford and Jerry Lewis commissioned Keane portraits of themselves. The art world was less impressed. In 1964, the *New York Times* wrote that Walter Keane "grinds out formula pictures of wide-eyed children with such appalling sentimentality that his product has become synonymous among critics with the very definition of tasteless hack work." The Keanes divorced the following year, and disappeared from the public eye.

Some years later, in 1970, Margaret went on a San Francisco radio program and revealed the truth — she had done all of the paintings by herself, but kept it a secret under threat of death from Walter, who wasn't nearly as talented. The dispute ended up in a Honolulu court in 1986, when a jury asked both Keanes to render big-eyed paintings right there in the courtroom. Margaret set up a canvas and whipped out a painting in less than an hour, but Walter claimed he couldn't because of a shoulder injury. She was awarded $4 million, but Walter was broke and couldn't pay up. In the 1980s, Margaret reopened the Keane Eyes Gallery in San Francisco, and the opening night gala was graced by a bouquet of flowers from Wayne Newton. She still lives in the Bay Area, and still paints the big eyes that captivated the world.

Keane Eyes Gallery
3036 Larkin Street
(415) 922-9309

# Blame It on the Nugget

O pportunists from all walks of life dashed to San Francisco in the mid-19th century. Ships headed to the Golden Gate from China, Australia, South America, and Europe. Dentists in Boston quit their jobs, shoved their families into a covered wagon, and headed west. Industrialists set up banks, railroads, and real estate offices. Shysters and con men materialized, accompanied by prostitutes, drunks, and gamblers. Nobody came here for the weather. They all came because of a little lump of metal that now sits under glass at the Bancroft Library on the UC Berkeley campus.

The gold nugget that launched the Gold Rush of 1849 actually has two names, Marshall's First Nugget, and The Wimmer Nugget. On the morning of January 24, 1848, a carpenter named James Marshall was working in a lumber mill owned by John Sutter, in the Sierra foothills. Marshall spotted a pebble the size of a pea, sitting in the water that powered the mill. The nugget was supposedly boiled in lye by the wife of mill worker Peter Wimmer. After it tested positive as gold, lumber workers quickly spent their free time looking for more of it. Historians suggest that if this particular nugget wasn't the first to be discovered, it was one of the first.

Newspapers went nuts over the discovery, and within months all the above-mentioned palookas showed up, in the largest peacetime migration in history. In one year San Francisco's population grew from 1,000 to 20,000. Very few ever got rich from mining gold, but the belief that one can change his life overnight just by moving here continues to this day.

A nugget eerily identical to the Gold Rush nugget

Bancroft Library
UC Berkeley campus
(510) 642-3781

# World's Oldest Jeans

**N**obody remembers Loeb Strauss. He was just one more 19th-century immigrant who moved to San Francisco and reinvented himself. But around the globe, people wear his legacy, because he changed his name to Levi Strauss, and began making pants out of denim.

The popular myth is that Strauss designed his pants for miners during the Gold Rush of 1849, fashioned out of the heavy brown canvas from their tents. In truth, Strauss didn't patent the clothing rivet until 1873, when his company started manufacturing copper-riveted "waist overalls," i.e., blue denim pants. By the 1920s, Levi Strauss pants were worn by laborers throughout the western states, who found the rough denim fiber a perfect surface upon which to strike a wooden match. Up through the 1950s Levi's were sold only west of the Mississippi River. Visitors from the East Coast would buy the pants and take them back home to amaze their friends — "Look! Real cowboy pants!"

As that pesky rock and roll crept into 1950s American culture, so did those goddamn juvenile delinquents. Their choice of clothing? Tight Levi's. The simple sight of a young boy or girl in blue jeans outraged parents and school administrators, and the company received angry letters decrying the crumbling of the nation's moral fiber. Communism and sexual deviancy always start with the pants.

By the 1960s and 1970s, blue jeans were the required uniform on high school and college campuses. Hippie girls embroidered their pants and jackets. Biker clubs' "colors" were stitched onto Levi's jackets. One tall tale circulated that Levi's was planning to market a separate line of pants and jackets featuring the Hell's Angels motorcycle gang colors.

But one blue jeans company wasn't going to be enough for San Francisco. Back in 1935, Benjamin Franklin Davis started manufacturing baggy utility pants with a distinctive little smiling ape logo. Davis had credentials to launch his Ben Davis line of jeans. His father was Jacob Davis, a Latvian immigrant who had worked for Levi's and supposedly invented their pocket rivet. The basic design has remained intact since then, and beginning in 1991, Ben Davis began attracting a huge secondary market of hip-hop kids through the X-Large store in Los Angeles, owned by members of the Beastie Boys.

Another entrant into the city's blue jeans wars was local real estate developer Donald Fisher and his wife Doris. Frustrated by their inability to find a well-organized blue jeans store (or so Donald says, anyway), the Fishers opened their own jeans retail company in 1969, with a single shop in the city's Sunset District, near what is now the San Francisco State University campus. In homage to the "Generation Gap," they named their little store The Gap. (Good thing they stuck with that slogan, otherwise we all might be wearing "Power to the People" jeans today.) The company now operates several hundred stores in countries

around the world, and owns Banana Republic, Old Navy, and GapKids, for those infants who prefer to drool onto a nice $80 pair of denim overalls.

Today, San Francisco claims the birthplace for three of the world's largest blue jeans companies. Don't bother trying to track down Ben Davis. They have no retail store, and aren't even listed in the phone book. The Gap, of course, is ubiquitous in almost every neighborhood, and in 1998 gained extra publicity for their famous semen-stained blue dress, worn by Monica Lewinsky during her nostril-flaring encounters inside the Clinton White House.

But since Levi's patented and perfected the modern blue jeans as we know them, they are the company that deserves the museum. Located in the original Levi's plant, which still makes jeans, the Levi Strauss Museum displays the oldest pair of jeans in the world. These so-called "Calico Mine Pants" were made by Levi's around 1890, and were discovered in 1948 in an abandoned silver mine in the Mojave Desert. This American treasure features rusted buttons, large holes in the seat and knee, and — decades before anybody heard of Monica Lewinsky — mysterious stains on the front. You should call the museum in advance to set up a tour.

Levi Strauss Museum
250 Valencia Street
(415) 565-9100

# Big House

On October 12, 1989, a Los Angeles jury recommended that devil worshipper Richard "Night Stalker" Ramirez, already found guilty of 13 murders, be sentenced to the gas chamber at San Quentin Prison. Ramirez told the court, "Big deal, death always went with the territory. I'll see you in Disneyland."

Although San Quentin sits just a short drive north of the Golden Gate, with a lovely view of the bay — provided you're near a window — it is definitely not Disneyland. This prison is the oldest in California, housing 5,400 male criminals, approximately 390

of whom are sitting around waiting to be executed on the state's only death row. Not exactly what you'd call the Magic Kingdom. But it does boast some exciting historical highlights, as well as a nice little gift shop and museum.

Kidnapper and rapist Caryl Chessman spent 12 years here on death row, watching his execution date change eight times. Finally, on May 2, 1960, he sat in the gas chamber hoping for another last-minute reprieve. Outside the prison, picketing in the rains, was a well-dressed, orderly crowd that included Marlon Brando, Shirley MacLaine, and Abbie Hoffman. The decision came to grant Chessman yet another appeal, but the judge's secretary misdialed the number, and in that time, the cyanide pellets dropped and Chessman was history.

On February 24, 1969, country singer and convicted pill-popper Johnny Cash brought guitarist Carl Perkins and the rest of his band inside the walls of San Quentin to record a live album of his music. Cash introduced himself to the crowd, cracking a few jokes that made clear he himself was no stranger to a prison cell. The band kicked into a boot-stomping groove, and when Cash sang the opening lyric, "San Quentin, may you rot and burn in hell!" the inmates roared and cheered — the noise can still send chills up the spine of any listener. The record sold 6 million copies, and was voted the Country Music Association's Album of the Year.

In 1971, Black Panthers leader George Jackson attempted to escape from the Adjustment Center, and was killed, along with three prison officers and two other inmates.

On October 3, 1996, wedding bells rang for Doreen Lioy, 41, and the afore-mentioned Richard Ramirez, 36, in the prison's main visiting room. The bride wore a white wedding dress with chiffon sleeves, and was accompanied by two attorneys. The groom wore starched prison blues with no restraints. After exchanging vows, the happy couple gave each other rings, and kissed. The bride is employed as a part-time editor for teen magazines, and

# Follies

the groom remains on death row. Because San Quentin does not allow conjugal visits for inmates sentenced to die, the couple enjoyed a limited honeymoon.

But enough name-dropping. Visitors can get a little taste of the Big House for themselves, by stopping into the prison museum. Check out a model of a prison cell, a miniature of the now-retired gas chamber, and mementos from the original gallows and The Dungeon, known as "The Hole." The store offers T-shirts, mugs, and other trinkets, as well as art objects made by inmates. Featured among the books for sale is *Cooking With Conviction*, a cookbook put together by the Kairos religious group, in support of their ministry. Be sure to sign the museum guest register, which sits on a podium once used to log the details of executions.

From San Francisco, take 101 north to Sir Francis Drake Boulevard, then take the exit to San Quentin. Pass the back gate, then get on Highway 17 heading east, and take the next exit, the last exit before the Richmond-San Rafael Bridge. Follow Main Street to the main gate of San Quentin and turn left into the parking lot for visitors. The museum is through the main gate on the right. Cameras, guns, knives, and bombs are not allowed inside. Call ahead to check for hours.

San Quentin Museum
Building #106, Dolores Way
San Quentin
(415) 454-8808

# The Black Bird

Dashiell Hammett lived in the city in the 1920s, working by day as a Pinkerton detective, and at night writing detective magazine stories and novels. Many of these tales were set in San Francisco, their hard-boiled tone a perfect match for the depressing, fog-bound streets. Like many writers of his era, Hammett eventually followed the money to Hollywood and cranked out screenplays, turning two witty alcoholics into the long-running series *The Thin Man*. But he's best known for his 1930 noir classic novel *The Maltese Falcon*, set in San Francisco and featuring detective Sam Spade. Since Hammett frequently ate at John's Grill, a restaurant on Union Square, he made his Spade character stop in for a meal at a Union Square restaurant, which was patterned after John's Grill. This detail has not been lost on the owners of John's. In business since 1908, the place has evolved into a shrine to Hammett and his books, and constitutes the only Dashiell Hammett museum in the world.

John's kitchen offers up "Sam Spade Chops," Spade's usual order of chops, baked potato, and sliced tomatoes. They also proudly serve "John's Steak," Maltese Falcon private label wines, and the "Bloody Brigid" cocktail in a souvenir glass. If you're feeling at all healthy, the menu includes "Jack LaLanne's Favorite Salad" (named for the fitness freak who once swam to Alcatraz while pulling a boat with his teeth).

The second floor has been decorated as a Maltese Falcon Dining Room. At the top of

the stairs sits a glass case containing Hammett books and a replica of the black bird (available for only $27.50, according to a waiter). One floor up, a former brothel is now the Hammett Den, where live bands get toes tapping on the Brigid O'Shaughnessy dance floor. Hammett-heads meet here periodically to discuss his novels, and gather liquid fortification for the Hammett walking tours (ask the staff for details).

Every wall throughout John's Grill is lined with photos and memorabilia from Hammett's life, from his perennial girlfriend, playwright Lillian Hellman, to Hammett authors and experts, and stills and dialogue snippets from *The Maltese Falcon*. (Two other film versions had appeared previously, but John Huston's version remained the most faithful to the book, and launched Humphrey Bogart's career as a leading man, after George Raft had turned down the role.)

Falcon freaks will salivate over other locations from the book, all within walking distance: The Geary Theater, where Joel Cairo takes in a show; the Palace Hotel, where Spade eats breakfast after getting kicked in the head; Spade's apartment building on Geary at Hyde; and his office at 111 Sutter and Montgomery.

Hammett once lived at 20 Dashiell Hammett Way, which cuts up Nob Hill off Stockton Street. Across the road a mysterious plaque is attached to an alleyway called Burrett Street, reading, "On approximately this spot Miles Archer, partner of Sam Spade, was done in by Brigid

# Peculiar Pacific Heights

Photo: Paul Trapani

From the outside, it appears much like a nondescript former French laundry in Lower Pacific Heights, which it once was, but inside the front door, the San Francisco Museum of Exotica completely overwhelms visitors. Every inch of the walls, floors, and ceilings of this 6,000-square-foot building is covered with collectible art and artifacts from all over the world. It will take a few minutes to adjust to the visuals, but eventually your eyes will focus on specifics — Bali masks, Turkish tapestries, Indonesian sculptures, African animal hides, objects from India, China, Nepal, Tibet, Iran, New Guinea, the Philippines. Anyplace on the planet you can imagine, owner John Wickett has probably visited and brought back some kind of memento. As is typical of local eccentrics, he allows his obsessions to run rampant, and continues visiting auctions and traveling abroad to add to the collection.

The 82-year-old Wickett has had several previous lives, growing up in a wealthy insurance family, owning businesses and real estate in San Mateo, working for charities and organizing debutante cotillions, before getting divorced and converting his assets to collectibles. Before opening this location ten years ago, he kept many of his artifacts in another mansion in Pacific Heights. Look closely at some of the "Swedish Erotica" porn films from the '70s, and you'll see Wickett items appearing as props in the background.

The museum hosts parties and events, at Wickett's whim, and if individuals are interesting enough, he'll even allow them to live there for free. Technically this gallery of oddities isn't open to the public, but it's listed in the phone book, so approach slowly and act interesting.

**San Francisco Museum of Exotica**
**2671 Sutter Street**
**(415) 885-4558**

O'Shaughnessy." No other words, or indication what it means.

The plaque was put together in the late 1960s by journalist Warren Hinckle and ad man Howard Gossage, to commemorate the approximate location of the first murder in *The Maltese Falcon*, when Archer is blown away by O'Shaughnessy in the opening pages. However, the tribute wasn't installed on Burrett until 1974. Two stories circulate why. Either permission was never granted until then, or the plaque was simply misplaced. Gossage had passed away by that time, but you can bet there was an official ceremony.

An added bonus of the restaurant, having absolutely nothing to do with Dashiell Hammett, are the many framed photos of local police officers, and a letter of appreciation from Hillary Rodham Clinton.

**John's Grill**
**63 Ellis Street**
**(415) 986-0069**

# Tattoo You

**H**ow many years has mankind dyed decorative patterns into the skin? Tattooist Lyle Tuttle wondered that, as he sat in his shop inking designs on drunken sailors, and 1960s rock stars like Janis Joplin, Joan Baez, and Jorma Kaukonen. As he traveled all over the world, he spent thousands of dollars collecting old examples of tattoos, storing them in boxes and suitcases. And now he owns the largest repository of tattoo artifacts in the world. The majority of his collection is packed away in a Cold War fallout shelter, but you can check out a small percentage of it at his tattoo parlor in North Beach.

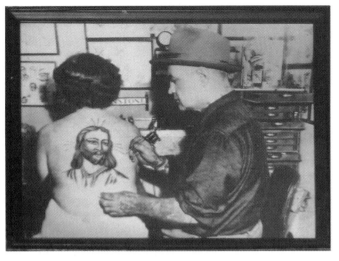

The Tattoo Art Museum features 5,000 sheets of hand-drawn flash, over 600 machines, and 2,000 artists' business cards. San Francisco's earliest tattoo artists are represented with photos and other memorabilia, some of which dates back to the turn of the century. Back in those days, tattoo people all built their own machines, and drew their own flash designs. Tuttle's collection also contains many-one-of-a-kind items. One walrus tusk, dated 1840, sports an image of a Marquesan Islander scrimshawed on it. His rarest piece is a sheet of butterflies, with "Naples, 1898" written on the side.

Tuttle admits he

**Tattoo Art Museum and Hall of Fame**
**Lyle Tuttle Tattooing**
**841 Columbus Avenue**
**(415) 775-4991**

Images Courtesy: Tattoo Art Museum

# Da Vinci's Masterpiece

Originally invented by Leonardo da Vinci in the 16th century, the camera obscura was thought at the time to be the instrument of the devil, and it was banned because the Greeks thought da Vinci could predict the future. Luckily the prohibition didn't stick, because Copernicus used the world's oldest camera to chart the stars, Renaissance artists created paintings using the principle, and much later, San Franciscans used the camera obscura to entertain visiting family members.

One of only a handful left, this West Coast version was built at the Cliff House in 1949 as a student project, patterned after the Encyclopedia Britannica's descriptions of da Vinci's original design. People didn't know what the camera was supposed to be or do, so owner George Whitney constructed the exterior to look more like an actual giant camera.

Made of a rotating mirror, a few lenses, and a parabolic curved screen, the camera obscura reflects 18 degrees of the view from the outside world. The screen takes six minutes to fully go around. Some people stay there for hours, watching the crisp images of surfers, sea lions, and flying birds. Photographer Ansel Adams would hang around the camera so often, they quit charging him admission.

The camera is open 11 a.m. to sunset every day, and costs $1, making it one of the best bargains in the Bay Area. Even if you're not interested in the principles of photography, rumor has it that it's also a great location for giving your boyfriend a blowjob.

**Camera Obscura**
**Behind the Cliff House**
**1090 Point Lobos Avenue at the ocean**
**(415) 750-0415**

doesn't collect many artifacts made after 1976, at which point he says the tattoo industry changed. People started staging conventions and other events, and the secret inner world became more accessible to the public. Along with various magazines and books came a rivalry among the city's various tattoo artists, so don't start asking one about the other, because you might not hear the end of it.

But despite the bickering, something about it will always be special.

"It's one of the human race's oldest art forms," Tuttle has said. "It was invented by the devil and it's not practiced by Ogar. The Tattoo Art Museum is dedicated to the art that art history forgot."

# Chapter Seven

# Get Outta Dodge

Photo: Paul Trapani

Yeah, it's a pretty postcard town. But even for those who live and work here — walking the charming little streets, stopping at the swell little cafes, enjoying all the other quaint little picturesque things — a steady dose of all this cute crap is bound to get on your nerves. "This isn't the real world," you find yourself muttering. "This is some sort of surreal diorama inhabited by psychos." And so, because this is America, you get in your car and drive away from that which bugs you. Within a few hours you're at a location far away from the hectic pace of the city, relaxing in peace and collecting your thoughts. Breathe fresh country air at the site of the most infamous act of cannibalism in modern history. Clear the head with a pleasant stroll through the only fully restored nuclear missile site in the United States. Bask in the sunshine as your remaining pocket cash hinges on a long shot at the state's oldest horse racing track. Or get a good massage and step into a natural hot spring pool with 50 pudgy, middle-aged nudists. Or, if you don't have a car, just walk down Haight Street, sample the wares offered by sales representatives from the underground pharmaceutical industry, and go home and turn up the Hendrix. But that's another book.

# Missiles

Courtesy: Nike Missile Site SF88L

**D**eadheads and nature lovers permeate Marin County, an area famous for mountain bikes, strong dope, healthy vegetarian food, and hot tub parties. Most of this mellow crowd has no idea they're living in the backyard of the only fully restored nuclear missile site in the country.

Imbedded in a hillside of the Marin Headlands, Nike Missile Site SF88L attracts a steady crowd of military veterans, their families, and Cold War freaks who yearn for the good old days of Commie paranoia. Precursor to the Patriot missile, media darling of the Persian Gulf "war," the Nike was part of our primary West Coast defense program. At one time, 11 such sites were sprinkled throughout the Bay Area, one even hidden in the hills of Berkeley, above the Commie-pinko U of C campus.

The SF88L base shut down in 1974, but when it opened 20 years earlier, this was home to the Nike-Ajax line of non-nuke missiles. With a range of 25 miles, the Ajax could shoot down a plane doing twice the speed of sound. In 1959 the military replaced the Ajax with Nike-Hercules, which carried a nuclear warhead and covered a range of almost 90 miles. The Hercules flew over 3.5 times the speed of sound, and reached an altitude of 150,000 feet, before leveling off and finding its target.

In the past few years, Nike fans have painstakingly restored this site, importing parts and gear from all over the country. A visitor's room displays a cross-section of a missile, and patches, monogrammed Zippo lighters, and other memorabilia. According to a guide, periodically the items have to be replaced.

Photo: Paul Trapani

U. S. ARMY

"Every time there's a gun show in San Francisco, we get burglarized." Visitors walk inside the olive-green launch control trailer, which tracked the missiles on radar screens. The cumbersome switches and blinking lights remind you of a cheap 1950s sci-fi movie, where a giant rubber tarantula ravages a small town, impervious to the futile attacks by the Air Force.

Groups are allowed to stand on a platform with one of the Nike missiles, and ride an electric elevator down to an underground bunker, where up to five Nikes were stored on rolling tracks, allowing them to be fired one after another. The guide explains that when they began restoration of the base, everything in this bunker was rusted from exposure, and the floor was covered in water. After the ride back up to level ground, the guide flicks a switch and the missile raises all the way up to launch position: an 88-degree angle. He says if the angle were actually 90 degrees, the booster rocket would fall back onto the site after separating from the main payload

# of Marin

portion of the rocket. People ooh and ah, and shake their heads in wonderment.

Half the fun here is listening to the old veterans spew statistics in defense of liberty:

One guy in a Nike missile cap quickly rattles off a bunch of speeds and altitudes, and concludes triumphantly, "This was the *first missile* to intercept an ICBM."

"With a 95 percent kill ratio, this was the most tested missile system on the planet," growls another tour guide with a big stomach. "It's a lot better than throwing rocks at 'em!"

When asked about the nuclear warhead capabilities, one volunteer jokes, "Obviously we can neither confirm nor deny the existence."

Despite all the posturing, America has never fired the Nike missiles in wartime. This doesn't mean that they're out of service. As is tradition, the United States generously sells off its old military weapons to other countries, so that more cultures may benefit from our outdated technology and blow each other up at discount prices. Somewhere on the opposite side of the globe, a Nike launch drill is in progress.

The real highlight of the Nike tour turns out to be the horny guard dog. Because old missiles and tracking equipment are static displays, base volunteers flesh out the tour with an exciting guard dog demonstration —provided by the local Park Service — which is designed to re-create the feel of German shepherds that patrolled the base when it was active. The Park Service still uses dogs, but at the Nike site, there's no reason to employ them. The pooches are strictly for show. The dog, named Vandor, was actually trained in Germany, and responds to commands in German only. After his trainer works him through an obstacle course, kids are allowed to come up and pet him. And when they do, the happy, panting Vandor grows an enormous pink Nike missile of his own. Red alert!

Photo: Paul Trapani

Nike Missile Site SF88L
Fort Barry, Marin Headlands
(415) 331-1540

# Naked, Crazy-
# Women Wine

**C**alifornia state law dictates that no Bay Area guidebook may be published without including something about the wine country north of San Francisco. (The adjectives "well-balanced," "dusky," and "amusingly presumptuous" should also appear somewhere in the text.) Luckily, one Sonoma County winery is appropriate for this book. The Bartholomew Park Winery is not only located in a beautiful natural setting, and produces award-winning wines, it's built on the spot of a State Farm for Delinquent Women, and one of its vineyards grows on land that once was a nudist colony.

The property's history of growing grapes dates back to the 1830s. A crackpot Hungarian nobleman named Agoston Haraszthy purchased the land in 1857, and his empire soon became the largest vineyard in California. Haraszthy eventually was forced to give up his wineries, and disappeared into the jungles of Nicaragua. A wealthy family purchased the land and built a Victorian mansion, which ended up the residence of one old woman and 200 Angora cats.

The state of California bought the grounds in 1920, and opened a home for prostitutes, drug addicts, and assorted "wild women." New tenants were brought in and fumigated in a receiving hospital, which is now the winery building. Although feminists of the era championed the efforts to take care of such women, neighbors protested the use of government money to house "narcotics addicts, inebriates, and women of the night." Sheriff's deputies regularly spent time investigating reports of escaped inmates, and chasing wayward women up and down the countryside. The hospital later served as a "Home for the Feeble-Minded." The Bartholomew family purchased the entire mess in World War II, and revived the winery business.

One of four Bartholomew vineyards, Denudos (Spanish for "nudes") is located on the site of a former nudist colony. As you roll the award-winning Merlot or Cabernet Sauvignon around on your tongue, keep in mind these grapes grew from the ground where naked people once reclined and splayed their hairy bodies to the sun. Mmmm.

The winery does not require employees to work in the buff, but in 1998 they did sponsor a Sonoma Valley nudist art festival and tasting party. Wine journalists shuffled around the grounds, sipping and ogling the nude models, who were being sketched and painted by local artists. And while it is generally not advisable to place reporters, free alcohol and naked people in close proximity to each other, apparently there were no arrests.

As with all Bartholomew stock, Denudos wines are hand picked and sorted, and only 3,000 cases are produced each vintage. Wines are not available in stores; they are sold only at the winery. If you show up naked, or dressed as a wayward woman — or both — you might even get a discount.

**Bartholomew Park Winery**
**1000 Vineyard Lane, Sonoma**
**(707) 935-9511**

# Ghost Ships

**A**n eerie sight greets the commuter who glances out the window while crossing the Benicia/Martinez Bridge on Highway 680 — the largest single collection of ships on the Pacific Ocean. Silhouetted against the sky are over 70 ships, tankers, missile cruisers, barges, and tugboats, totaling over 2,000 years of active service in every war and military conflict since World War II. People usually refer to this boat Purgatory as the Mothball Fleet, but the government would prefer to call it the National Defense Reserve Fleet.

Other such fleets are in Beaumont, Texas, and James River, Virginia, and all provide auxiliary support during military actions. During the Persian Gulf War, 79 ships were called into service, including two from here. Just in case America must quickly go overseas to fight another war that lasts 100 hours, a team of 71 workers inspects the fleet every day for leaks, and oils the engines.

In the meantime, the Coast Guard uses the ships to train fire-fighting crews. Marines practice attacking them with helicopters. Their hulls are kept corrosion-free with a low-voltage electrical charge. A new ship is added every few weeks, and vessels determined to have no other use are sold for scrap.

Some have stories. The Navy tugboat *Hoga* rescued sailors during the 1941 Pearl Harbor attack. The *Jeremiah O'Brien* Liberty Ship is the only one of the fleet ever to leave under its own power, and not only did it leave, it made it all the way across the Atlantic for the 50th anniversary of D-Day (the *O'Brien* now sits on San Francisco's Embarcadero, open for tours). Recently saved from the scrap yard and refurbished, the *Red Oak Victory* cargo vessel was named for Red Oak, Iowa, the town with the highest number of casualties per capita in World War II. Another member of the fleet, the *Glomar Explorer*, was originally built by Howard Hughes for the CIA, to recover a sunken Soviet submarine off the coast of Hawai'i. The mission failed, but the *Glomar* has been resurrected for oil exploration.

So when you pass by this proud fleet of retirees, stiffen your back and give them a salute. If it weren't for these loyal servants of Uncle Sam, you'd be speaking goddamn German today. Or Japanese. Or Italian. Or Russian. Or Korean. Or Vietnamese. Or Farsi. Or Granadian. Or....

**Mothball Fleet**
**Suisun Bay**
**Off the 680 freeway at Benicia**

# Battle of the Biceps

The small town of Petaluma, 30 miles north of San Francisco, is known mainly for its chicken and egg industry, the kidnapping/murder of a young girl named Polly Klass, and its most famous export, actress Winona Ryder. All of this is overshadowed, of course, by the annual world wristwrestling championships.

Each year, bulging biceps from all over the world descend on Petaluma to compete in the tournament that started the organized sport. Since 1961, people have been coming here, putting their elbows on a table, and grunting it out for the world title. Winners take home $5,000 in cash and prizes.

Courtesy: World Wristwrestling Championships

If you've never watched professional wristwrestling (it was televised for 16 years on ABC's *Wide World of Sports*) it's something you have to see at least once. Like boxing or "Toughman" bar competitions, it's a sport that anyone can do, regardless of background. Many of the stars have nicknames like "The Iceman," and when they're not engaged in their 10-second bouts, they are getting shoulder massages, or walking around wearing a little sock-type sleeve around their wrestling arm. Often there's an enormously fat pig farmer who enters the competition, and wins because he's just so damn big and heavy. The woman wrestlers, in particular, are vicious-looking. Steer clear of them.

The best element of this sport, and one that makes it worth checking out, is its audience. A level of pure bloodlust emerges in a crowd assembled at a wrist-wrestling event. They scream bloody murder at each victory, and cheer on their favorite competitors. At one event on Fisherman's Wharf some years ago, sponsored by Yukon Jack whiskey, a crowd member rushed up to a competitor from Canada who had just been defeated and hollered in his face, "That's why you lost in Vietnam!"

World Wristwrestling Championships
P.O. Box 156
Petaluma, CA 94953
(707) 538-1113

# Nude Hot Tubs!

A stocky nude man in his 50s strides proudly across the courtyard of Harbin Hot Springs. His entire back, arms, and legs are covered with fuzzy hair that has turned mostly white, with intermittent dark patches. If he's aware he looks like an aging snow leopard, padding along a forest path, he gives no indication. He hangs his towel over a rail with the ease of someone who has done it a thousand times, and steps into a communal soaking pool. He sinks down under the surface and comes back up, his splotchy fur glistening with droplets of water.

Since the 1880s the clothing-optional Harbin resort has attracted people like Mr. Leopard, seduced by the natural spring tubs. Guests choose from a communal warm pool, a freezing cold pool, and a scalding hot pool that nobody can stand for more than five minutes. The idea is to rotate amongst the three in some kind of order that is healthy, invigorating, and life-affirming.

Brochures may advertise the springs' healing properties, but everyone knows Harbin's primary attraction is the infamous relaxation technique known as the "watsu." Supposedly a combination of water flotation and shiatsu massage, the watsu basically involves one person floating on her back (ideally, a young naked woman), with another person (oh, say, a horny old naked hippie guy) gently supporting her by the neck and the small of the back, swirling around and around in the communal tub, until all inhibitions break down and the young woman finds herself in an R.E.M. state of altered consciousness, clutching the back fur of Mr. Leopard and moaning like she's experiencing a simultaneous orgasm and enema. It probably feels good, but it sure looks weird.

Harbin also features arts and crafts, and a cafe with fresh organic food. On weekend nights, live music and a drum circle echo up and down the hills. Massage and other bodywork experts offer their services daily, in a row of little wooden rooms. To pick a masseuse, guests thumb through three-ring binders with résumés and photographs of all the massage practitioners, then pick the best-looking one. Call first before you make the drive. The hotel rooms fill up quickly, but you can always bring a sleeping bag and camp out on the redwood decks.

# Shit-Faced for Free

U sed to be, if you wanted to drink a beer, you cracked open a can of fill-in-the-blank and guzzled it down without worrying about things like taste. But in our new improved modern society, beer drinking has reached the fetish appeal — and price — of fine wines. People read beer magazines, go to beer tastings, and keep their own beer mugs in little cabinets at snotty beer bars. Ironically, one of the snotty beers indigenous to San Francisco, Anchor Steam, actually started as a working man's beer. It almost went out of business, until the company was saved by the sales of dishwashing machines. But there's a place in the city you can drink a whole bunch of it for free — the brewery tour.

Steam brewing developed in the mid-19th century, an adaptation of ale brewing techniques to a new type of yeast, producing a draft-only brew heavier in carbonation than the Austrian lagers popular at the time. The cool, moderate Bay Area climate allowed brewing at ale temperatures. Anchor was first brewed in San Francisco in 1896, as an attempt to develop a uniquely American style of "steam" beer. It was a blue-collar beer, sturdy and carbonated, and at one time 25 brewers produced it throughout the city. In 1934, the Anchor Brewing Company formed, becoming the first steam beer brewery to open after Prohibition, as well as the nation's first microbrewer. For years, it was another special little secret of the isolated Bay Area.

Sales of Anchor lagged in the 1960s, as gigantic pilsener-style brewers like Bud and Miller led the market. In the mid-'60s, a Stanford graduate and beer aficionado (occasionally they overlap) named Fritz Maytag was sitting in a San Francisco bar, having an Anchor, when the bartender informed him the company was going under the following week. Maytag said to himself, "No, it's not." He sold some shares of his family's business — which happened to be the Maytag family appliance fortune — and bought the brewery. Beginning with one employee, he focused on getting Anchor Steam back on track, and it's now the sixth largest "craft brewer" in the nation, producing 100,000 barrels every year. Each holiday season the company produces a limited amount of Christmas Ale, and depending on the batch that year, it's the lip-smacking favorite of beer geeks around Northern California.

Anchor can now be found in most bars in San Francisco, but if you want to make the pilgrimage back to the source itself, you can take the company brewery tour and get a heat on for free. Visitors are advised to make reservations as far in advance as possible — at least two weeks in advance.

Anchor Steam Brewery Tour
1705 Mariposa Street
(415) 863-8350

# A Taste of Sake

**M**any Americans have sipped from porcelain Sakazuki cups of heated sake, usually while wolfing down pieces of raw fish at a brightly lit sushi restaurant. But what few know is that California is the Sake Freak Zone — 60 percent of the nation's sake is consumed in San Francisco and Los Angeles. It makes sense, therefore, that California boasts five of the country's seven sake breweries. The largest, Takara Sake, takes up an entire city block of Berkeley, and visitors can go taste the products for free.

From noon to 6 p.m. every day, a steady stream of college students, tourists, and sake aficionados quietly stroll into the tasting room to understand more about the world of sake — not to mention the free buzz. Most are disappointed to discover the brewery is spacious and minimal, and not a party palace. No vomiting or bikini contests. You taste the 10 types of sake available, watch a 15-minute video about the history of sake, and wander the adjoining Sake Museum to check out the ancient wooden tubs and tools.

The tradition dates back 2,000 years to Japan, where sake was initially used only for holy religious events, and each village had its own sake master. Modern brewers have honed the method down to a science, fermenting precise amounts of Sacramento Valley rice and Sierra Nevada spring water. Professional tasters sample the raw sake concoction, adding other batches if necessary, and when it passes final inspection, the sake is bottled. Depending on the type, sake is best either at room temperature, heated to slightly above room temperature, or chilled to 50 or 55 degrees.

Takara brews many variations, including rice and plum-based wines, and a cooking sake, but its best-seller is Sho Chiku Bai Classic, America's #1 sake, which is served in Japanese restaurants. A recent visit to the brewery found that the plum-flavored varieties are as devastating as any flavored liqueurs, and should be avoided unless a dessert is sitting in front of you. But try the Ginjo, their premium blend made from special polished rice, which tastes like a fine tequila. And then drive home with a big smirk on your face.

**Takara Sake USA Tour**
**708 Addison Street, Berkeley**
**(510) 540-8250**

# Playing the Ponies

CalTrain commuters riding south from San Francisco will watch them climb aboard — old guys with porkpie hats and bad sport coats, younger guys in logo caps and windbreakers, sitting in the padded seats, gazing out the windows at the passing scenery, that faraway gleam in their eyes. Thirty minutes from the city, they will all stand up at once, as the train slows to a stop at the Bay Meadows horse track. It's time to play the ponies.

Opened in 1934, Bay Meadows is the longest continually operating track in California, and claims to have introduced the Daily Double and the photo-finish camera to horse racing. Star jockeys over the years have included Bill Shoemaker and the current winningest jockey in the country, Russell Baze. The track's publicity department is quite innovative in attracting folks to the sport, with free T-shirt and gym bag nights, and every Friday, drink specials and live concerts. Throughout, the sandwiches are excellent, and the beer is cold. Like every track, the atmosphere hums with a weird vibrancy of potential — in less than two minutes, someone could be set for life, or completely ruined. If you don't smoke cigars, it might be a good time to start up.

Up in the grandstand, a group of Asians crowd around one of the 160 video monitors, watching horses hit the home stretch — *shit! shit! shit! shit! shit!* — and then they collectively groan and turn away, suddenly silent. No stereotypes, just an observation. Underneath the grandstand, gamblers sit in big rooms, intently watching video screens of the Santa Anita track results. Members of the Turf Club quietly exhale when somebody drops thousands on one horse. It's only money, but still, nobody's goofing off or cracking jokes.

At the end of the day, the porkpie hats and baseball caps climb back aboard the Gamblers' Express, that same gleam still in their eyes. A few wear brand-new Bay Meadows caps. As long as they didn't bring the deed to the ranch, tomorrow is another day.

Bay Meadows
2600 South Delaware Street, San Mateo
(650) 574-RACE

# Between the Windmills

At the very end of the United States, two windmills stand guard over the Pacific, originally built to pump water for Golden Gate Park. The shorter one, the Dutch Windmill, was finished in 1902, and the Murphy Windmill was completed three years later. On most days, a breeze blows off the waves of Ocean Beach, up and over the picnickers, surfers, and rollerbladers, and ruffles the hardy shrubs between the windmills. Inside this shrub thicket runs a dirt pathway, which functions as the meeting place of the most secret organization in the city — the San Francisco Men's Botany Club.

As near as one can tell, that's what it appears to be. Lone male scientists saunter down this path, or linger in the trees, inspecting and identifying the local flora and fauna indigenous to the region. Such field trips are informal, and seem to be at the whim of each member. As with many male clubs, women and children are frowned upon. Sometimes it just has to be a guy thing.

There are no organized bus schedules.

Occasionally these botanists will chat amongst each other, perhaps discussing a raccoon sighting, or a particular strain of sand grass, but for the most part they keep to themselves, and avoid conversation with non-botanists. You can't blame them. If you're deeply engrossed in a favorite hobby, you don't like to be bothered with silly questions, either.

Daytime field activities of the Men's Botany Club can be exhausting. Many members bring their own refreshments in coolers. Some sit on logs or benches, resting between botanical discoveries. The sun worshippers go shirtless, while others wear tight pants so as not to snag and damage a rare Spanish moss.

Nocturnal excursions are even more secret, members preferring the light of the moon to illuminate Nature's evening wonders. Low-level lighting eliminates the amateurs, leaving only the seasoned botanists who can identify nomenclature by touch.

**Golden Gate Park Windmills
Ocean Beach**

Photo: Sharon Selden

# Indians on Alcatraz

**S**helves of tour guidebooks will describe the general history of Alcatraz, the escape-proof prison built on a rock outcropping in the middle of San Francisco Bay, with Al Capone, "Machine Gun" Kelly, "The Birdman of Alcatraz," and all the rest of it. Less documented is the 19-month occupation of "The Rock" by American Indians. And anybody who has the balls to offer $24 for the entire island deserves an entry here.

Since the Civil War, Alcatraz had operated as a prison. Besides the harsh weather and complete isolation, inmates could also hear the sounds of partying carry across the waters from San Francisco. That's got to wear on you. Attorney General Robert Kennedy closed the prison in 1963, after a congressional committee discovered that the costs of operating Alcatraz equaled the expense of putting up guests at New York's exclusive Waldorf Astoria hotel. For the next six years, Alcatraz sat unoccupied in the middle of the bay, until November 20, 1969, when a group of American Indian activists pulled up boats to the darkened island and declared it theirs by first right.

Led by college student Richard Oakes, the Indians offered a treaty to the white man. They would purchase the island for $24 in glass beads and red cloth. Fully aware that Manhattan Island was sold for only $12, the Indians adjusted the price for current land values, and claimed that their offer of $1.24 per acre was actually more than the 47 cents per acre the white men were paying California's Indians for their lands.

Prior to this maneuver, Indian activism had been centered in small geographic areas, focusing on specific issues like illegal trespassing on Indian lands, and denying Indians access to their hunting and fishing areas. The Alcatraz occupation was different, a reclamation of land on a global scale that brought the attention of the world's media. Over the next 19 months, hundreds of Indian people lived on the island, and thousands more watched it on television, cheering on the occupation. It had been a long time since Indians felt such pride for their culture. Irritated, the government pondered what to do. The FBI was instructed not to intervene.

Photo: Paul Trapani

The Indians settled into their new life on The Rock, and decorated the buildings with slogans like "YOU ARE ON INDIAN LAND." The occupiers called their new-found cultural pride "Indianness," and for the first time they felt free from government control. The island celebrated "Liberation Day" on May 31, 1970, and two months later, the first baby was born on the island.

As time went on, the hierarchy of leadership began changing. Many of the Indians who were students returned to school, and were replaced by Indians who were not involved with the initial occupation. Non-Indians moved onto the island. Tensions grew. Occupants knew they could be removed at any time.

Secret negotiations took place. The Indians were offered a portion of Fort Miley as an alternative site to occupy, but refused. They wanted full title to Alcatraz, and to

# Buns by the Bay

Ahh, the simple joy of ripping one's clothes off and spreading out buck naked on the beach like a lazy house cat. Northern California may not have the balmy climate of the Caribbean, but we do have plenty of coastlines where nudists can sunbathe away without fear of imprisonment.

Describing every single isolated spot would fill half this book, and dedicated naturalists already know where they are, but we will tell you that the Bay Area's most popular clothing-optional hangout is Baker Beach. Located just below the Golden Gate Bridge, Baker will see up to 500 sun worshippers on a warm day, many of whom will be unabashedly displaying their genitalia. Some local nude beaches are predominently occupied by gay males, but Baker attracts any and all types. Once you hike down to the beach, just keep walking towards the bridge until it starts getting nude. Find yourself a spot, spread out a blanket, and don't forget the sun block.

**Baker Beach**
**Below the Golden Gate Bridge**

• • • • • • • • • • • • • • • • • • • • • • • • • • • • • • • • • • • • • • • • • • • •

establish a university and cultural center. The government then shut off all electrical power to the island, and removed a barge that had been providing fresh water. Life grew more chaotic. A fire broke out, and several buildings were destroyed. Blatant drug use was everywhere, and people fought over authority. To raise money for food, Indians stripped and sold copper from the island's plumbing and electrical connections.

In January 1971, two oil tankers collided in the entrance to the bay. Although the lack of an Alcatraz light or foghorn was not to blame, the accident was enough for President Nixon to green-light a removal plan. Six months later, on June 11, 1971, federal agents and special forces waited until Alcatraz was nearly empty, and stormed the island, removing five women, four children and six unarmed men.

Was it a success? As a result of the Alcatraz protest, many of the approximately 74 occupations of federal facilities and private lands that followed were either planned by or included people who had been involved in the island, from the BIA headquarters takeover in 1972, to the June 26, 1975, shootout between American Indian Movement members and FBI agents on the Pine Ridge Reservation in South Dakota. Alcatraz is thought of as the catalyst for this new activism, and gradually, U.S. government policy began changing towards Indians.

Today the island is part of the Golden Gate National Recreation Area. An excellent cell-house audio tour (recorded by former inmates and wardens), takes visitors through the history of The Rock. Each Thanksgiving and Columbus Day, the International Indian Treaty Council — an organization of indigenous peoples from North, Central, South America and the Pacific — hold Sunrise Ceremony on Alcatraz. The event is open to the public.

**Alcatraz Island Tours**
**Red & White Fleet**
**Pier 41 at Fisherman's Wharf**
**(415) 546-2805**

# Weird Computer Junk

**B**ecause San Francisco is home to *Wired* and 539 other computer magazines, and Silicon Valley is the world headquarters for almost every computer company, and the surrounding Bay Area is rife with Internet publications and HTML design firms, walking down any street means you'll nearly be run over by a sport-utility vehicle driven by a khaki-pants in fashion eyewear who's simultaneously talking on a cell phone and receiving a faxed menu from the hottest new Thai restaurant.

But what about the other end of this exciting and lucrative field, the ones who aren't living out a Douglas Coupland fantasy? The people who don't care about being yuppies, but who just *really, really like* computers? The folks who can start with a plastic tower shell, and build their own computer *at home*? There wouldn't be any khaki-pants yuppies without these guys toiling away in the back room. *They're* the real heroes. And every month you can find them at Robert Austin Computer & Internet Expo, a traveling computer parts show that alternates between Oakland's Convention Center and San Francisco's Cow Palace.

The first thing you'll observe, after filling out an official VIP form that asks for your e-mail address, is how quiet, polite, and efficient the expo seems. Booth after booth, room after room, the fix-it guys constitute the best-behaved crowd you've ever seen at any convention. Essentially, this event is as dull as the computer industry itself. People stroll the aisles in an orderly manner, serenaded by tinny, upbeat music blaring from little workstation speakers.

What's most interesting about the atmosphere is the apparent synthesis of the best elements of a Radio Shack store and a fish market. But instead of flopping fish or turtles crawling out of buckets, there's bins of connectors and transistors and memory chips and all sorts of weird little junk that goes inside your computer somewhere. Peruse the tables of 25-cent mousepads, $8 keyboards, outdated computer manuals, computer dustcovers, do-it-yourself computer tower shells, and your mind races. Who buys all this crap? Is it stolen? Do these things even work? Are these parts left over from some liquidation sale of an early Microsoft competitor that collapsed in a pile of lawsuits? The implied message seems to be, "Here are the products, go ahead and sift through them, and if you can make any of it work, we'd like to know how you did it."

Just as the 8-track cartridge had its glory years, so goes the CD-ROM format of data storage and retrieval. Many booths display racks of old CD-ROM titles, priced to move. *The Magic Death, Falcon AT, Learn to Do Windows '95* by John Dvorak, *Floor Plan #D Design Suite, Daryl F. Gates Police Quest: Open Season, WarCraft II: Tides of Darkness.* You might as well be flipping through vinyl records at the Goodwill.

Although computer language is universal among all cultures, with all the excitement, the English language often gets left behind. "Beat anyone price" boasts one handwritten sign in front of a pile of memory upgrades. A adult CD-ROM title *Happy Time* instructs, "Just Type Setup. For Adult Only."

The optimist will leave the expo knowing that even though he wasn't able to find a replacement "w" key for his Apple Lisa keyboard, there will be another show next month.

**Robert Austin Computer & Internet Expo**
**(800) 243-7041**

# Toasted at Trader Vic's

T he name Trader Vic's evokes images of thatched-roof huts and hula-dancing luaus on the beach, but the origin of the international chain of Polynesian-style restaurants is much less exotic than it sounds. A restaurateur named "Trader" Vic Bergeron started his career in the 1930s, serving steak and chicken at an Oakland beer joint called Hinky Dink's. Bergeron kept his place lively with potent tropical drinks, and entertained customers by sticking an ice pick into his wooden leg.

In 1937, Bergeron returned from a trip to a Hollywood restaurant flush with ideas, and reverted Hinky Dink's to a tropical theme. He changed the menu to Chinese food with a South Pacific twist, and added fish netting, canoes, tiki statues and wooden masks to the walls. Business took off, in part because of America's hunger for exotic sophistication, and an increasing interest in Polynesian culture brought over from G.I.s after World War II. Another Trader Vic's opened in San Francisco, then the chain spread to hotels throughout the rest of the world.

The San Francisco version served as a famous celebrity watering hole for decades, before closing for good in 1994, but the first-ever restaurant in the chain remains in the Bay Area. Originally on San Pablo Avenue in Emeryville, it was moved to its present location in the late 1960s.

> ### Menehune Juice
> 1 lime
> 1/2 ounce orange curacao
> 1/4 ounce rock candy syrup
> (same as simple syrup)
> 1/4 ounce orgeat syrup
> 2 ounces light Puerto Rican rum
>
> Squeeze lime juice over shaved ice in a mai tai (double old-fashioned) glass; save one shell. Add remaining ingredients and enough shaved ice to fill glass. Hand shake (just to mix it — don't strain the ice out). Decorate with one spent lime shell, fresh mint, and a menehune.
>
> — from Trader Vic's Bartender's Guide, 1972

As you enter this shrine of tiki kitsch, you're greeted by two massive split-oak, wood-burning ovens. Periodically, staff emerge from the kitchen, climb up a short ladder, and deposit raw meat inside them. As a waiter wearing a blue blazer and fresh handkerchief whisks you to a table, you notice the views of the bay out the window are excellent. Is the food good? Who knows? You're having the dreaded Scorpion Bowl cocktail. Two hours later, your head swimming from rum, the waiter's words come back to you: "Don't worry, we'll take care of you." You look up and realize there is a giant wooden canoe hanging above your head, in one of the most earthquake-prone areas in the world.

Two more reasons to stop at Trader Vic's: hot moist towels furnished at the table, and for the Anglophiles, framed portraits of Queen Elizabeth and Prince Philip.

**Trader Vic's**
**9 Anchor Drive, Emeryville**
**(510) 653-3400**

# Cannibal Campground

**W**e scowl in disgust at modern-day flesh eaters like Jeffrey Dahmer, the Milwaukee chocolate factory worker who lured men to his apartment and then hacked them up for dinner. Cannibals were more resourceful in the 19th century. Members of the Donner Party ate their friends and family simply because they were hungry. This tragic and gruesome saga of the American West is now commemorated with a nice monument, park, and camping facilities. And if you have a car, it's not far at all.

As people migrated westward across the U.S., two brothers from Illinois, Jacob and George Donner, organized their own expedition of 89 Midwestern farmers and adventurers, which left Independence, Missouri, in April of 1846. When the caravan of oxen and wagons reached what is now Wyoming, a guide named Lansford Hastings whipped out a leaflet and insisted he knew a shortcut to California. The Donners said hey, sounds great to us, and followed the cutoff through Utah into Nevada.

Unfortunately, the route was actually a brutal trek through severe desert conditions. They arrived at the Sierras late, and camped at what was known as Truckee Lake. The winter snows descended upon them, trapping them without food, and little knowledge of how to hunt and fish. Thanks a lot, Lansford Hastings.

In January 1847, a few of the emigrants broke through over the 7,000-foot pass, and summoned relief parties. In March the first team came upon the group. Nearly half were dead from starvation or cold. The 47 pioneers still alive survived by boiling ox hides into a foul-tasting paste, eaten the dog, and eventually turned to their dead friends and relatives, cooking the flesh and making it into soup.

The grisliest tale of cannibalism was related by a Captain W.O. Fallon, whose rescue party found a sole survivor, German-born emigrant Lewis Keseberg. Previous relief parties left the ailing Keseberg behind with two others, George Donner and his wife, Tamsen. Fallon's party was shocked at the sight of a robust Keseberg, sitting in front of a pot of soup, surrounded by picked-over corpses. Creepier still, Keseberg appeared to be demented, and acting pretty flippant about the whole cannibal thing. He insisted that he hadn't killed the Donners, he'd only eaten them after they had died, and there's a big difference. Despite this line of reasoning, Keseberg was put on trial for murder in a Sacramento court. Although acquitted, he spent the rest of his life pelted by rocks as he walked the streets.

Donner Memorial State Park is located 100 miles east of Sacramento along the I-80 freeway, and is built upon the site of the Donner cabins. Historical postcards, posters, maps, and books are available at the Emigrant Trail Museum. A Pioneer Monument measures 22 feet high, the same height as the snow that trapped the Donner Party. An adjoining campground features tables and stoves, for those who wish to re-create the cannibal experience.

If anything positive could be gleaned from this tragedy, it's nice that the Donner family did eventually end up with their name attached to a mountain pass, a state park, and a ski area.

**Donner Party Emigrant Trail Museum**
**Donner Memorial State Park, I-80**
**(530) 582-7892**

# Bombs in our Backyard

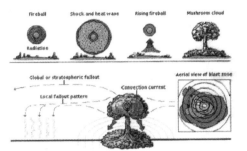

S outheast of Berkeley and Oakland, Interstate 580 runs through hillsides of strange high-tech windmills. This is the largest wind-farm in the world, silently generating electricity. Cows wander the surrounding pastures, and farmers plow the fields with tractors. Plunked down in the middle of this idyllic Norman Rockwell valley is the laboratory that gave birth to the hydrogen bomb.

Lawrence Livermore Laboratory is one of two facilities in the U.S. that develops new and exciting nuclear weaponry. Oh, Livermore scientists also work with magnetic and laser fusion energy, non-nuclear energy, biomedicine, and environmental science, but the coolest aspects of the lab are the new things that blow other things up.

And like most aspects of weapons technology, the laboratory's origins spawn from a typically American climate of paranoia, competition, and egomania.

After the Russians tested their first A-bomb in 1949, two members of the U.S. atomic bomb project at Los Alamos, New Mexico, met to discuss what this meant. The Soviets were going to kick our ass in the Cold War unless they did something fast, to protect the free world from Commies — and also to create some important, high-paying jobs for themselves. Nobel laureate scientist Ernest Lawrence and physicist Edward Teller thought another nuclear weapons lab could compete with Los Alamos and be able to handle future projects. Besides, Teller had worked with J. Robert Oppenheimer, father of the A-bomb, and the two egos could barely stand to be in the same room together.

Lawrence pitched the idea of a second weapons lab to the Atomic Energy Commission. The government said okay, and created the Livermore branch of the UC Radiation Laboratory at the college in Berkeley. In September 1952, the Lawrence Livermore weapons laboratory formally opened its doors on the site of a former naval air station in Livermore. Livermore has developed scary new weapons ever since, including Teller's H-bomb and the Strategic Defense Initiative (SDI) "Star Wars" program.

The Visitor's Center, located on Greenville Road just outside the laboratory's East Gate, is open every weekday afternoon, and offers displays on lasers, chemistry, energy, bioscience, and "national security." Tours of the actual lab must be planned in advance, but include a peek at Nova, the world's largest laser.

**Lawrence Livermore National Laboratory Visitor's Center**
**7000 East Avenue, Livermore**
**Tours (925) 422-4599**

# Ghosts and Mobsters and Mermaid Prostitutes

**B**uilt in 1900, the eight-acre Brookdale Lodge resort sits hidden away in the mountains outside Santa Cruz. Surrounded by redwoods are condos, cabins, a motel, a cafe, and a bar.

The main restaurant features an actual stream, built in the 1920s, that runs through the middle of the dining room, and was included in "Ripley's Believe It or Not." The creek's water is stocked with fish, and tourists are encouraged to feed them bits of bread from the tables.

Such a unique, isolated location is obviously going to attract rogue elements.

Celebrities used the Brookdale as a bacchanalian getaway pad. Over the years, Hollywood partiers included Joan Crawford, Howard Hughes, Hedy Lamarr, President Herbert Hoover, Marilyn Monroe, and Rita Hayworth. Walter Matthau and Shirley Temple dropped by. The Inkspots released an album, "recorded at Beautiful Brookdale Lodge."

But the Brookdale has a much seedier side. It was also a mobster hangout, especially during Prohibition. One wall of the lodge's Mermaid Room is plate-glass, and offers an underwater view of the swimming pool. In the old days, working girls dressed as mermaids would frolic in the water, wearing numbered tags. The gangsters would sit in the bar having drinks, and select the fish they wanted. Mermaid and mobster would rendezvous, and walk through an underground tunnel across the road to a more discreet cabin.

In addition to a rich tradition of celebrities, illicit hooch, gangsters, and prostitutes, the place is also haunted by ghosts. Many people died at the lodge during the gangster days, and a little girl drowned many years ago in the dining room creek. (Perhaps she was trying to escape mermaid duty by swimming back upstream.)

Spirits are said to wander the lodge to this day. Doors slam for no reason. The jukebox and TV suddenly crank up. Toilet paper rolls unwind simultaneously in both the men's and women's rooms. Sounds of laughter drift from the empty billiard room.

In the lobby of the lodge sits a display case of old clippings about the ghosts, and playbills from one-acts that have been staged about the spirits.

The psychic activity may also be responsible for more severe acts. One of the original lodge buildings burned to the ground in 1952, killing five people. A flood and another fire ravaged the business further. The property fell into disrepair, attracting squatters and drug dealers.

In 1989, a San Francisco police officer and his family stepped in, purchased the resort, and over the years have completely renovated it. The Brookdale now hosts weddings and corporate events, and the bar features niche market musical acts such as the Fleetwood Mac tribute band Rumours. These days, when tourists drop by, instead of watching drunk gangsters chase prostitutes, they can tap their toes to an ersatz yet eerily lifelike version of "Rhiannon."

**Brookdale Lodge**
**11570 Highway 9, Brookdale**
**(831) 338-6433**

# Explore Yourself

A few hundred years ago, five hours south of what is now San Francisco, the Essalen Indians lived along the coast, fishing the ocean and hunting in the Santa Lucia Mountains. They were probably pretty happy campers, but not in the chief's wildest dreams could he imagine his bucolic Big Sur surroundings would evolve into catnip for radical therapists, who would build an "educational center devoted to the exploration of unrealized human capacities."

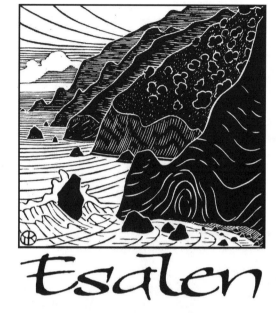

*Esalen*

Since 1962, thousands have flocked to the 27-acre Esalen retreat and paid good money for seminars about bodywork, primal therapy, biofeedback, intuitive development, and other components of what has become known as the "human potential" movement. Prominent psychiatrists and psychologists dropped by early on, from Fritz Perls to Ida Rolf and Alan Watts. Stories circulated of sex orgies and acid parties, and where there's drugs and sex, there's usually celebrities.

Members of the Beatles stopped in and cavorted in the clothing-optional hot springs. Hunter Thompson and the staff of *Rolling Stone* magazine were kicked out for partying too much. Even Charles Manson paid a visit in 1969, looking for new recruits for his little LSD/race war/Armageddon project. On August 5 the hippie con man pulled his stolen bakery van into the Esalen driveway. Leaving a 17-year-old hitchhiker girl asleep in the vehicle, Manson took his guitar inside and played some of his songs for everybody. For a "sensitivity retreat," the reaction was apparently less than sensitive. Manson later told a friend that some of the Esalen staff pretended to be asleep, while others said, "This is too heavy for me." Manson left, chagrined.

Three days later, on August 8, Manson Family members dropped by the home of Sharon Tate, and slaughtered the occupants. Coincidence? Probably.

Esalen can't promise such excitement these days, but their classes are just as esoteric. Typical titles include "To Be Ripe to Die, To Be Ready to Live," "The Story of Your Life: Becoming the Author of Your Experience," "Cultivating Resilience," and "Facilitating Deep Process Using the Penniston Protocol Alpha/Theta Brainwave Training Technique." For those desiring more intensive workshops, Esalen also offers a 26-day Ongoing Residence Program. Don't drop by unannounced, or the guard will stop your car at the gate and tell you to turn around.

**Esalen Institute**
**Highway 1, Big Sur**
**(408) 644-8476**

# Museum of Dudes

The clichéd image of Santa Cruz usually includes downtown street kids playing guitars badly, or a nightclub full of people high on 'shrooms, bouncing to a band and spilling their microbrews. But this small town also contains one of the best surfing spots on the West Coast, and is home to the Santa Cruz Surfing Museum, the first of its kind in the world.

The museum is located in a small lighthouse just off the legendary surf break known as Steamer's Lane. A short walk away is a statue of the Unknown Surfer, depicting a clean-cut guy standing in front of a board. Whenever a local surfer dies, ritual dictates that someone hang a lei around the neck of the figure.

Museum visitors are immediately greeted by a monitor playing surf videos, displays of surf club patches, old surf movie posters, and dioramas of sandy beaches decorated with antique swim fins and pre-World War II surfboards. Photos line the walls of surfing greats throughout the decades, including Duke Kahanamoku, the U.S. 1912 swimming gold medalist who first brought surfing to California from Hawai'i. Visitors learn that back in the 1930s, the Santa Cruz Surfing Club rode 11-foot, 100-pound boards made out of solid redwood, many constructed in high school wood shop classes. One such plank stretches up to the ceiling, dwarfing the boards of current local surf gods like Peter Mel.

The most unnerving display is the map of area shark attacks, in which a section of coastline has been filled with colored dots to indicate man's unfortunate encounters with predatory elasmobranch fishes. Prominent in this display is a news photo of Eric Larsen, sitting in a hospital bed, raising up his bandaged arms and hands. On July 1, 1991, Larsen was surfing north of Santa Cruz at Davenport Landing. In six feet of water, a great white shark attacked him, thinking he was a seal, then swam around and chomped him again. Larsen smacked the shark away, struggled back onto his board, and caught another wave all the way into the beach. A 16-year-old kid found him dazed and collapsed on the sand, and called for help. Larsen was rushed to a hospital. He had lost over half his blood, and the wounds were so deep the shark's teeth had actually scratched his bones. In 10 hours of surgery, doctors used metal staples and over 400 stitches to piece him back together. Another odd fact: In college, he lived down the hallway from me.

Santa Cruz Surfing Museum
Mark Abbott Memorial Lighthouse
1305 East Cliff Drive, Santa Cruz
(408) 429-3429

# Henry Miller Mambo

**A** true wild man of literature, Henry Miller exemplified the term "lust for life" — especially a lust for women — but even after several of his books were published in Europe, no United States publisher would touch him. His first-person style of barely controlled chaos was seen as too weird and perverted. In 1943 he wrote letters to *The New Republic*, begging for food and clothing in exchange for his watercolor paintings. After the magazine published the letters, money started rolling in, and the following year he moved to Big Sur, helping to establish the area as an artists' colony. For the next two decades Miller lived the life of a literary icon, writing, painting, and playing nude ping-pong with young women. But continual visitors and houseguests drove him and his wife to move to Pacific Palisades. His banned book *Tropic of Cancer* was finally published in the U.S., followed by the rest of his early autobiographical books. Miller eased through his remaining years, painting every day and writing occasionally, until his death in 1980.

Courtesy: Henry Miller Library

His longtime friend Emil White took it upon himself to convert his own home into a library devoted to Miller, and the Big Sur Land Trust has now assumed managerial duties of the library. Redwoods guard the entrance, and poetry festivals and art shows are held out on the big green front lawn. Guests can find naked women posing for photos on the wooden deck, or curator Magnus Torén strumming guitar. Besides selling Miller books, videos, and postcards, the library publishes a regular newsletter, and maintains a web site to connect Miller fans around the world. Recent additions to the library include two Miller paintings obtained from the estate of one of his friends, actor Vincent Price.

**Henry Miller Library**
**Highway 1, Big Sur**
**(408) 667-2574**

# Build It and

Six hours south of San Francisco, and five miles in from the Pacific Ocean, sits the world's most opulent mansion, built by newspaper kingpin William Randolph Hearst. He named his estate La Cuesta Encantada, which means "The Enchanted Hill," but people mostly referred to it as Hearst Castle. Today it could be called "Construction Deficit Disorder," because despite three decades of steady work, the buildings were never completed. This 165-room estate sprawls over 127 acres, and includes way too much of everything, including an 18,000-square-foot Roman pool. (As anyone in California knows, you can't skimp on the pool. ) Just to let us know how insignificant our lives really are in comparison, we can now take a guided tour and tromp through the second largest private home in the world.

Courtesy: Hearst Castle

The son of a mining industry millionaire, Hearst built his career initially on newspapers, starting with the *San Francisco Examiner*. His empire spread to at one time include magazines, radio, film, and theater productions. (When Orson Welles' classic *Citizen Kane* was released, based on the life of Hearst, ads for the movie were refused in all Hearst-owned newspapers. William

# They Will Come

Randolph Hearst III reportedly never even heard the film existed until he attended college.)

In between making more money than God — an estimated million dollars per day — Hearst was also a compulsive art collector, traveling the globe acquiring more items for his treasure trove. Eventually, he needed a permanent place to stash the goods.

In 1919 he hired San Francisco architect Julia Morgan to design the ultimate residence, overlooking the Pacific, on a ranch owned by the Hearst family. For the next 28 years, Morgan worked on the project. During construction, workers hauled slabs of stone up the mountain by horse-drawn carts.

The estate grew to include belfries, marble statues, billiard rooms, and even a private zoo, stocked with exotic animals. Hearst crammed as much of his art into the buildings as they would hold, from ancient tapestries to rugs, vases, furniture, and oil paintings. As tourists walk in awe through the rooms of collectibles, guides explain that his tastes ran to European because at the time he was shopping, it was cheap to obtain. Nobody in Europe was interested in centuries-old furniture or art from his own country.

Unlike his 1990s media-mogul counterpart, Bill Gates, Hearst possessed a lust for life, and generously threw parties — some continuing for days — that attracted celebrities and dignitaries from all walks of life. Social events were hosted by Hearst's longtime mistress, Marion Davies, who lived at the castle. People would visit for a weekend, and end up staying for weeks on end. No public drunkenness was tolerated, however. Legendary boozehound Errol Flynn was asked to leave the same day he arrived.

(Another story goes that in the 1980s, when party regular Cary Grant revisited the castle after many years, staff walked him around the grounds. When Grant entered the enclosed swimming pool, gilded in gold, his eyes lit up, as memories of late-night trysts drifted back to him.)

The castle was the vacation destination for Hearst family members, including a pre-kidnap Patty Hearst, as well as housing the old man's business office. In 1947 he moved to Southern California, where he died, fat and sassy, in 1951. His family gave the property to the state to be made into a park. Which means that all of us are free to stumble into the visitor's center for a "Castle Burger" and a delightful pocket comb memento.

**Hearst Castle**
**San Simeon**
**Reservations (800) 444-4445**

# The Grim Reaper Revue

The Bay Area area has an odd perspective on death. Perhaps it's because the town has no cemetery — all the stiffs are hauled off and buried outside city limits. Or maybe because our beautiful Golden Gate Bridge also is the number one suicide location in the world. Kicking the bucket is definitely something different here. As with every other basic ritual of life, death is a deeply moving, personal process, but since we're in Northern California, it gets over-emphasized to the point of obsession. An abnormal love of a common household pet. An elegant Art Deco building in which to stash Grampa's bone dust. A mass suicide, orchestrated by a mad preacher in sunglasses. A taxidermied mouse dressed up like a vampire. If you are considering tagging your own toes, as it were, you could do much worse than dying in San Francisco. Jumping off the bridge offers an incredible view, and the discount caskets are among the cheapest in the nation. As you'll see, whether you're a rock star, the President, or an eccentric homeless weirdo, death isn't merely inevitable — it can also be very entertaining for the rest of us.

# Coffin King

We hear familiar discount slogans such as "Factory direct — no middleman," "Free delivery," or "Savings up to 50% or more," and the usual products come to mind — used cars, stereo equipment, home appliances. Since 1996, San Francisco has also heard these price-busting promises associated with the morbid topic of human coffins. According to Casket Wholesale Centre owner Frank Loui, it's just service to the consumer. Business is so popular he's expanded the enterprise and opened more stores, attracting customers by running ads on local radio stations. As far as he knows, he's the cheapest in the Bay Area.

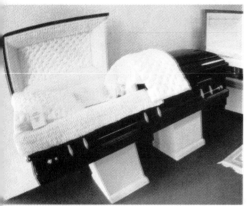

Photos: Sharon Selden

Loui's commercial brainstorm occurred while working as an office manager for law firms. After experiencing five family funerals in six years, he went through the bills and realized casket prices were by far the most expensive cost. And you can't have a funeral without a casket. Convinced this niche needed to be filled, Loui approached casket manufacturers, and struck deals to bring down the prices. He can't mention the names of his suppliers, but the majors won't have a thing to do with him, he says, because they're in bed with the funeral directors, and he's ruining their lucrative arrangement.

Casket Wholesale will also do referrals for discount flowers, headstones, and funeral plots, but it's the coffins that stand out inside the flagship showroom in the Mission District. Usually, Loui stocks around 30 caskets, priced from $595 up to $12,888 for a fancy 96-ounce behemoth (usually bronze jobs run about 48 ounces; he claims his are "the most in the country"). On average, his prices are about half of what a funeral home charges. If the customer wants to cremate, any casket can be used. Poplar is a good wood for burning because it's naturally soft. Most cremation services will rent a casket for the presentation, then return it and torch the corpse. Loui has a no-rent policy. You pay for it, and it's yours to keep.

If you want to take Loui up on his word, and purchase the cheapest casket in the Bay Area, a couple of options present themselves. Lovingly crafted from cloth-covered particle board, the $595 model features an oval-shaped top, and the "Moleskin" model is even cheaper, at $350. The top isn't oval-shaped, however, and Loui admits, "Your face is smashed right up against the top."

**Casket Wholesale Centre**
**301 Valencia Street**
**(415) 552-8766**

# Killed by Cops

**E**ach day, tourists stroll blithely through Fisherman's Wharf, spraying money before them — a mediocre seafood meal, an "Alcatraz Swim Team" T-shirt, a reading light from Barnes & Nobles. For a refreshing dose of reality, all they really need to do is walk up to the entrance of the Longshoremen's Hall. In front of the doors to this building, two body outlines are painted on the sidewalk, the hearts of each marked with fresh blotches of red paint. No, they weren't shot while shoplifting baskets from Cost Plus. Howard Sperry and Nicholas Bordoise were union workers killed by police in the middle of the bloody General Strike of 1934.

In February 1934, the International Longshoremen's Association held their West Coast convention in San Francisco, and produced a list of demands for their shipping boss employers — a pay raise, a 30-hour week, no more corrupt hiring practices, a ban on new technology that reduced jobs, and restructuring of current grievance management. When the shipping companies refused, strikers shut down the port of San Francisco. San Francisco's Industrial Association used police and strike-breakers to move cargo off the port, and things got violent. July

Photo: Sharon Selden

5, 1934, became known as "Bloody Thursday." Hand-to-hand fighting broke out all over the Embarcadero waterfront, and rioters dropped rocks from the Bay Bridge onto police cars. The National Guard charged 2,500 troops into the mob with tanks, firehoses, shotguns, and tear gas. Sperry and Bordoise were killed, and hundreds were injured, but the strike proved effective. The big shippers lost millions. By July 31st the strike had ended, with the unions declaring partial victory on wages and hours, and a joint management agreement for hiring halls.

Constructed in 1959, the current Longshoremen's building has been the site of everything from boxing matches to LSD parties. In January 1966, Ken Kesey and the Merry Pranksters sponsored the Trips Festival, featuring the Grateful Dead and a bunch of hippies with overhead projectors. But 65 years later, Wharf visitors could care less about Howard Sperry or even Ken Kesey, unless they were selling souvenir baby bibs that read, "I got crabs at Fisherman's Wharf."

**Longshoremen's Hall
400 North Point Street**

# Stuffed Mice

You're a lowly mouse, a scurrying little simpleton of no consequence. You have absolutely nothing going for yourself other than the fact you happen to live in the Bay Area. Your brief time here on Earth is dictated from birth. You are bred in captivity and raised in a cage, to eventually wind up a lump of mush inside the belly of a boa constrictor. But if you were to have a brain larger than, say, the size of a pea, you'd realize your life doesn't have to be that boring after all. You could be rescued from your place on the food chain, get stuffed with cotton balls, and be transformed into a beautiful work of art — for instance, a teeny vampire, accompanied by your very own miniature coffin!

An outlet for such mice exists. Those with an appetite for such delightfully sick artifacts can hustle on down to Paxton Gate, one of San Francisco's oddest retail outlets, which specializes in what the store's owners describe as "treasures and oddities inspired by the garden and the natural sciences." In this case, the twin extravagances of petrified animals and high-end gardening tools. Visitors find themselves gawking at the bizarre juxtaposition of jungle beetles and expensive pruning shears, but more often than not, they will stop and marvel at the mice — rodents reincarnated into personae from all walks of life. How about a half-pint doctor, complete with stethoscope? Or a mohawked punk rocker holding a tiny can of Bud? Perhaps even Hamlet, captured in mid-soliloquy, a mouse skull clutched in his paw?

The mastermind behind these mutations is a woman named Jeanie M., a San Francisco multimedia professional by day, who after dark turns into, as far as she knows, the nation's only mouse taxidermist. For the past five years, she has collected mice from snake dealers and resurrected the little tykes into a myriad of cute and creepy gift ideas. She tells me her most popular requests are religious icons.

"Virgins of Guadalupe, lots

of popes, lots of nuns," she says. "Catholics are fucked up."

But even if you aren't a catechism-damaged member of God's Army, you can still appreciate the fine detail inherent in a mouse lovingly dressed as Dracula, Satan, or a dominatrix wielding a cat o'nine tails. As would anyone. Just look at 'em!

Before entering this exciting field, Jeanie M. produced the annual underground sensation known as the Roadkill Calendar, a self-explanatory project that eventually took up too much time. As one can imagine. She says her father steered her toward taxidermy, and after taking a few basic lessons, is now off and running, cranking out mice for five stores across the country. If customers are too sensitive to owning a dead mouse metamorphosed into a winged angel Christmas ornament, she also will do squirrels and other animals that legally can be stuffed. She does draw the line at rats, however, because they're too intelligent, and would rather have them as pets.

For those readers anxious to replicate this at home, stuffing a dead mouse is trickier than it seems. Most taxidermied animals keep looking their best via an armature, a blob of plastic vaguely in the shape of the beast, upon which the skin is then slid onto. Add a couple of glass eyes, and voilá! Your very own bobcat! (Or bighorn sheep, or whatever.) Unfortunately, armatures aren't available for smaller critters like rats and ferrets, and such species are traditionally preserved by freeze-drying. This process may be fine for fat-cat institutions like the Smithsonian, but for the average field mouse, it's a bit pricey. Jeanie M. solves this problem by stuffing her creations with cotton, using string and a wire frame to retain the body's shape. Such cost-saving measures have allowed her to crank out over 1,000 mice (beginning at $38 a pop), and she receives orders from 10 to 50 at a time. Even Henry Ford would be impressed.

Paxton Gate
824 Valencia Street
(415) 824-1872

**THE GRIM 173 REAPER REVUE**

There's a reason you see a lot of flower shop vans and granite monument companies when driving through Colma. Half a million people reside here, but only 1,103 are actually alive. For the past century, ever since San Francisco outlawed burials in 1902, Colma has functioned as the city's primary boneyard. Years ago, diligent workers dug up every cemetery within the city limits — except the Presidio and Mission Dolores — hauled off the moldy corpses, and replanted them under Colma's gentle hills. Tombstones that remained were broken up and used to line the pathways of Buena Vista Park in the Upper Haight. As bodies kept migrating south, Colma got really, really quiet.

Although a long drive from Hollywood, the City of Souls is not without its celebrity highlights. Head south on 280, take the 82 exit at Daly City, and keep an eye peeled for Death Row, aka El Camino Real. Star billing of the Hills of Eternity Memorial Park (1301 El Camino Real; 650-756-3633) is the snazzy tombstone of Wyatt Earp, legendary U.S. Marshall of the O.K. Corral shootout in Tombstone, Arizona. Drive through the middle and around the circle, and look for the C. Meyer mausoleum. Get out of your car, take a right, and walk down the path almost to the end. His marker should be just left of the B.H. Levy tomb, and will be decorated with a toy sheriff star and poker chips, maybe a stale cigarette. Before ending up food for worms in his wife's family plot, Earp made a celebrated stop in San Francisco. On December 3, 1896, he refereed a prizefight at the city's Mechanics Pavilion. Earp was sued for allegedly fixing the fight, then beat the charges, and paid a $50 fine for carrying a pistol without a permit. Directly across the road from Earp is the Home of Peace Cemetery (1299 El Camino Real; 650-755-4700). At the end of the path, one row to the left, lives the domed mausoleum of Levi Strauss, King of the Blue Jeans.

In the left rear of Woodlawn Memorial Park (1000 El Camino Real; 650-755-1727), next to the tall white William Hamilton monument, rests San Francisco's original eccentric nutbag, Emperor Norton. In 1859, a once-successful businessman named Joshua Abraham Norton bottomed out, financially as well as mentally, and wrote to a newspaper, announcing a name change. He would hereafter answer only to Norton I, Emperor of the United States and Protector of Mexico. For over 20 years Norton wandered the streets of the city, wearing a hodgepodge military uniform, often accompanied by a couple of stray dogs. Even in those days, the town humored such loonies. Restaurants gave him free meals. Businesses accepted the currency he had printed up. The city's charter provided an annual stipend to keep him in proper clothing. After Norton collapsed

# Souls

dead of a heart attack one night, on the corner of California and Grant streets, his memorial service was attended by 30,000 people.

Norton is remembered today with two peculiar annual ceremonies. On the 100th anniversary of his death in 1980, the California fraternal order/drinking organization known as E Clampus Vitus got shit-faced and ate crab meat. Every January 9th since then, approximately 400 big fat bearded drunk guys converge on Colma and re-create this magic ritual. The following month, hundreds of drag queens descend upon the same grave to celebrate the crowning of the Emperor and Empress of San Francisco. For over 20 years, octogenarian drag entertainer Jose Sarria, aka Empress I the Widow Norton, has presided over the elaborate, five-hour bejeweled coronation. Just in front of Norton's gravestone, another marker has already been reserved for Sarria, the original Empress Norton.

At the rear of Olivet Memorial Park (1601 Hillside; 650-755-0322), located more or less in the center, a large monument salutes our nation's circus performers, so "that they may rest in peace among their own." The Showfolks of America organization is based in Florida, but for some reason chose Olivet as the site to honor their brethren from the days of the Big Top. Erected in 1945, this colorful memorial is hard to

miss, being decorated with a bright yellow clown.

Colma also boasts its unsubstantiated folklore. When Tina Turner's dog died, the shimmy-queen singer supposedly wrapped the animal in one of her fur coats and planted it in an unmarked grave at Pet's Rest (see following entry). And a member of the Hell's Angels was reportedly buried alongside his beloved Harley, in a location that has never been disclosed because enterprising thieves might dig up the bike.

A lone outpost of alcohol on the Colma landscape, the Old Molloy's tavern (1655 Mission; 650-755-1580) has kept gravediggers well lubricated since opening as a hotel in 1883. The Molloy family has managed the business for over 60 years, and decorates the walls with priceless historical memorabilia, including the original bell phone from the speakeasy/brothel days. Visitors should watch for the traditional Irish wakes, pie-eyed gravediggers headed back to work, and one night a month, the viciously competitive trivia contest.

# Bedtime for

**A** peculiar offshoot in the culture of death, pet cemeteries invite a variety of emotions and opinions, from grief and compassion to scorn, hilarity, and in the end, solace. Like it or not, many people are extremely attached to their pets, and when those eyes of unconditional love close shut for the final sleep, the only honorable course of action left is to provide the animal a proper burial. Fortunately, three of the finest critter cemeteries in the nation are located within the Bay Area.

Pet's Rest Cemetery and Crematory (1905 Hillside; 650-755-2201) carries the distinction

of being Colma's most visited cemetery, and began back in 1946. A Cypress Lawn Cemetery employee named Earl Taylor kept hearing requests from people who wanted their pets included in the family lots. Earl got together his wife, Julia, and a few other folks, converted a bee house into a small chapel, and opened Pet's Rest. Since 1972 it's been owned and operated by the Taylors' daughter and her husband. Sitting on two acres, Pet's Rest provides eternal sanctuary for over 13,000 pets pushing up daisies, from dogs and cats to monkeys, cheetahs, and goldfish. According to staff, it's also a singles scene. Grieving pet owners develop friendships while visiting the cemetery, and a few have even gotten married.

Pet's Rest offers complete service, from picking up your dead pet, to building or ordering the casket, inscribing a small granite marker, and digging the grave. Blankets, toys, or other personal items are allowed to be buried with the animal, and lawn burials can be arranged in single lots, double lots, or group lots for families with several pets. But prepare to flash some cash. One small pet, i.e., a canary, can cost $400 for the lot and $75 for a pine box. A lot and custom casket for an extra-large pet can run over $1,000. Whichever plan you choose for Brandy or Muffin, keep in mind that Pet's Rest charges a nominal annual fee of 30 bucks for each grave.

The most unusual pet cemetery would have to be in the former Presidio military base (Crissy Field Avenue, underneath the Golden Gate Bridge on-ramp). Opened originally by the base veterinary clinic, this final bivouac for doggies, kitties, and birds dates back to World War II, and for years was maintained by the Boy Scouts. Most markers are poignantly homemade and crudely inscripted, but the grounds' condition says somebody is obviously still maintaining the place. Few animals are interred here since the base closed a few years ago, making the cemetery a pet lovers' time capsule.

# Poochie

The pet cemetery milieu is not without tragedy. Errol Morris' brilliant 1978 documentary film *Gates of Heaven* tells a heart-wrenching story of paraplegic Floyd McClure, who fulfills his lifelong dream to open a pet cemetery in Los Altos, just south of San Francisco, and then loses ownership of the property. Morris had never directed a film before, but after reading news articles about 300 dead animals being dug up from Foothill Pet Cemetery and relocated north to Bubbling Well Pet Memorial Park (2462 Atlas Peak Road, Napa; 707-255-3456), the fledgling filmmaker was touched enough to record the emotional aftermath.

Opened in 1971 by Calvin Harberts, Bubbling Well employed various members of the Harberts family, including the long-haired son Danny, who jammed on electric guitar in between digging pet graves. He described the nuance of his profession for Morris' camera:

"You don't want to make it too large because you don't want to waste space, and you don't want to make it too small because you can't get the thing in there."

Today, Bubbling Well boasts over 10,000 little buddies "at rest" in acreage overlooking the Napa Valley vineyards. A variety of burial areas beckon the remnants of your pet. The Garden of Companionship offers a Gentle Giant section for large

breeds, a Kitty Curve for the felines, and separate regions for Champions and Mighty Midgets. The Foothill Garden, for pets weighing less than 30 pounds, includes all the animals relocated from the ill-fated Foothill cemetery. Bubbling Well will post a tribute on the Internet, so that the vast cyber-space audience may share in the grief of your dead animal. The cemetery web site contains no mention, however, of either the Harberts family or the film by Errol Morris.

# City Hall Carnage

**D**esigned in 1915, San Francisco's fancy-schmancy City Hall building features a gold-leaf dome modeled after St. Peter's in Rome, Baroque staircases, and marble corridors. And in 1978 it was also, apparently, a good place to kill the mayor and a city supervisor.

A one-time successful Wall Street investment analyst and theater nerd, the charming and witty Harvey Milk moved to San Francisco, opened a camera store on Castro Street, and used the storefront as his political headquarters. In 1977, he won a seat on the Board of Supervisors, and a liberal gay political power structure gained national attention.

A former state senator, George Moscone was elected mayor by a thin margin. He was not only liberal, he was outwardly pro-gay, and even signed a gay-rights bill into law with a lavender pen given him by Milk.

The pro-gay political agendas of Milk and Moscone did not sit well with homophobic Dan White, the 32-year-old son of a working-class Irish family. A former Golden Gloves boxing champ, White had already served his city as a police officer, firefighter, and city supervisor. He was frustrated and depressed.

Nine days after the Jonestown mass suicide, White crawled into City Hall through a basement window on the McAllister Street side, to avoid the metal detector. Armed with his police special .38 and extra hollow-point bullets, he paid a visit to Mayor Moscone, to ask if he could be reappointed as a city supervisor. The mayor mixed them two drinks, and told him no. White shot him in the chest and the arm, then finished him off with two rounds to the side of the head. Leaving the drinks untouched, White then walked into Milk's office, and immediately shot him three times in the chest, stomach, and back. As with Moscone, White ended the visit with two execution-style shots into the back of Milk's head. White left City Hall, met with his wife, and then surrendered to his friends at the Northern Station of the San Francisco Police Department. As he was booked, reporters discovered later, some of the officers were smirking and making jokes.

News spread quickly of the shootings. Many offices and businesses closed. By evening 50,000 people had walked down Market Street to City Hall in a silent, candle-light march. A lone trumpeter played "Blowing in the Wind." Joan Baez stood on the steps and led the crowd in a singalong. For days following the murders, San Francisco police were seen wearing "Free Dan White" T-shirts, and heard singing "Danny Boy" over the police radio frequency. According to a county jail employee, while awaiting trial, White threw all of his prison dinners in his toilet. Instead, he was brought roast beef sandwiches, ice cream, and chocolate. He demanded linens on his bed, and was the only prisoner with a private shower. He never showed any remorse, but did confide to a nurse, "I guess they were nice guys. Too bad it happened."

Six months later, on May 21, 1979, White's verdict was returned by a jury — voluntary manslaughter, with special circumstances. White's attorneys successfully argued diminished capacity, in what would become known as the infamous "Twinkie defense": Because White had consumed so many Twinkies, the spongy snack cake had altered his blood sugar level to the point that he was not in control of his actions. White looked at a maximum of seven years behind bars.

That night another crowd gathered at City Hall, which erupted into the "White

# The Art of Death

Ghia Enterprises runs several sideline businesses, but it's the Third Street gallery that death fans know and love — the city's only combination casket/urn store and fine art gallery. In addition to hosting regular touring art shows, owner Alex Ghia also sells caskets and urns. But there's a twist. He hires artists to customize them, and give a funeral an extra, personalized touch. An entire room in the gallery is reserved for one-of-a-kind items, from caskets covered in graffiti and psychedelic art, to urns decorated like King Tut or the Virgin Mary. One urn has been incorporated into a free-standing music box that when its door is opened, starts playing "How Dry I Am."

The gallery keeps odd hours, but if you can get ahold of Ghia, the man is full of interesting information about the funeral industry. He says that the 1965 satirical film *The Loved One* (based on the novel by Evelyn Waugh) portrayed the industry as being so heartless and greedy, that enraged funeral directors attempted to destroy every print in the country.

Another conscientious member of the death business, Ghia scoffs at the insane prices most funeral homes charge, and gladly directs people to low-cost alternatives. And if you feel like throwing a soiree in a strange surrounding, the gallery has been known to host private parties, serving beer from a keg displayed inside a coffin.

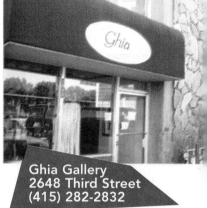

**Ghia Gallery**
**2648 Third Street**
**(415) 282-2832**

• • • • • • • • • • • • • • • • • • • • • • • • • • • • •

Night" riot. The angry mob trashed the building, and set police cars on fire. Cops retaliated by charging into Castro District bars and beating gays with clubs. Despite the protesting, White walked out of prison after five months, a free man and due to conjugal visits with his wife, a new father.

The convention center South of Market was later christened Moscone Center in honor of the slain mayor. Harvey Milk's memory is kept alive by several books, films, an opera, a band, a civil rights academy, and a bar/restaurant, located on the same spot as his camera shop (see museum chapter).

But people still debate why Dan White committed the murders. A campaign brochure from his run for supervisor holds a clue: "I'm not going to be scared out of San Francisco by splinter groups of radicals, social deviates, and incorrigibles...There are thousands upon thousands of frustrated, angry people such as yourselves, waiting to unleash a fury that can and will eradicate the malignancies which blight our city."

Photo: Sharon Selden

In 1985 White committed suicide, gassing himself in the garage of his home.

**San Francisco City Hall**
**1 Dr. Carlton B. Goodlett Place**
**(415) 554-4000**

# Sympathy for Altamont

They may have boasted of being the greatest rock and roll band in the world, but the Rolling Stones have had problems with their concert documentaries. Renowned photographer Robert Frank filmed their 1972 American tour, but the resulting *Cocksucker Blues* was so full of overt sex and drug use it was never released. Three years earlier, the Maysles brothers filmed a Stones concert at Altamont, east of San Francisco. Instead of the ultimate hippie groovie-movie, *Gimme Shelter* essentially exposed the ugliness underneath the peace and love, culminating in a dramatic on-camera murder.

The Stones were scheduled to play December 6, 1969, at Sears Point Raceway, just north of San Francisco. Also on the bill were the Grateful Dead, Crosby, Stills, Nash and Young, Santana, the Flying Burrito Brothers, and Jefferson Airplane. But Filmways Corporation suddenly demanded the film rights to the documentary, so with only 24 hours time, San Francisco attorney Melvin Belli engineered the move of the entire concert to Altamont, an old oval racetrack out near Livermore, in the East Bay. Altamont appeared ideal: It didn't have a film company contract, and could use the publicity.

The concert went off, a giant petri dish of 400,000 kids, all high out of their minds. So many people were freaking out on acid that paramedics and doctors from the local free clinics ran out of Thorazine in half an hour. Hell's Angels provided security, and were suggested to the Stones by members of the Dead, who assured everyone the bikers would work free in exchange for beer. The atmosphere grew weirder. Scuffles broke out in the crowd and onstage. The Jefferson Airplane's Marty Balin was knocked unconscious.

Vintage Altamont flyer; courtesy San Francisco Rock Posters & Collectables

In the middle of this monstrous hippie freak-out, the Stones took the stage, and as they played "Sympathy for the Devil," a young black man named Meredith Hunter approached the stage with a pistol. A Hell's Angel pounced on him, pulled a knife and stabbed him to death. The song chugged to a halt. Mick Jagger yelled at Keith Richards to stop playing, and pleaded with the mob, "People, why are we fighting?" The Grateful Dead landed in helicopters, saw what was going on, and left immediately. To round out the tragedy, one person drowned in an irrigation ditch, and two more were struck and killed by vehicles.

The Altamont Raceway is still in use, and the Stones are still touring, but these days, if someone dies at one of the band's concerts, it's most likely from forgetting to take his heart medication.

Altamont Raceway
17001 Midway Road, Livermore
(925) 373-7223

# Zodiac Killer

On the evening of October 11, 1969, San Francisco police let the most infamous serial killer in Bay Area history slip through their hands. Taxi driver Paul Stine picked up a fare on Geary in front of the theaters, and drove to an address in Presidio Heights. Teenagers at a party looked out the window and saw a cab parked across the street. The driver and passenger seemed to be struggling in the front seat. The passenger then got out of the cab and left. Somebody called the cops. Within two minutes a patrol car arrived, and stopped a stocky guy walking down the street. The man told officers he'd seen someone waving a gun, running in the opposite direction. The cops drove off, completely unaware their friend was actually the Zodiac killer. Authorities later returned to the blood-smeared cab. The meter was still running. So is the legacy of the Zodiac.

Beginning in 1966, a man calling himself the Zodiac terrorized the Bay Area in a bloody, bizarre killing spree. Authorities confirmed eight attacks with two survivors; he claimed at least 37. The murder victims were usually young people, often killed near a body of water, usually on Friday or Saturday night, during a new or full moon. The Zodiac used both knives and guns, and occasionally wore a bizarre-looking hood and tunic he had fashioned himself. Many others reported escaping from him, or experiencing strange interactions with a heavy-set man in a white car.

In the great pantheon of American serial killers, the Zodiac was perhaps the first to recognize and become obsessed with his own media attention. He wrote many letters to the *San Francisco Chronicle*, some of which included snips of Stine's shirt. His mail continued through 1978, always with his trademark double postage, upside-down stamps, and the introduction, "This is the Zodiac speaking." Some of his correspondence was printed in an obscure combination of astrological symbols. He quoted lyrics from *The Mikado* by Gilbert and Sullivan, and wrote letters on the anniversaries of his attacks. One note included a critique of the film *The Exorcist*, which he called "a satirical comedy," and ended with a scorecard: "Me-37 SFPD-0."

For several years, police ran around the Bay Area trying to find the Zodiac. At one point, 50 cops and a number of detectives were working on the case.

Hollywood recognized the potential for a great story. Clint Eastwood's *Dirty Harry* used Zodiac facts faithfully in the script, even down to the style of handwriting in the letters. Steve McQueen patterned his character in *Bullitt* after the main Zodiac investigator, SFPD Detective Dave Toschi. In *Legion*, his sequel to *The Exorcist*, William Peter Blatty based his "Gemini Killer" character on the Zodiac, as did Armistead Maupin with his "Tinkerbell" killer in *Tales of the City*.

Despite all the media attention, the manpower involved, and the efforts of many investigative reporters — including *Chronicle* editorial cartoonist Robert Graysmith, who authored the definitive Zodiac book — no arrests were ever made in the case. An astrological expert did determine that the Zodiac was probably a Taurus.

Zodiac Killer Location
3898 Washington Street
at Cherry

# People's Temple

**E**verybody asks the same question. What would compel 1,000 people to leave San Francisco, move to a jungle in Brazil, and kill themselves on orders from a sweaty man who looked like Elvis Presley? The Jonestown deaths of 914 people have permanently scarred the Bay Area, driven the finest conspiracy theorists completely crazy, and prompted 20 years of jokes about Kool-Aid parties. This largest mass suicide in history started with a monkey salesman in Indiana.

Born to a Ku Klux Klansman, young Jim Jones showed his religious leanings early. By age eight, he could quote long passages from the Bible, and at 12 was preaching to other children, and practicing faith healings on stray animals. He became a Methodist

minister, but was defrocked for his interracial appeal, so he made money on the side by selling imported monkeys for $29 apiece. He founded The People's Temple Full Gospel Church in 1956 in Indianapolis, offering a church for every color of the rainbow. Parishioners were convinced to believe in themselves, and feel good about belonging to something, even if it was a church run by a monkey salesman. But by 1965, the state was onto Jones' phony faith healings.

His black Caddy led a caravan out to California, stopping first in Ukiah and then arriving in San Francisco, where Jones settled in the black Fillmore ghetto. The city's political structure courted his fundraising efforts, and especially his buses of voters who drove around the city, casting ballots as many times as necessary. Mayor George Moscone appointed him to a position on the housing board. He met for dinner with Rosalyn Carter, and was photographed with then-Governor Jerry Brown and future Mayor Willie Brown. He claimed 20,000 followers, but actual figures were closer to 3,000.

Jones' behavior grew more fraudulent and increasingly weird. He would shake a Bible above his head, then throw it to the floor and holler to his congregation: "Too many people are looking at *this*, and not at me." After Martin Luther King was assassinated, Jones smeared chicken blood on his face and clothes, and appeared before his flock, claiming he was shot. He was arrested in a porno theater. He started in with the cocaine and the young chicks, and hired a cosmetician to make himself look more like Elvis Presley.

But things were deteriorating. A paternity suit was filed against him. A magazine exposé appeared in 1977. Jones convinced everyone to move to Guyana, where the People's Temple had previously leased 27,000 acres in the jungle. One thousand people lived at Jonestown (or as the media began to call it, a "jungle outpost"), worked in the fields, and ate a diet of rice and beans. Rumors spread of public beatings. Jones spoke on a PA system for hours at a time, and conducted "White Night" drills with phony poison, in preparation for a possible raid by CIA mercenaries.

In November 1978, Congressman Leo Ryan flew to Guyana on a fact-finding mission, to investigate allegations of human rights abuses. During his visit, people slipped Ryan notes, and somebody put a knife to his throat. To the reporters, Jones appeared disturbed and agitated. As Ryan's group prepared to depart the Port Kaituma airfield, gunmen opened fire. Ryan, three news guys, and a potential defector were killed, and 11 others were wounded. Later that day, Jones ordered the final White Night drill, and the grape Flavor-Aid was passed around, with screaming babies receiving mouthfuls via syringes. He rambled on into the PA system, and people died, hearing their leader's final words:

"Take the potion like they used to take in ancient Greece, and step over quietly...Let's be done with it. Let's be done with the agony of it."

Anyone who tried to escape was shot. The final tally: 914 corpses, including 276 children. Jones was discovered shot in the head, with amphetamines, Percodan, and a personal refrigerator full of food among his possessions.

Now it was conspiracy theory time. A few insisted it was the work of the Soviets, because shortly before the massacre two People's Temple members supposedly moved $500,000 from Jonestown to the Soviet embassy!

Or, it was the CIA, because they were first to report news of the mass suicide, and among the wounded was U.S. embassy official Richard Dwyer, who was identified in the 1968 edition of *Who's Who in the CIA*, and during Jones' final sermon, the recording supposedly captures Jones' voice saying, "Get Dwyer out of here!" and Jones lieutenant Larry Layton survived the suicide, and Layton's father was a U.S. Army biochemist in charge of chemical warfare, and his brother-in-law was reportedly a CIA mercenary in Angola!

Or, it was a mind-control experiment, because large amounts of psychoactive, i.e., mind-control, drugs were found after the suicides, and Leo Ryan's office later received a paper from a UC Berkeley professor, detailing how the CIA's MK-ULTRA mind-control program did not end in 1973, as the CIA had told Congress, but had been transferred from hospitals and prisons to the less obtrusive arena of religious cults!

Or, it was a mass murder, because the Guyanese coroner testified that as many as 700 of the victims were not suicides, and appeared to have been killed!

In 1980 the House Permanent Select Committee on Intelligence announced they found "no evidence" of CIA involvement at Jonestown. Yeah, right.

Twenty years after the suicide, a television crew flew back to Jonestown with Jim Jones' two sons, who had missed the White Night because they were out of town playing basketball. The only evidence of the town still standing, out of all the buildings and farms, was a single palm tree, which had stood next to the main pavilion building. Everything else was gone. Jones' sons hacked through the tall jungle grass, searching for memories, evidence that anything had even existed. And then they abruptly discovered — coincidentally, at the exact moment a camera was filming — the vat that held the cyanide-laced potion.

Over 400 Jonestown victims are buried in Oakland's Evergreen Cemetery, and a memorial service is held for them every November. The Temple site is now a post office.

**People's Temple site
1859 Geary Boulevard**

# Good Night, Garcia

Serenity Knolls Treatment Center, a few minutes north of San Francisco, August 9, 1995, 4:23 a.m. A night nurse checked on patient Jerome John Garcia, and discovered he had stopped breathing. Two days earlier, the Grateful Dead guitarist had driven himself to Serenity Knolls, after ducking out of the Betty Ford Center a few weeks before. Death was by heart attack, due to a recurring weight problem, junk food, diabetes, and of course, years and years of acid, cocaine, booze, and heroin. Nevertheless, a preliminary coroner's report listed "natural causes." He was only 53.

Health problems were nothing new to Garcia. He collapsed in 1986 and was rushed to a hospital in a diabetic coma. Upon recovering, he proudly switched from Camel cigarettes to a filtered brand. In 1991 he again checked into a hospital, suffering from exhaustion. Police once discovered his BMW parked in Golden Gate Park; inside he was shooting up heroin, and supposedly had a half-eaten cake sitting on the seat next to him. And in January 1995, seven months before his death, he smashed his brand-new BMW 525i into a retaining wall on Highway 101 outside Mill Valley.

But even though Garcia's life spiraled down in later years, the Bay Area treated his death as the passing of an international hero, which in a sense, he was. The mayor wore a Garcia necktie, and ordered all flags in the city lowered to half mast. Computer users couldn't log onto Internet accounts because of so much traffic. Newspapers and magazines published special Garcia and Deadhead tribute issues, spinning the story of the musical prodigy from Palo Alto who became Captain Trips, the invincible party-animal king of the extended noodling guitar solo.

On the night after his death, the Haight-Ashbury immediately became the focal point for the world's media, as it had 30 years earlier. Garcia had once again contributed to the neighborhood's reputation, except instead of the birth of hippies, it was the death of an era. Hundreds of Deadheads descended upon Haight Street, blocking traffic so that buses couldn't even make it through. Television vans squeezed into the mob, jettisoning reporters into the pot smoke to do their stand-up reports. Drum circles materialized on streetcorners, and those who didn't have drums kept time on beer bottles with their car keys. As people came onto their acid, they drifted towards Golden Gate Park.

Fans had constructed a shrine at the intersection of Haight and Ashbury, with fresh roses and scraps of paper. During the rush-hour chaos, two kids in flannel shirts stared at the Grateful Dead lyrics that had been scrawled on the sidewalk.

"It's about love, man," one murmured.

"It's about weed," corrected his friend. "Weed and LSD."

# Old Bones

The oldest building in the city, and founded by Spanish settlers, Mission Dolores was built in 1791, and not much has changed. The original redwood logs still hold up the roof. The structure has withstood four major earthquakes. Mission Dolores Basílica, the larger church next door, still marries and buries people. And speaking of death, just around the corner sits the town's first graveyard.

Tombstones date back to 1785, many of them historical figures who loaned their names to city streets — the first governor (Arguello), the first mayor (de Haro), the leader of the first settlers in the area (Moraga).

But none of this really matters, unless you're an Arguello fetishist — usually distinguishable by their clipboard and worried expression. What's important in visiting the cemetery is to soak up the calming yet sinister ambiance. The place looks like something straight from voodoo New Orleans — incredibly creepy even in the sunlight, with overgrown trees, little iron fences, and chipped grave markers weathered by centuries of storms. You can imagine the yarking hounds from hell coming over the wall, fangs flashing white with froth, looking for Gregory Peck from the '70s film *The Omen*. And that's worth a couple bucks' donation.

**Mission Dolores Cemetery
Dolores Street at 16th Street
(415) 621-8203**

# Killer

Built in 1937, San Francisco's landmark Golden Gate Bridge rises majestically 40 stories into the sky, its International orange color and Moderne design attracting tourist cameras from all parts of the globe. At mid-span, the roadway hangs 260 feet above the water, a height requested by the Navy to allow its battleships sufficient room to pass. A round-trip stroll across the 1.2-mile structure takes about an hour, and presents an amazing view of the entire bay. Closed-circuit cameras and emergency phones are positioned along the walkway, but it doesn't matter. They're going to jump anyway.

If California is the end of the migration west, the Golden Gate Bridge signifies the end of the trail of broken dreams, when a move, a career change, a complete personal reinvention just doesn't help you turn the corner. Not only can San Francisco boast consistently high statistics for alcoholism, heroin addiction, and AIDS, we claim the highest suicide rate of any American city, and the most popular suicide spot in the world.

Before the bridge was even completed, it was killing people. By the time the city proclaimed Opening Day on May 27, 1937, 10 men had already died in a scaffold collapse. Not three months later, war veteran Harold B. Wobber walked away from his job on a barge, strolled onto the bridge, chatted with a tourist, then launched over the side. He would be the first of over 1,000 who have chosen to end life with a final flair.

From the railing it's a quick four-second ride, approaching 80 mph at impact, with the force of hitting concrete. Most are killed instantly. The body count eclipsed 1,000 in 1995, when newspapers stopped listing the number after each jump, hoping to thwart thrillseekers. No such luck.

Some plan ahead, buying a

Photo: Sharon Selden

one-way ticket to San Francisco, with the bridge specifically in mind, because to them it's the most glamorous way to go. Others leave this world quietly, slipping over in the night. Those in a hurry simply park their car in the middle of the bridge and let somebody else deal with it.

One couple took turns posing for pictures along the walkway, then the man handed the camera to his girlfriend, crawled onto the railing, and leaped to his death. A 72-year-old man scribbled a final message to the world: "Survival of the fittest. Adios — Unfit." A young father from Fremont threw his 3-year-old daughter over the bridge, and then followed

her. In the early 1990s, after a dog jumped off the bridge, the *San Francisco Chronicle* screamed "Dog Suicide," and traced the animal's final route through the city with a dotted line. Roy Larson Raymond, entrepreneur and founder of the Victoria's Secret lingerie empire, kissed the world goodbye in 1993, 11 years after selling the company.

Occasionally someone weathers the leap, usually with broken bones and internal injuries. The first survivor was #35, 22-year-old Cornelia Van Ireland, who took the plunge in 1941 and spent the next two months in a hospital.

Jumping off the bridge has prompted its share of folklore. Jumpers are said to sit or

stand on the walkway way too long, and frequently look straight up in the air before they leap. More people supposedly dive from the city side because the view is better. One ridiculous rumor circulated that a majority of the survivors were wearing Levi's jeans, which cushioned their impact. During the 1970s, a group of sick-humored artists named themselves The Suicide Club, and threw a party every time a person hopped the rail.

Periodically there is talk of installing an anti-suicide barrier, but it's usually shouted down by opponents who claim it will ruin the beauty of the bridge. So for now, the Golden Gate retains its original grandeur, unencumbered by an ugly barricade, and littered with the souls of those who left life with an exclamation point.

So why? Psychologists have pondered this for years. First of all, it's accessible. Anybody can walk onto a bridge. And you can't beat the cost. You don't need a prescription, or have to spend several days waiting for a gun permit. It's over rather quickly, and it's almost guaranteed that you'll die. And there's the element of the mystique. Whatever attracts humans to take pictures of the bridge, or stroll across its span, also beckons others to cash in the chips. We may never understand or explain why so many jump from the Golden Gate, but you have to admit, it's a nice-looking bridge. And according to one local psychiatrist, San Franciscans' most common fear is Gephydrophobia, a fear of crossing bridges.

**Golden Gate Bridge
Highway 101**

# Heartstop Hotel

**B**uilt in 1904 by millionaire Charles T. Crocker and his friends to provide adequate accommodations for their pals, the original St. Francis Hotel featured electric grills that cooked a steak in five minutes, and pipes that dumped ocean water into the Turkish baths. Official hotel history boasts of President Nixon's midnight Oreo cookie craving, Ethel Barrymore's pet chimpanzee, and the lobby's grandfather clock that dates back to 1907. But it doesn't mention that the hotel appears to be completely cursed to a lifetime of death and mayhem.

On September 5, 1921, tubby silent film comedian Roscoe "Fatty" Arbuckle threw a Labor Day weekend gin party in suites 1219, 1220, and 1221 that resulted in the death of actress Virginia Rappe. The rumor circulated that he raped her with a Coke bottle, and nasty headlines in the *Chronicle* and *Examiner* attacked and convicted him immediately. Three trials later, Arbuckle was absolved of guilt in her death, but it was too late. He changed his name to Will B. Good, his career tanked, and he died penniless in 1933. (Rappe's ghost is said to haunt the Moss Beach Distillery south of Pacifica on Highway 1.)

In another gin-related death, on October 23, 1950, Al Jolson arrived in San Francisco from entertaining the troops in Korea. While waiting to tape a radio program with Bing Crosby, he ate a seafood dinner at Fisherman's Wharf, then returned to his St. Francis suite for some hands of gin rummy with friends. At 10:30 p.m., he called a break, complaining of chest pains, and The Jazz Singer cashed in from a coronary occlusion.

On September 23, 1975, President Gerald Ford exited the hotel, no doubt still jumpy from an attempted assassination three weeks earlier in Sacramento by Manson Family member Lynette "Squeaky" Fromme. A nursing school dropout named Sara Jane Moore squeezed into the crowd, pointed a .38 pistol at Ford, and fired twice. An alert ex-Marine named Billy Sipple grabbed her arm and deflected the bullet's path. As his reward for saving the president's life, Sipple was later revealed in the press to be a homosexual.

For a final thrill, the high-rise elevator #4 is the best moving view in the city.

Westin St. Francis Hotel
335 Powell Street at Union Square
(415) 397-7000

# Check-out Time

Originally built in 1875, the Palace Hotel advertised itself as the largest and most luxurious hotel in the city, and began attracting famous guests from all over the world, from Oscar Wilde to Rudyard Kipling, Bing Crosby, Will Rogers, and Prince Philip. Some had better luck than others. After a lifetime of alcohol and women, Hawai'ian party-boy King David Kalakaua died in his suite of kidney disease in 1891. Opera star Enrico Caruso survived the 1906 earthquake by running out of the building clad only in a towel, and vowed never to set foot in the city again. But for our purposes, the Palace marks the deathbed of President Warren Harding.

Elected to the White House in 1920, people knew the former newspaper publisher as friendly and handsome. And in Washington, that often leads to fooling around on your wife. This particular strumpet lived in Chicago, her name was Nan Britton, and she bore him a child. But Harding also had other worries. News leaked to the press about a possible Teapot Dome Scandal, involving an oil field in Wyoming. In 1921, Harding's secretary of the Interior secretly leased the field to an oilman, got caught, and was convicted for taking bribes and sent to prison for a year.

Throughout this ignominy, Harding prepared to win a second term. Britton moved to Washington to be closer to him, and they began seeing each other both at the White House and at homes of friends. Mrs. Harding discovered the rekindled affair, and approached a government agent named Gaston Means, asking about a lethal "little white powder" that could be slipped into a person's food or drink.

The Hardings returned from a vacation to Alaska, stopped in Vancouver, and the president became ill with what was thought to be food poisoning. Although everyone in their entourage ate the same food, nobody else felt sick. The Hardings continued to San Francisco by train, and on July 29, 1923, checked into the Presidential Suite of the Palace Hotel. Despite the ministrations of his personal physician, on August 2, the president suddenly died in his room.

Did his wife poison him, or did he simply die of a heart attack following years of high blood pressure? Unfortunately, the Sheraton Palace downplays the entire business — no special suite, no cleverly-named dishes on the menu. Nothing.

# Ice Ice

**W**e've always been fascinated by the idea of life after death. As science progressed through the 20th century, the ultimate science-fiction plot emerged. Freezing a human being would be a nifty way to preserve a body for later revival — if not the entire person, at least a person's physical consciousness, their "self," their memory and personality. The revolutionary field of cryonics hopes to make this fantasy a reality.

Only a handful of legitimate cryonics organizations exist in the world, and three just happen to be located in the Bay Area. The largest and most elaborate of the three, San Leandro-based Trans Time provides complete suspensions and caretaking for its cryonics patients, as well as those from the International Cryonics Foundation in Stockton, which has no such capabilities. (The third organization, Cupertino's American Cryonics Society is membership only and doesn't get along with Trans Time, so it contracts out its suspensions and caretaking to an organization in the Midwest.)

Scientists have been freezing bull sperm since 1949, but it took until 1964 and the publication of the book, "The Prospect of Immortality," for people to seriously ponder freezing *homo sapien*. Michigan physics teacher Robert Ettinger suggested in his book that if human beings were to be frozen after death, then someday in the future, technology would be able to repair, revive, and rejuvenate them.

Courtesy: Alcor

The book generated great excitement, and in early 1967 someone decided to give it a go. A California psychology professor named James H. Bedford died of cancer, and according to his dying wish, his body was frozen in liquid nitrogen at 321 degrees below zero Fahrenheit. But most people never saw or heard of Bedford. The biggest publicity for cryonics came from the persistent rumor that Walt Disney was secretly frozen after his death in 1966.

Within a few years after Bedford's big freeze, the industry saw major setbacks. The Cryonics Society of California, started in the mid-1960s, began offering "cryonic interments," freezing several dozen people and stashing the bodies in a cemetery crypt in Chatsworth, California. Constant infusions of liquid nitrogen grew so expensive that the "clients" were secretly allowed to thaw out, and their discovery prompted great outrage in the community. Some even compare the Chatsworth disaster to the cryonic equivalent of the Challenger space shuttle explosion.

Some years later, in 1987, an Arizona cryonics firm called Alcor suspended a woman named Dora Kent (head only). After a coroner retracted his initial conclusion of death from pneumonia, suspicious deputies confiscated patient records and attempted to take Kent's head for autopsy. Alcor refused to reveal the head's location. The following week,

# Baby

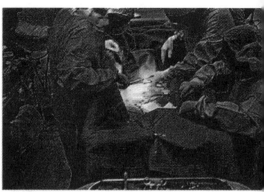

coroner's deputies, police, and a SWAT team again entered Alcor's offices and removed computers, records, and other items. The case spent years in the legal system, before all charges against Alcor were dropped. The company steadfastly insisted that none of its patients were thawed during the commotion.

With such controversies, it's not surprising there were only three intact bodies frozen at liquid nitrogen temperatures in the United States, including Bedford, still slumbering in a vacuum-insulated bottle. It was time to start experimenting with lower species.

Alcor performed America's first successful dog freeze, a German Shepherd named Dixie who "experienced the privilege (and the peril) of having all her blood washed out and replaced with a synthetic solution and then being cooled to 4° C. For four hours she was held at this temperature: stiff, cold, with eyes flattened out, brain waves stopped, and heart stilled. Then, she was reperfused with blood, warmed up and restored to life and health." Dixie made a total recovery.

More animal experiments also proved successful. In 1987 ACS and Trans Time revived a beagle after "total body washout and cool-down." They named him Miles, after the character in the Woody Allen movie *Sleeper*, and one of the doctors adopted him as a pet. In 1992 another company, BioTime, froze and revived a baboon in Berkeley, with no signs of brain damage.

A handful of humans are already frozen whole, and others with more limited means have opted for the head only. Some people started out as whole bodies, but when finances ran out, were decapitated and only their heads were saved. Several hundred people are now legally signed up to get frozen upon their death.

So what happens? Moments after cardiac arrest and pronouncement of legal death, technicians begin cooling the body. It is whisked to a special lab and hooked up to a heart-lung machine, which pumps oxygen to living tissues while the blood is drained and replaced with chemicals. The body is transferred to a liquid-nitrogen-filled upright vacuum-insulated flask. Bodies are placed in the flask head-downward, so that in the event of a problem, the feet will thaw first. A special fund, hopefully set up with life insurance money, is then activated to pay for "perpetual care."

Interested parties who live in the Bay Area can make reservations through Trans Time. Incorporated in 1972, they operate a full-service cryonics laboratory and storage facility. Like other cryogenics firms, Trans Times encourages potential customers to plan ahead, and get the paperwork out of the way. A $150,000 minimum donation for whole-body suspension should cover costs of maintaining your body after death. You can also sign on as a Trans Time Emergency Responsibility Donor, which means the company's 24-hour team will be "on call" to freeze you as soon as you drop dead.

No human being has yet been successfully revived, but don't let this get you discouraged. Keep your sense of humor. One joke circulating among the cryogenic community goes something like this:

Q: How many cryonicists does it take to change a light bulb?

A: Four. One to ensure that the light bulb is certifiably dead, one to perfuse it with cryoprotectants, one to slowly cool it to liquid nitrogen temperature, and one to wait two hundred years for technology to advance sufficiently to revive it.

# Tree-Stump Urns

**A**nother example of Bay Area overachievers: California may lead the nation in number of cremations every year, but San Francisco claims the largest facility for cremated ashes on the West Coast. The century-old Neptune Society Columbarium not only contains the cremains of 10,000 people, it probably also houses this coast's largest collection of urns shaped like tree stumps.

Commissioned by the Oddfellows Cemetery, the 1898 circular domed mausoleum was designed by British architect B.J.S. Cahill with a combination of Greek and Roman influence, and incorporating a 75-foot-high rotunda. Protected from real estate development by the Homestead Act, the building passed from one organization to another, and eventually fell into disrepair. The Neptune Society purchased the structure in 1980, moved their offices next door, and began restoring the artwork and beautiful stained glass windows.

Three floors display a cornucopia of urns, from silver and gold soup tureens to championship cups and simple metal cubes. Fraternal orders are strongly represented by the Freemasons and the Omaha-based Woodmen of the World, an organization of life insurance salesmen, whose urns are shaped like greyish-green tree stumps, spiffed up with a logging symbol. Relatives often accent urns with personal items of the deceased, such as teddy bears wearing reggae hats, a bust of W.C. Fields, or a sculpture of a hippo. Urn space is currently available.

Wills and last dying wishes often dictate the deceased's cremains to be strewn outdoors, but loved ones should think this one through carefully. The past two decades have not provided the best publicity for the cremation distribution biz. In 1984, rather than scatter ashes from his airplane, Amador County pilot B.J. Elkin simply dumped over 5,000 sets of cremains on his property. Family members sued Elkin and received a $32 million settlement, in part because he commingled the remains, and they couldn't be sorted out. That same year, Contra Costa County pilot Al Vieira launched his own ash-scattering business, but apparently took a cue from Elkin, and soon began stockpiling his payloads in a rented storage space. Sheriff's deputies discovered the ersatz mausoleum in 1997, filled with the remains of 5,067 former human beings. Again, relatives took the pilot to court, but even though attorneys reached a tentative $4.17 million settlement, the point became moot when Vieira shot himself to death.

The lesson here, obviously, is don't trust a California cremation charter pilot. A

recent state law now allows residents the right to scatter cremated remains anywhere on land with permission of the property owner, or anywhere at sea, 500 yards or more from the coastline. To ensure your loved one's cremains receive a proper resting place in the great outdoors, you can leave it to licensed professionals. The Neptune Society (of which the Columbarium is a member) will take loved ones aboard their sleek 60-foot yacht, the *Naiad*, and scatter the ashes at sea.

**San Francisco Columbarium**
**1 Loraine Court**
**(415) 752-7891**